CHAPTER 5 THE DRAGON HOURGLASS

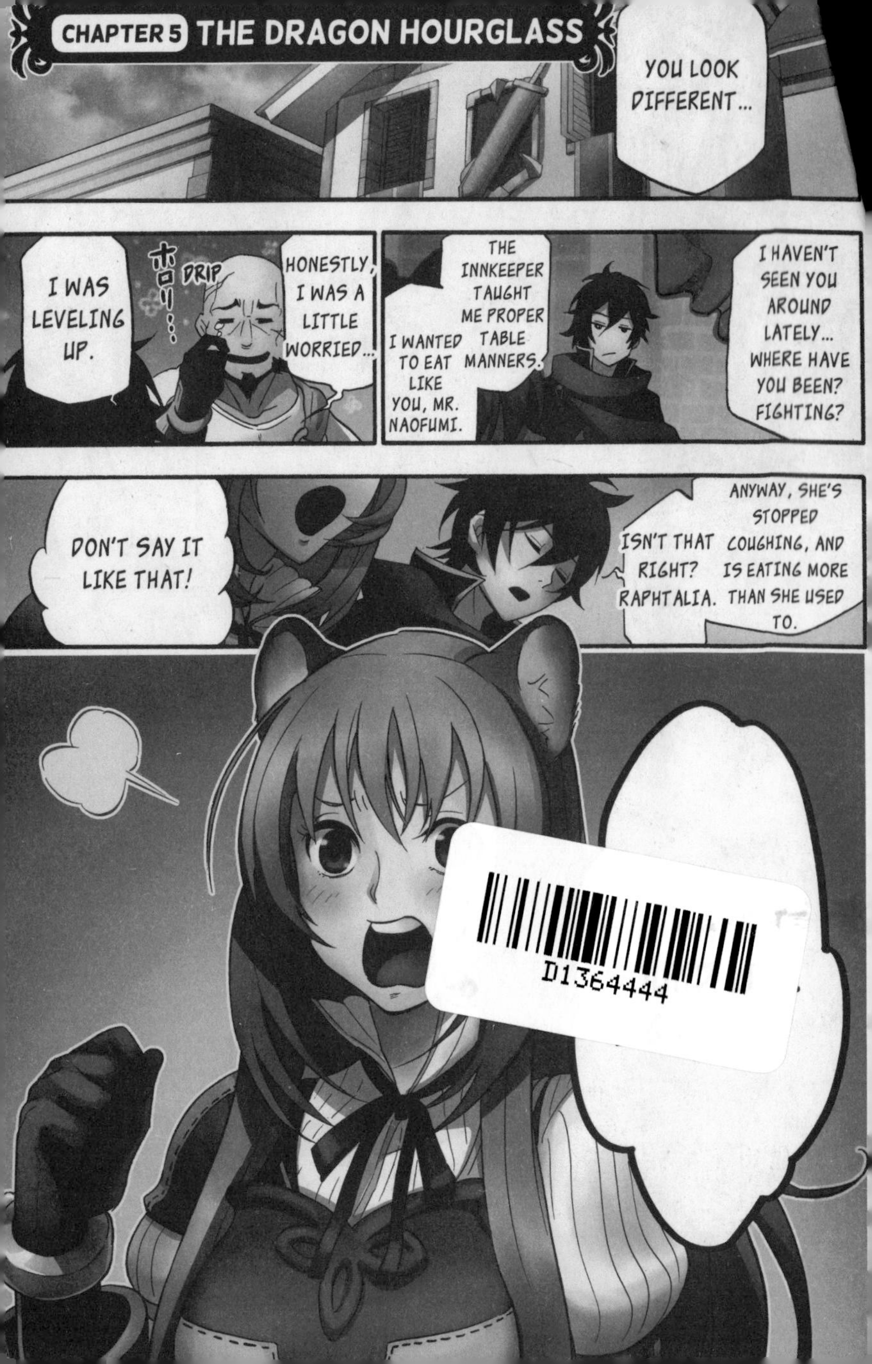
YOU LOOK DIFFERENT...
I HAVEN'T SEEN YOU AROUND LATELY... WHERE HAVE YOU BEEN? FIGHTING?
THE INNKEEPER TAUGHT ME PROPER TABLE MANNERS.
I WANTED TO EAT LIKE YOU, MR. NAOFUMI.
HONESTLY, I WAS A LITTLE WORRIED...
ホロリ…
DRIP
I WAS LEVELING UP.
ANYWAY, SHE'S STOPPED COUGHING, AND IS EATING MORE THAN SHE USED TO.
ISN'T THAT RIGHT? RAPHTALIA.
DON'T SAY IT LIKE THAT!

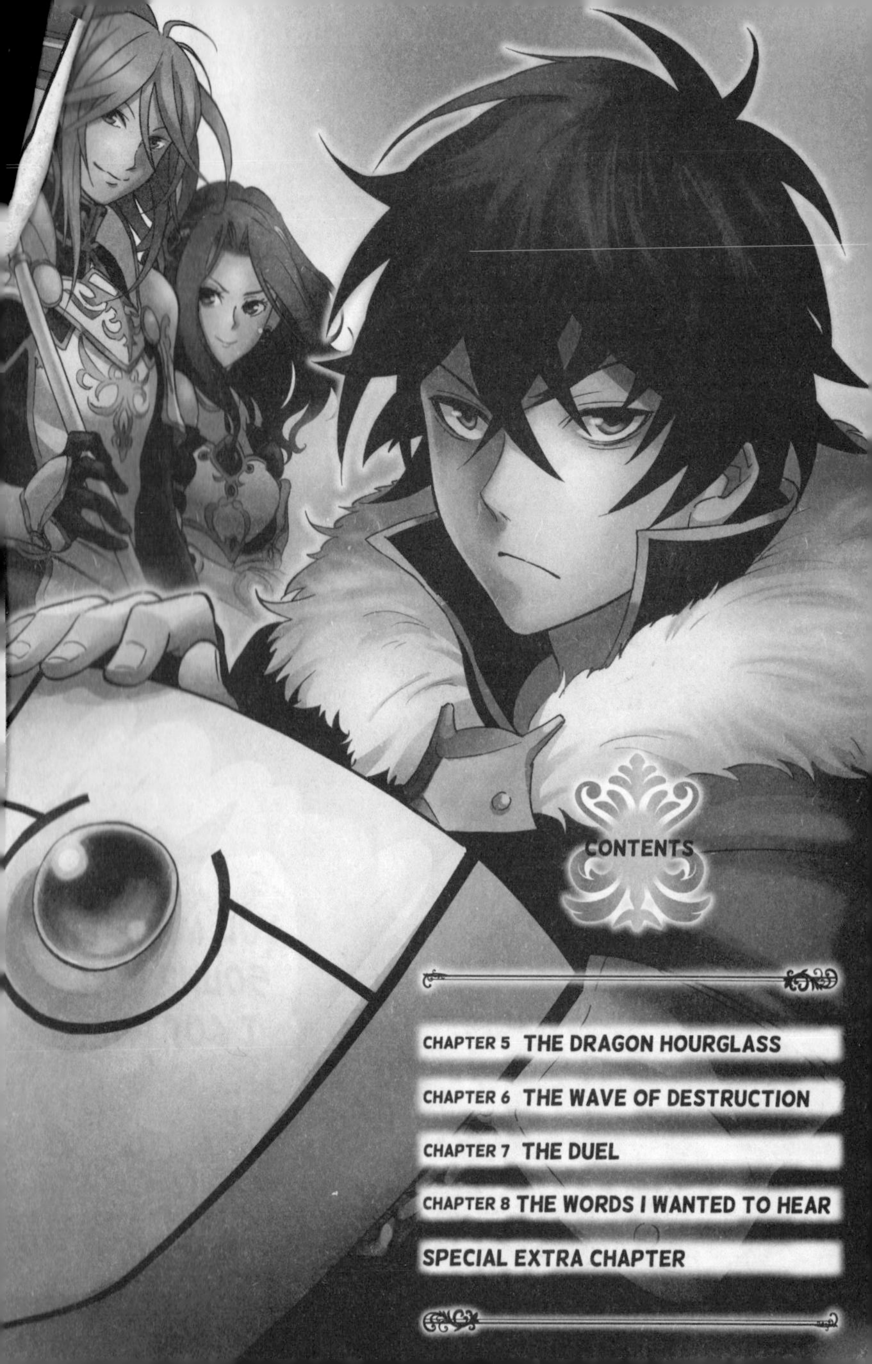

CONTENTS

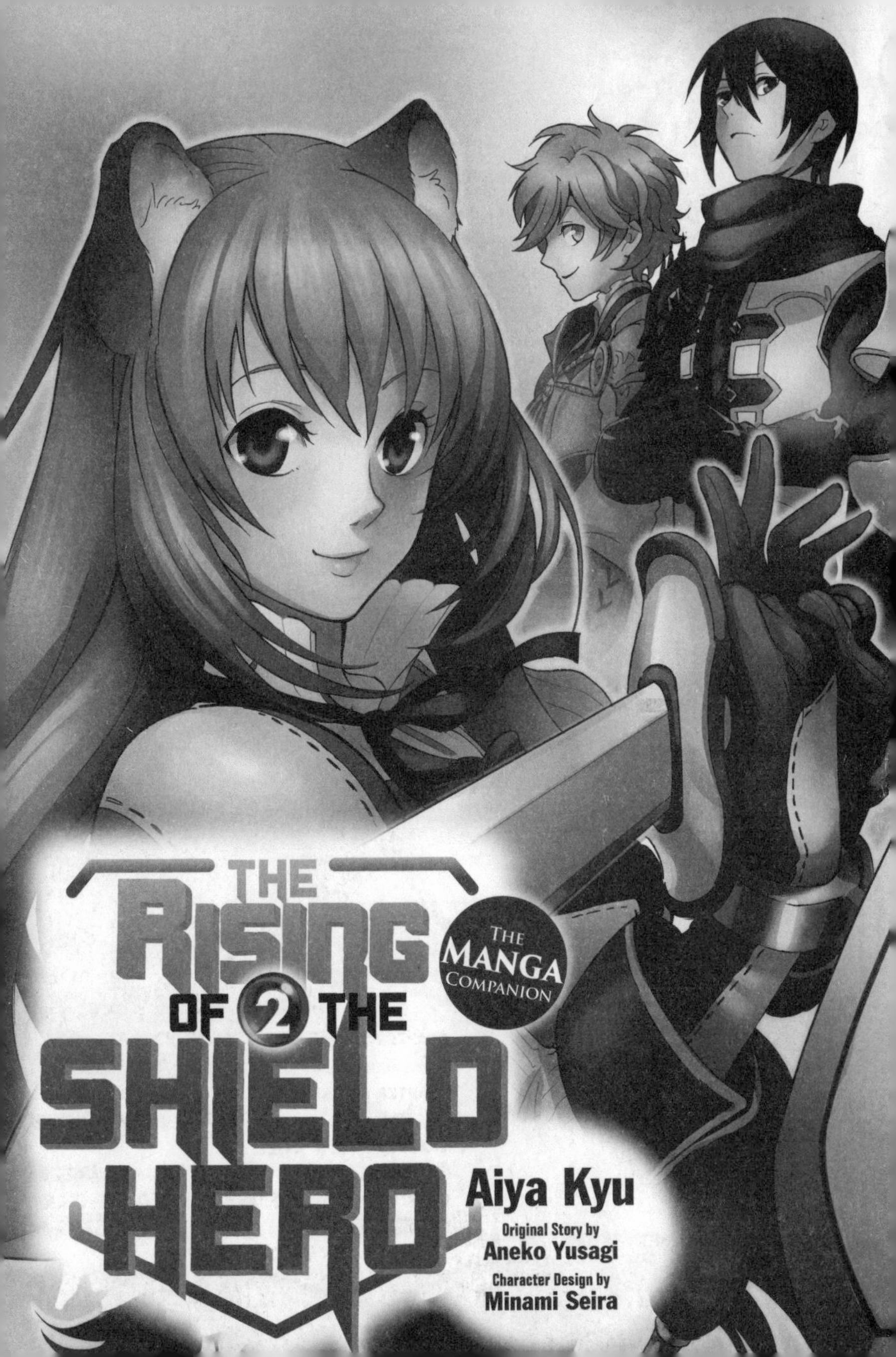
THE RISING OF THE SHIELD HERO
2
THE MANGA COMPANION
Aiya Kyu
Original Story by
Aneko Yusagi
Character Design by
Minami Seira

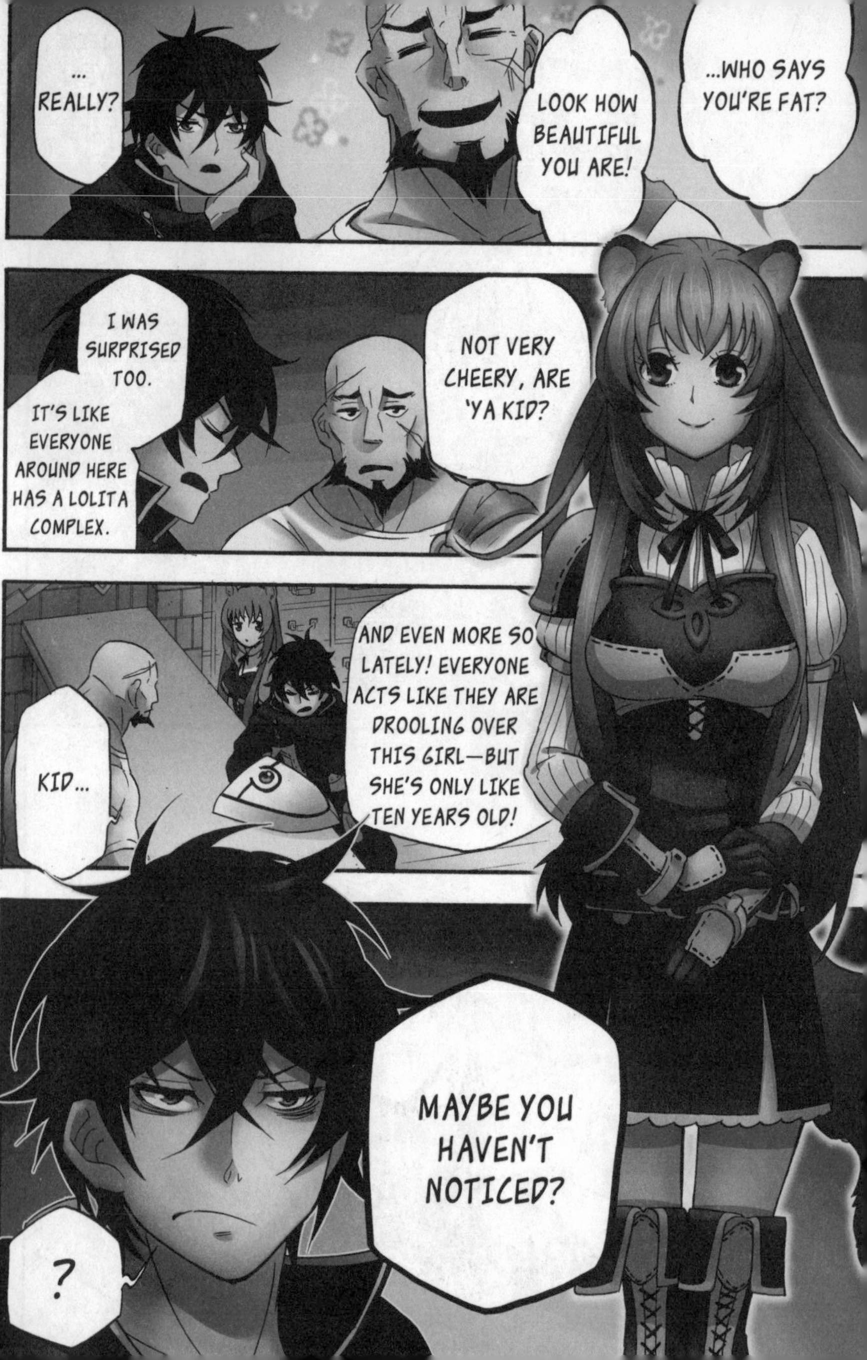
...WHO SAYS YOU'RE FAT?
LOOK HOW BEAUTIFUL YOU ARE!
... REALLY?
NOT VERY CHEERY, ARE 'YA KID?
I WAS SURPRISED TOO.
IT'S LIKE EVERYONE AROUND HERE HAS A LOLITA COMPLEX.
AND EVEN MORE SO LATELY! EVERYONE ACTS LIKE THEY ARE DROOLING OVER THIS GIRL—BUT SHE'S ONLY LIKE TEN YEARS OLD!
KID...
MAYBE YOU HAVEN'T NOTICED?
?

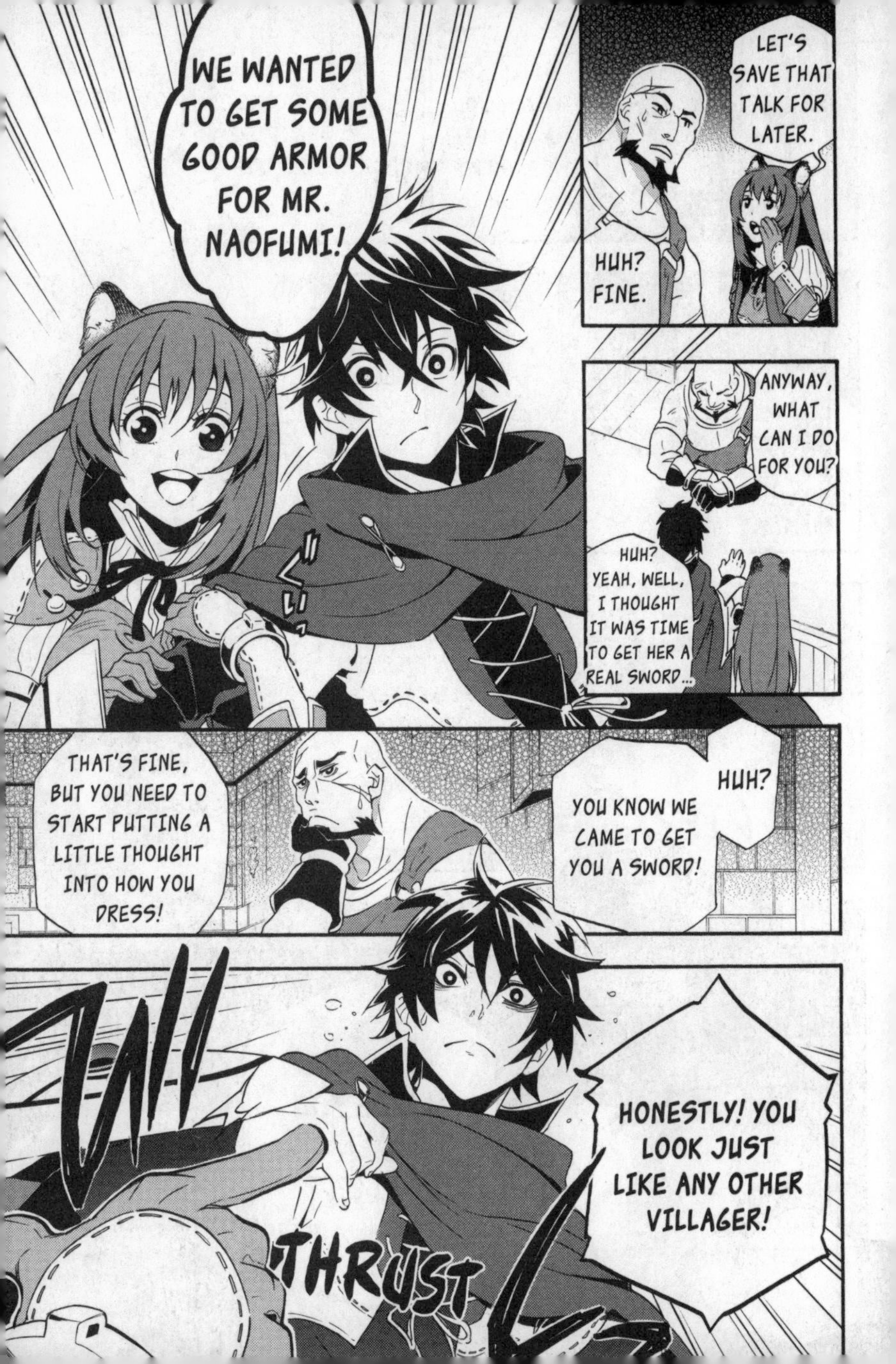
LET'S SAVE THAT TALK FOR LATER.
HUH? FINE.
ANYWAY, WHAT CAN I DO FOR YOU?
HUH? YEAH, WELL, I THOUGHT IT WAS TIME TO GET HER A REAL SWORD...
WE WANTED TO GET SOME GOOD ARMOR FOR MR. NAOFUMI!
HUH?
YOU KNOW WE CAME TO GET YOU A SWORD!
THAT'S FINE, BUT YOU NEED TO START PUTTING A LITTLE THOUGHT INTO HOW YOU DRESS!
HONESTLY! YOU LOOK JUST LIKE ANY OTHER VILLAGER!
THRUST

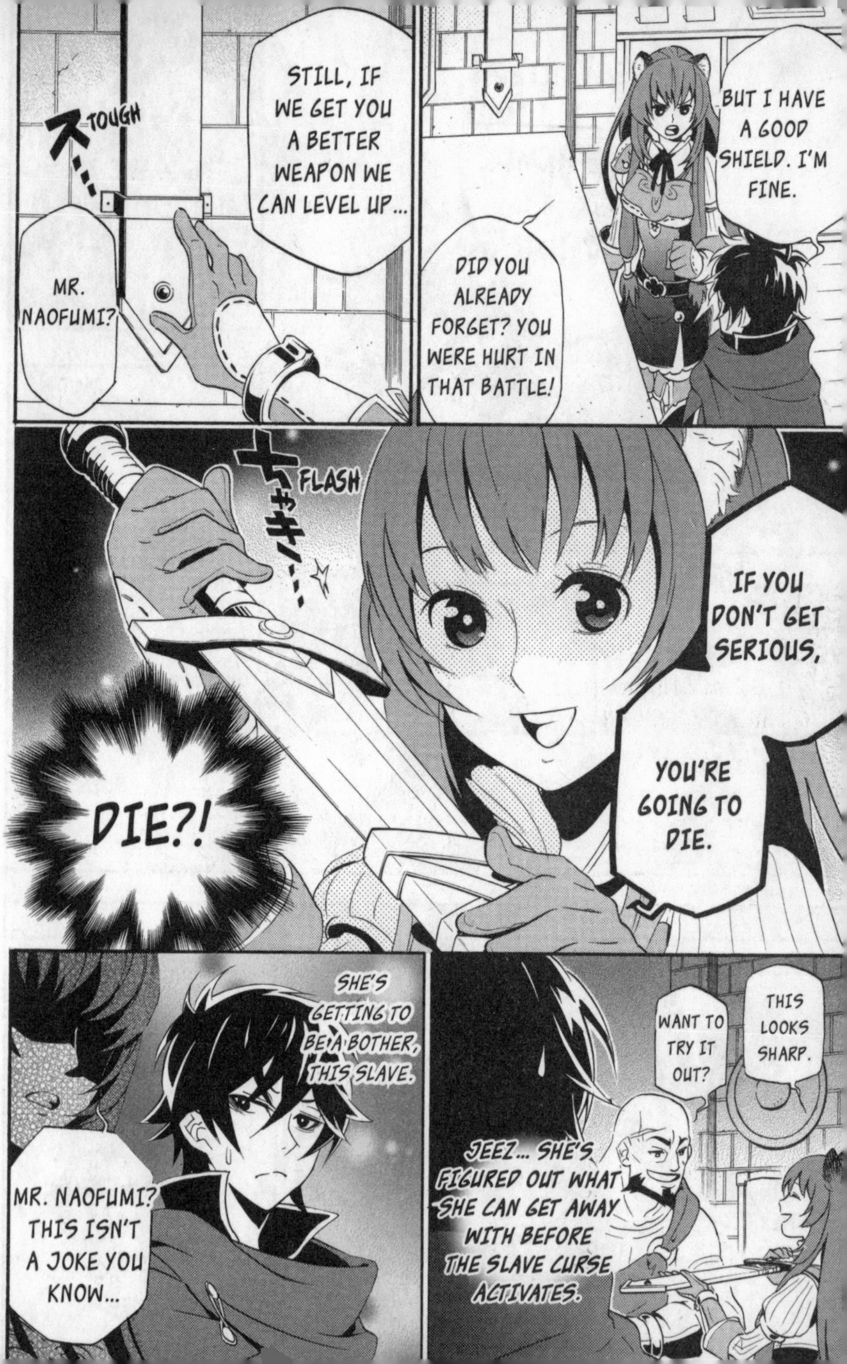
BUT I HAVE A GOOD SHIELD. I'M FINE.
DID YOU ALREADY FORGET? YOU WERE HURT IN THAT BATTLE!
STILL, IF WE GET YOU A BETTER WEAPON WE CAN LEVEL UP...
TOUGH
MR. NAOFUMI?
IF YOU DON'T GET SERIOUS,
YOU'RE GOING TO DIE.
FLASH
DIE?!
THIS LOOKS SHARP.
WANT TO TRY IT OUT?
JEEZ... SHE'S FIGURED OUT WHAT SHE CAN GET AWAY WITH BEFORE THE SLAVE CURSE ACTIVATES.
SHE'S GETTING TO BE A BOTHER, THIS SLAVE.
MR. NAOFUMI? THIS ISN'T A JOKE YOU KNOW...

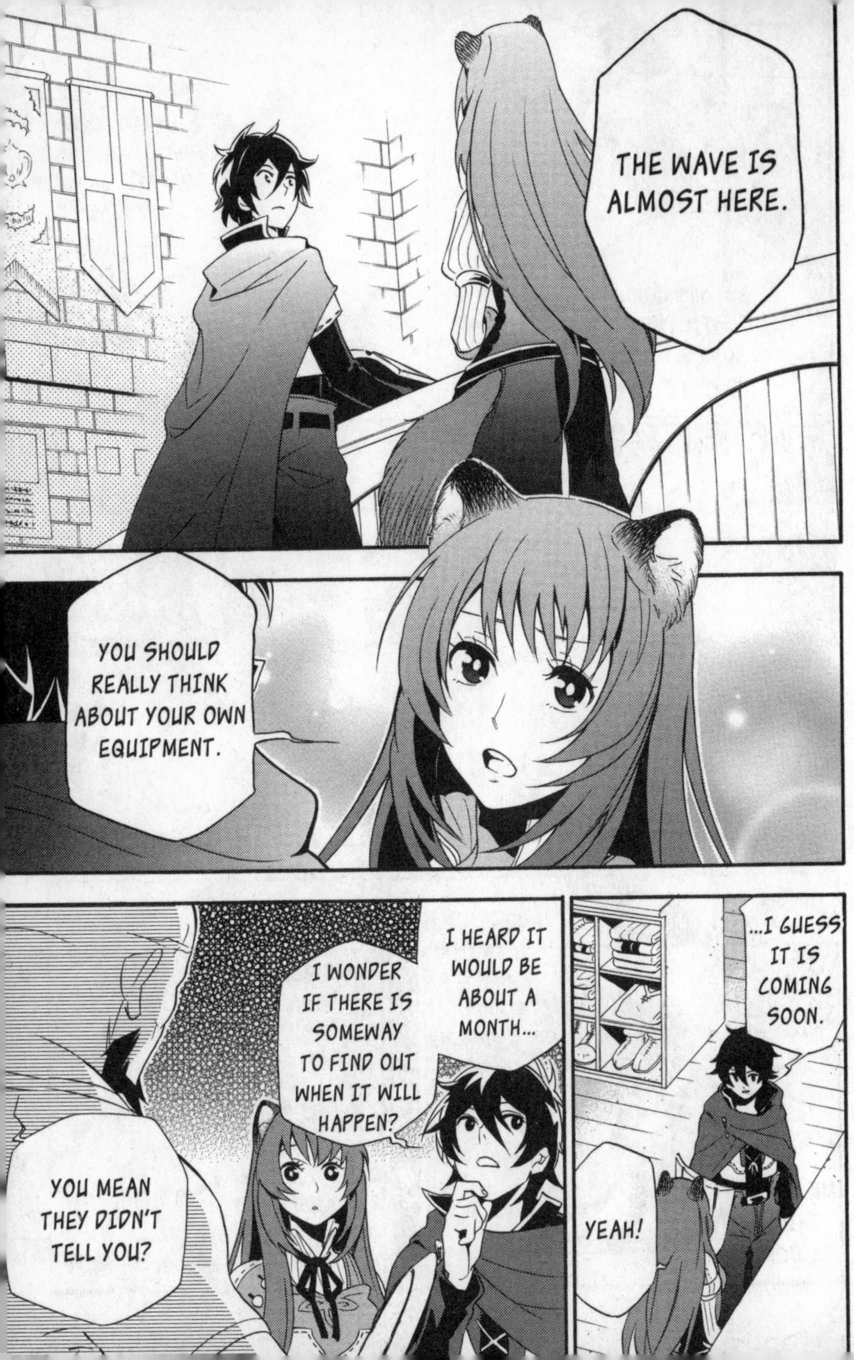
THE WAVE IS ALMOST HERE.
YOU SHOULD REALLY THINK ABOUT YOUR OWN EQUIPMENT.
...I GUESS IT IS COMING SOON.
YEAH!
I HEARD IT WOULD BE ABOUT A MONTH...
I WONDER IF THERE IS SOMEWAY TO FIND OUT WHEN IT WILL HAPPEN?
YOU MEAN THEY DIDN'T TELL YOU?

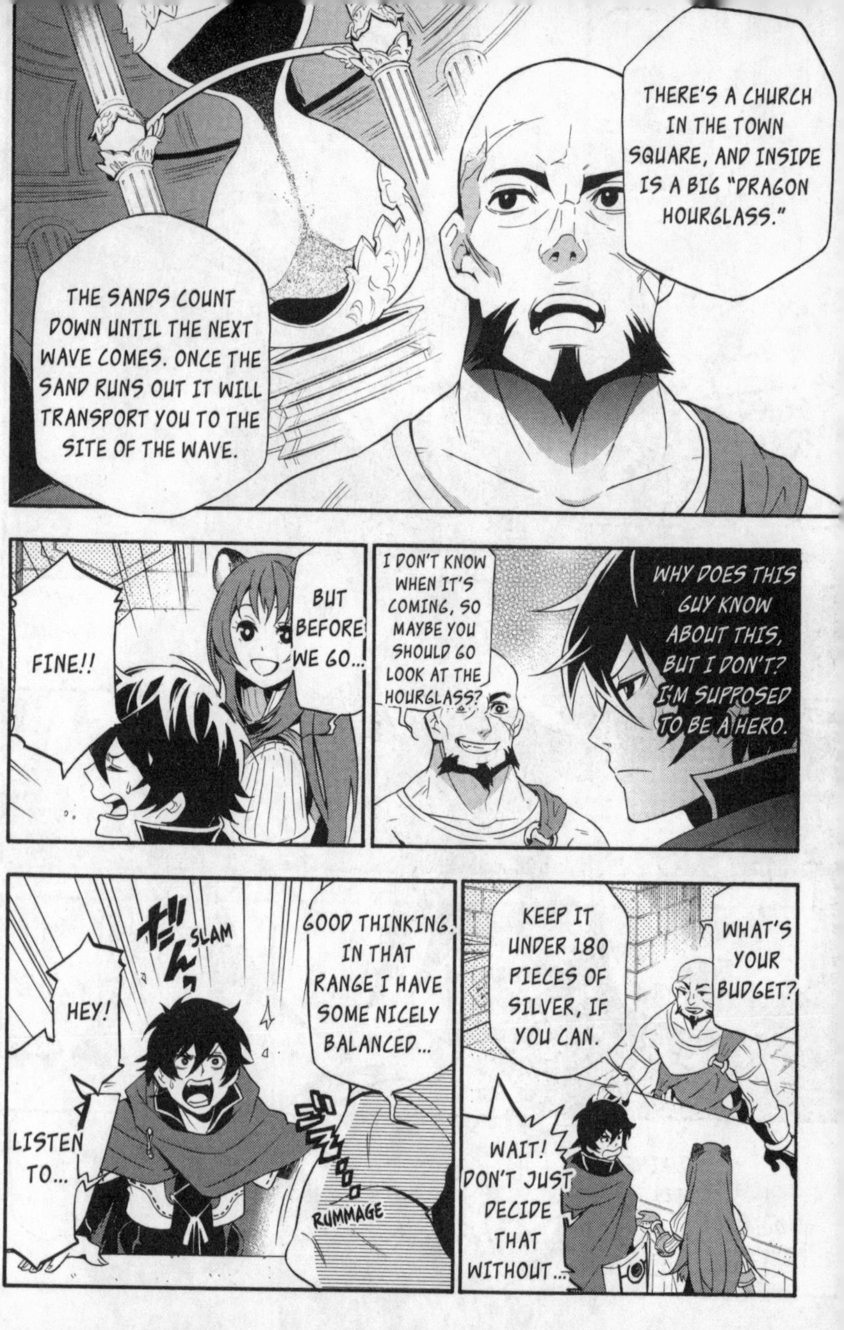
THERE'S A CHURCH IN THE TOWN SQUARE, AND INSIDE IS A BIG "DRAGON HOURGLASS."
THE SANDS COUNT DOWN UNTIL THE NEXT WAVE COMES. ONCE THE SAND RUNS OUT IT WILL TRANSPORT YOU TO THE SITE OF THE WAVE.
WHY DOES THIS GUY KNOW ABOUT THIS, BUT I DON'T? I'M SUPPOSED TO BE A HERO.
I DON'T KNOW WHEN IT'S COMING, SO MAYBE YOU SHOULD GO LOOK AT THE HOURGLASS?
BUT BEFORE WE GO...
FINE!!
WHAT'S YOUR BUDGET?
KEEP IT UNDER 180 PIECES OF SILVER, IF YOU CAN.
WAIT! DON'T JUST DECIDE THAT WITHOUT...
GOOD THINKING. IN THAT RANGE I HAVE SOME NICELY BALANCED...
SLAM
HEY!
LISTEN TO...
RUMMAGE

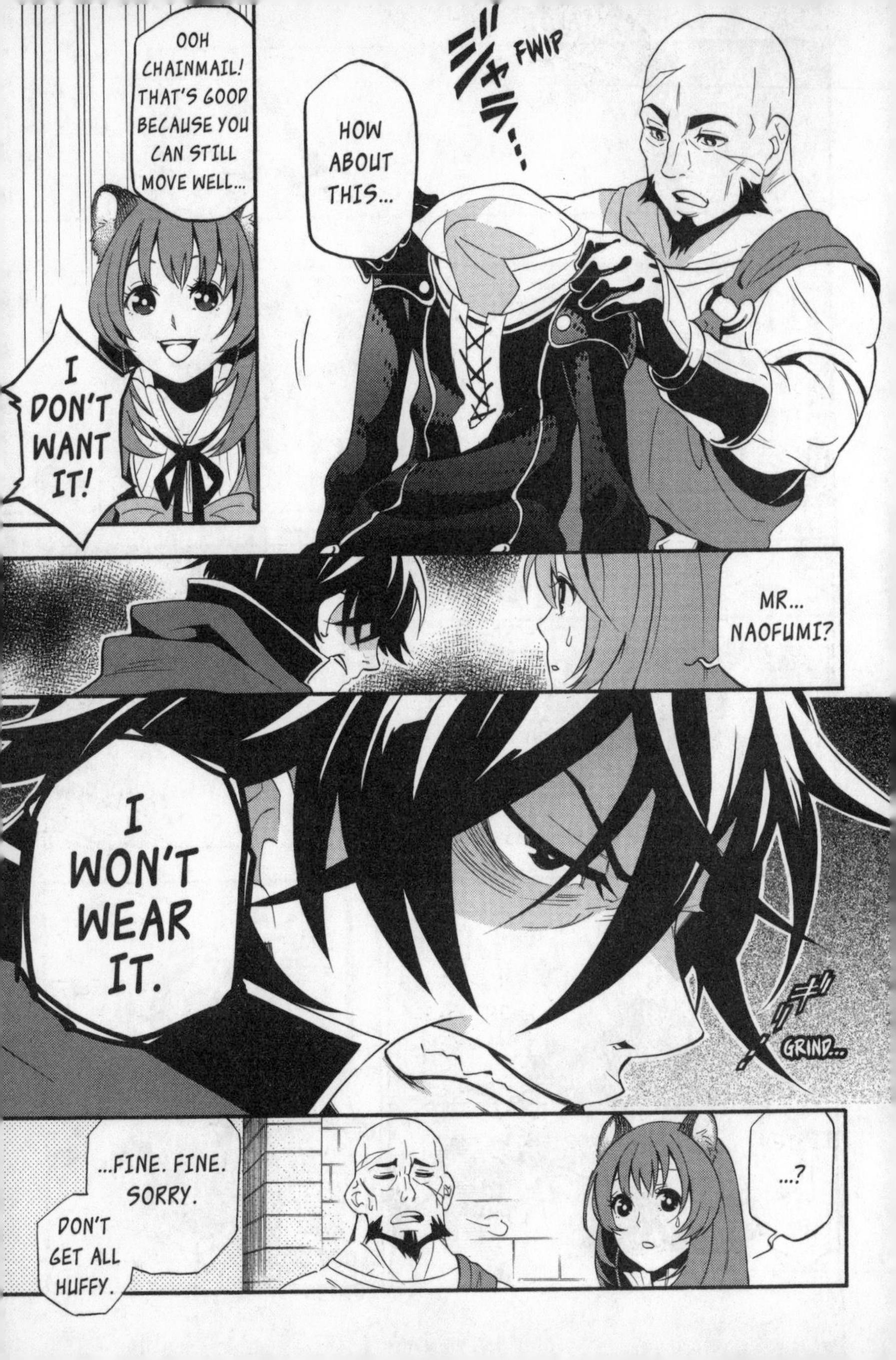
ジャラ…
FWIP
HOW ABOUT THIS...
OOH CHAINMAIL! THAT'S GOOD BECAUSE YOU CAN STILL MOVE WELL...
I DON'T WANT IT!
MR... NAOFUMI?
I WON'T WEAR IT.
ギリ
GRIND...
...?
...FINE. FINE. SORRY.
DON'T GET ALL HUFFY.

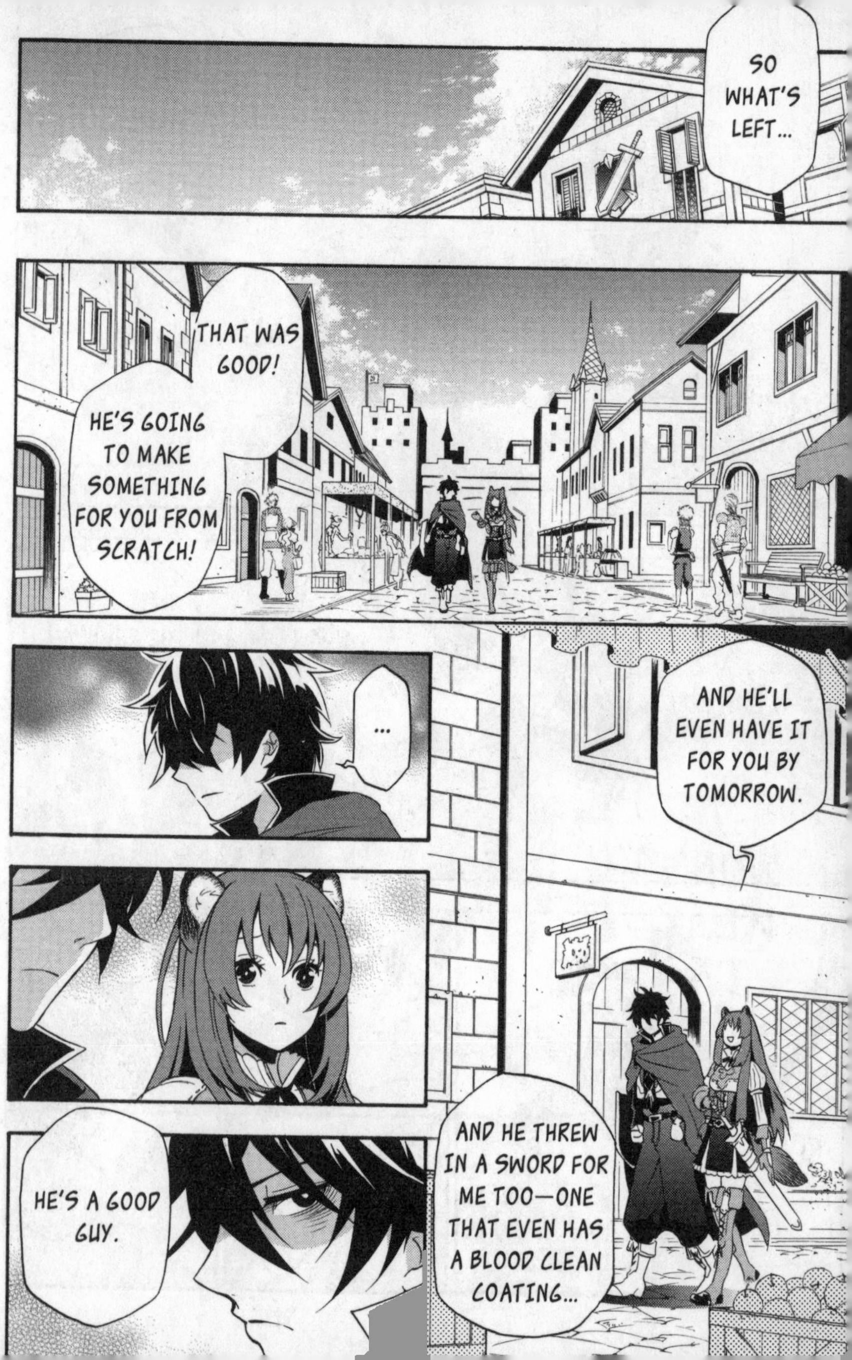
SO WHAT'S LEFT...
THAT WAS GOOD!
HE'S GOING TO MAKE SOMETHING FOR YOU FROM SCRATCH!
AND HE'LL EVEN HAVE IT FOR YOU BY TOMORROW.
AND HE THREW IN A SWORD FOR ME TOO—ONE THAT EVEN HAS A BLOOD CLEAN COATING...
...
HE'S A GOOD GUY.

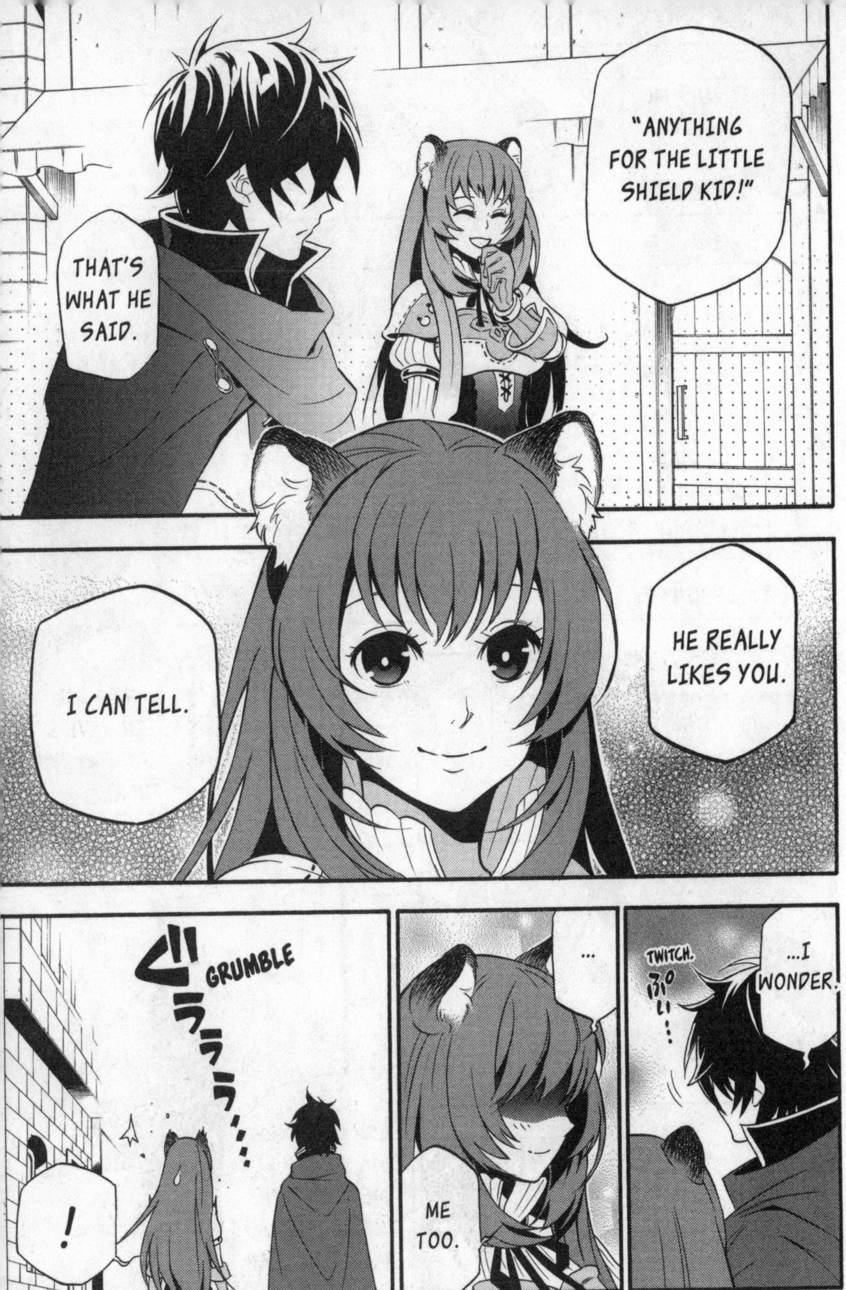
"ANYTHING FOR THE LITTLE SHIELD KID!"
THAT'S WHAT HE SAID.
HE REALLY LIKES YOU.
I CAN TELL.
...I WONDER.
TWITCH.
...
ME TOO.
GRUMBLE
!

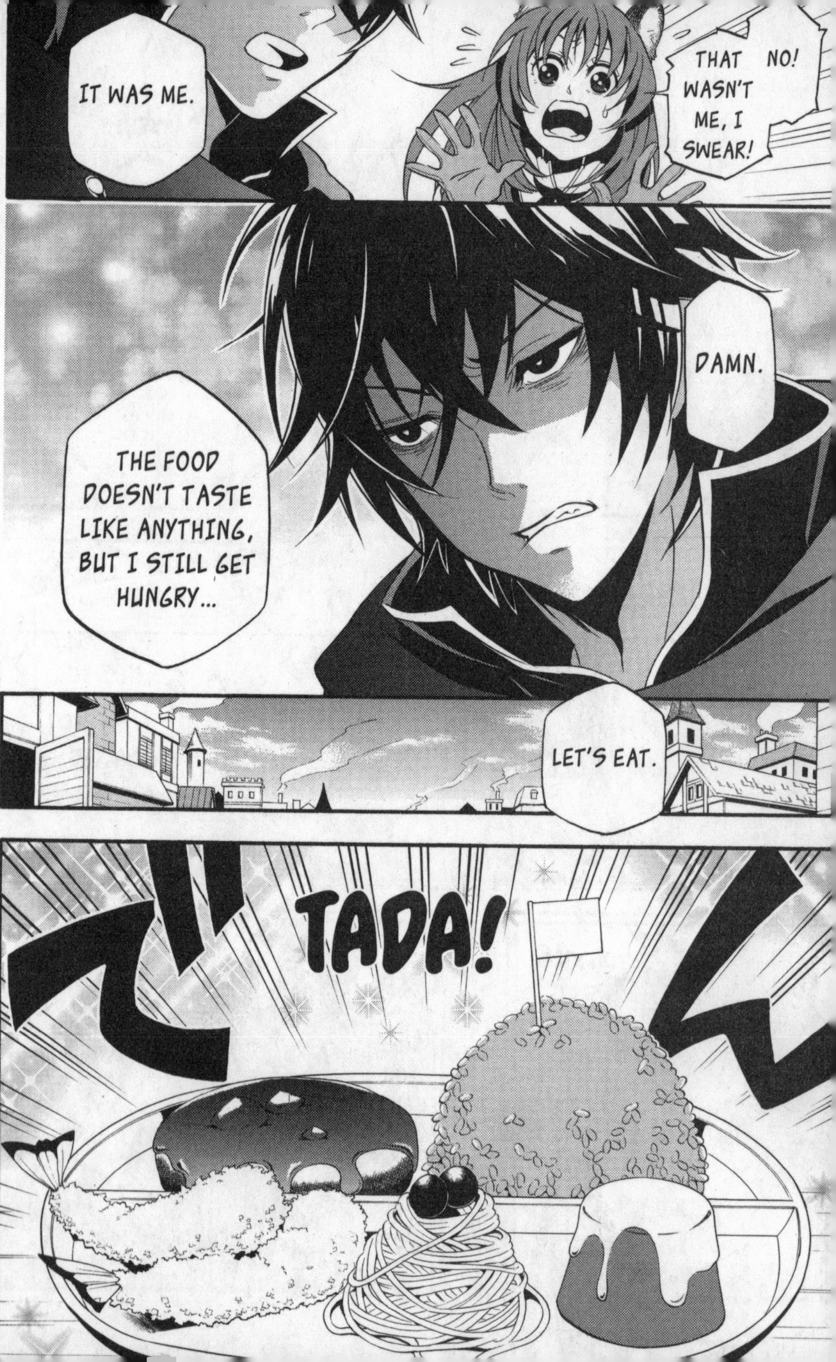
NO! THAT WASN'T ME, I SWEAR!
IT WAS ME.
DAMN.
THE FOOD DOESN'T TASTE LIKE ANYTHING, BUT I STILL GET HUNGRY...
LET'S EAT.
TADA!

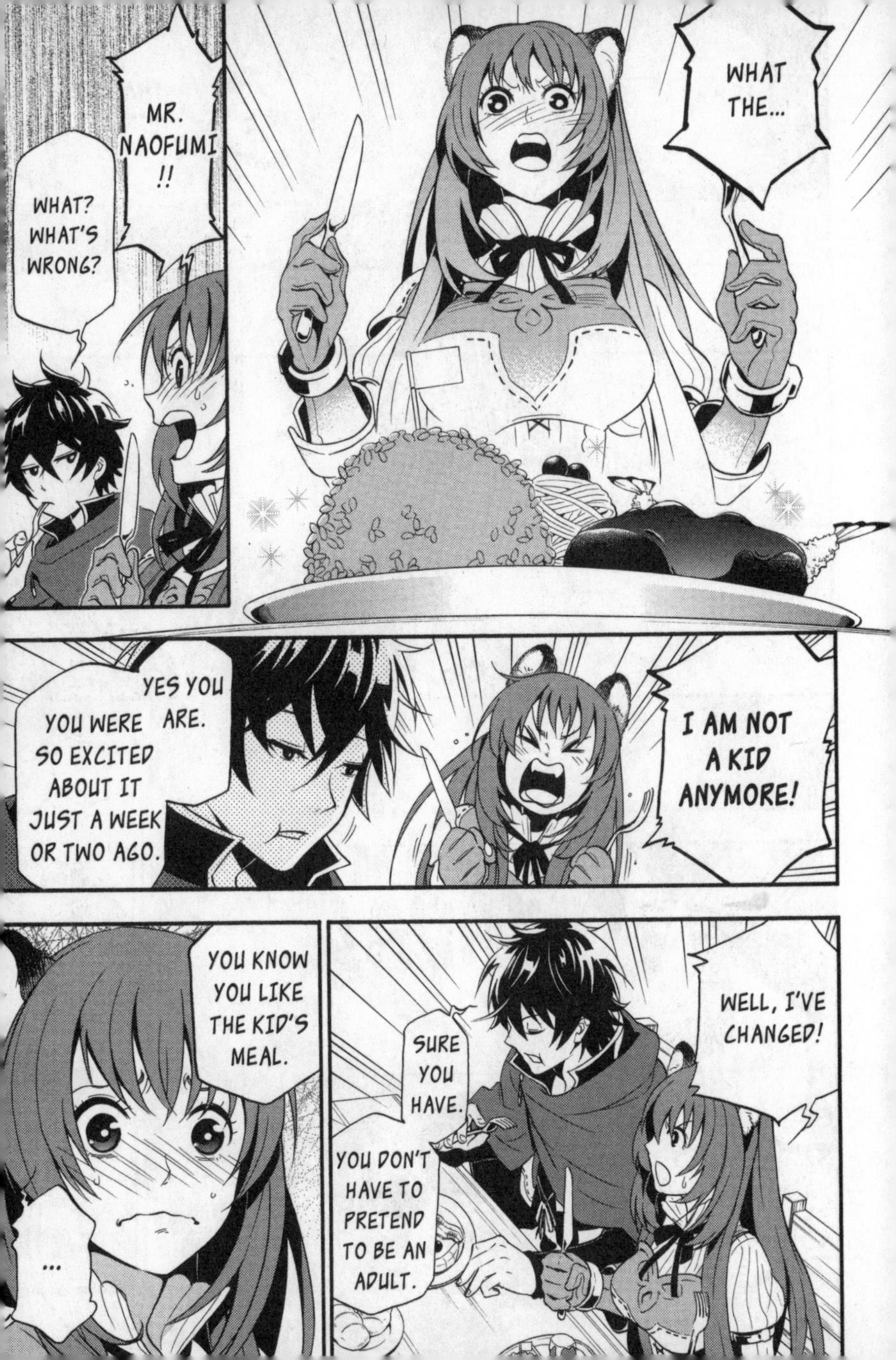
WHAT THE...
MR. NAOFUMI !!
WHAT? WHAT'S WRONG?
I AM NOT A KID ANYMORE!
YES YOU ARE.
YOU WERE SO EXCITED ABOUT IT JUST A WEEK OR TWO AGO.
WELL, I'VE CHANGED!
SURE YOU HAVE.
YOU DON'T HAVE TO PRETEND TO BE AN ADULT.
YOU KNOW YOU LIKE THE KID'S MEAL.
...

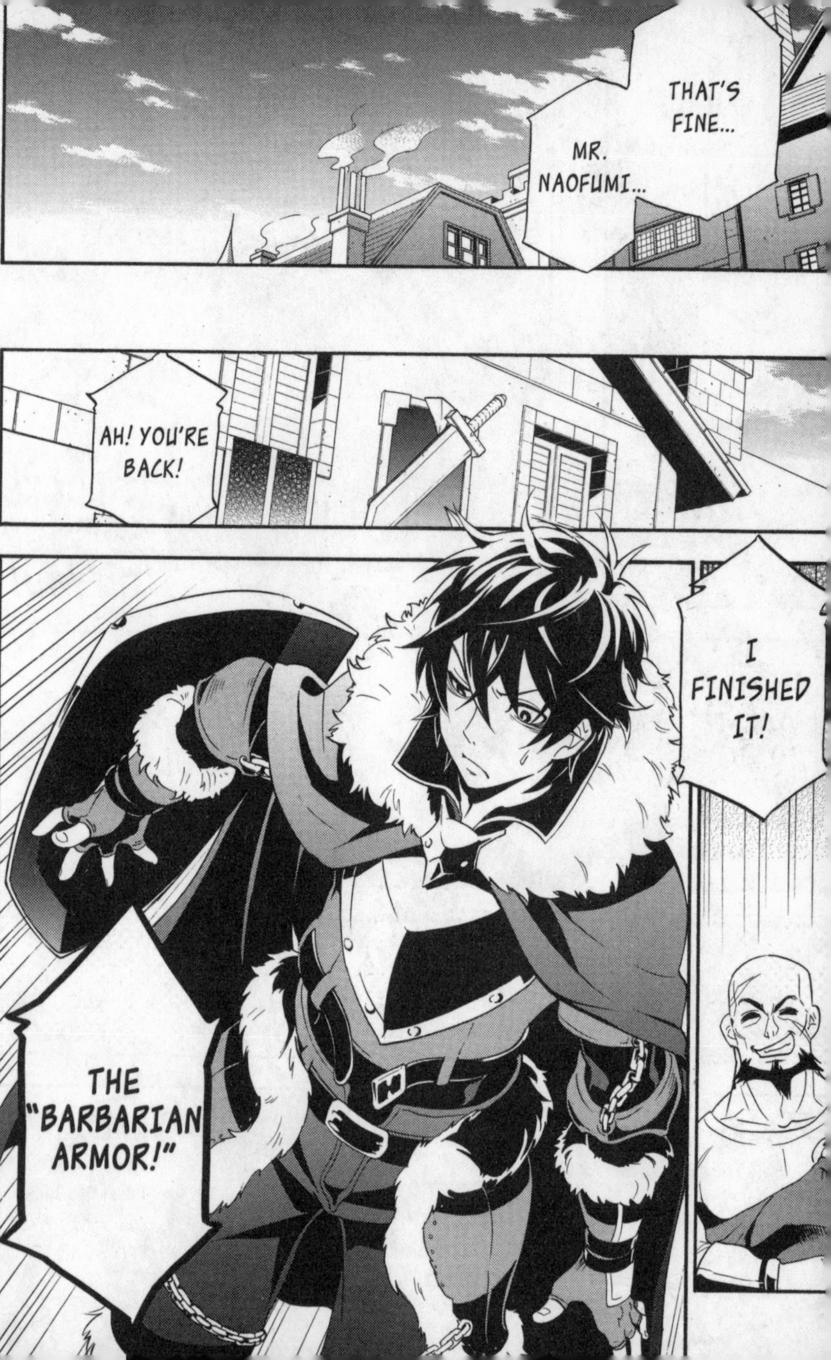
THAT'S FINE...
MR. NAOFUMI...
AH! YOU'RE BACK!
I FINISHED IT!
THE "BARBARIAN ARMOR!"

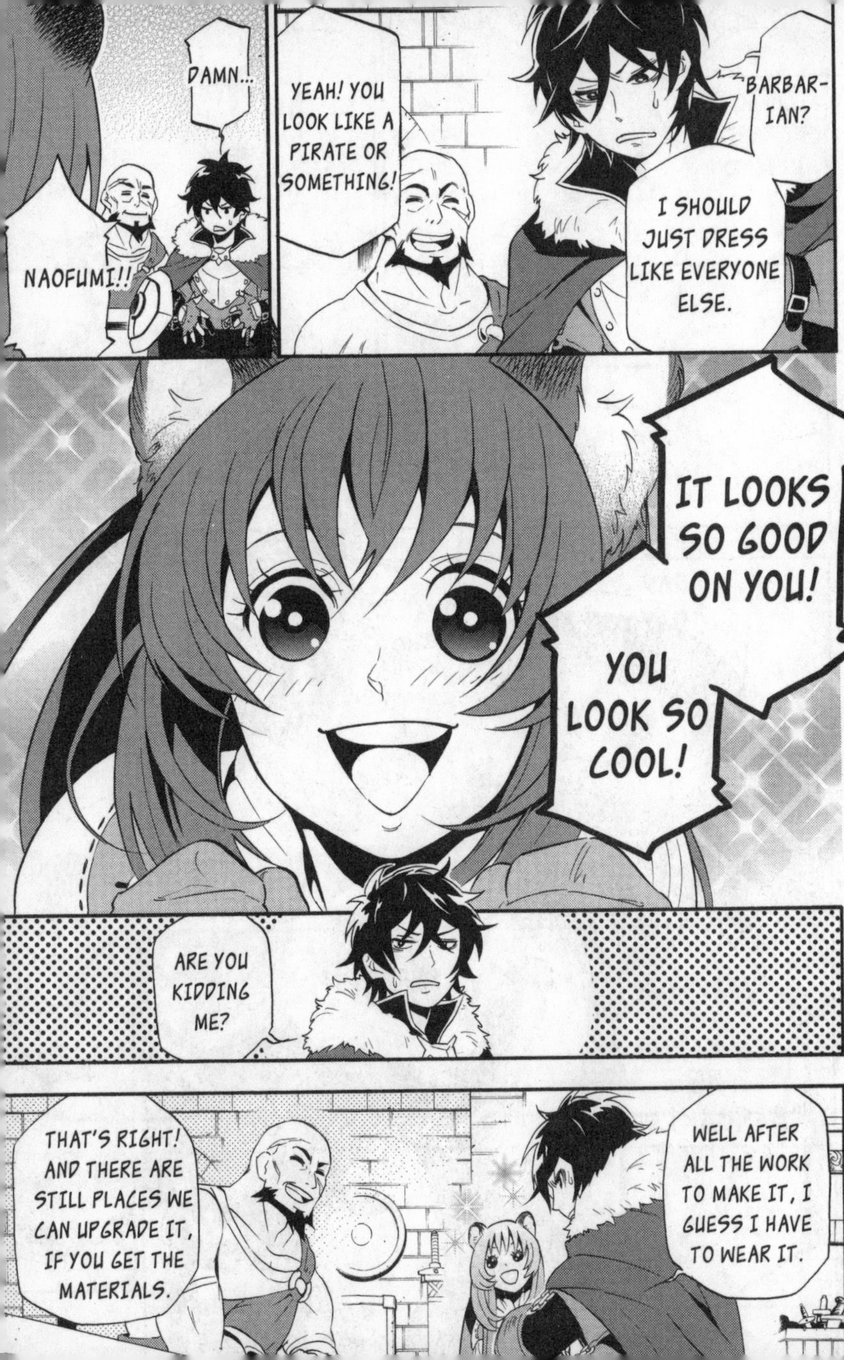
BARBAR-IAN?
YEAH! YOU LOOK LIKE A PIRATE OR SOMETHING!
I SHOULD JUST DRESS LIKE EVERYONE ELSE.
DAMN...
NAOFUMI!!
IT LOOKS SO GOOD ON YOU!
YOU LOOK SO COOL!
ARE YOU KIDDING ME?
WELL AFTER ALL THE WORK TO MAKE IT, I GUESS I HAVE TO WEAR IT.
THAT'S RIGHT! AND THERE ARE STILL PLACES WE CAN UPGRADE IT, IF YOU GET THE MATERIALS.

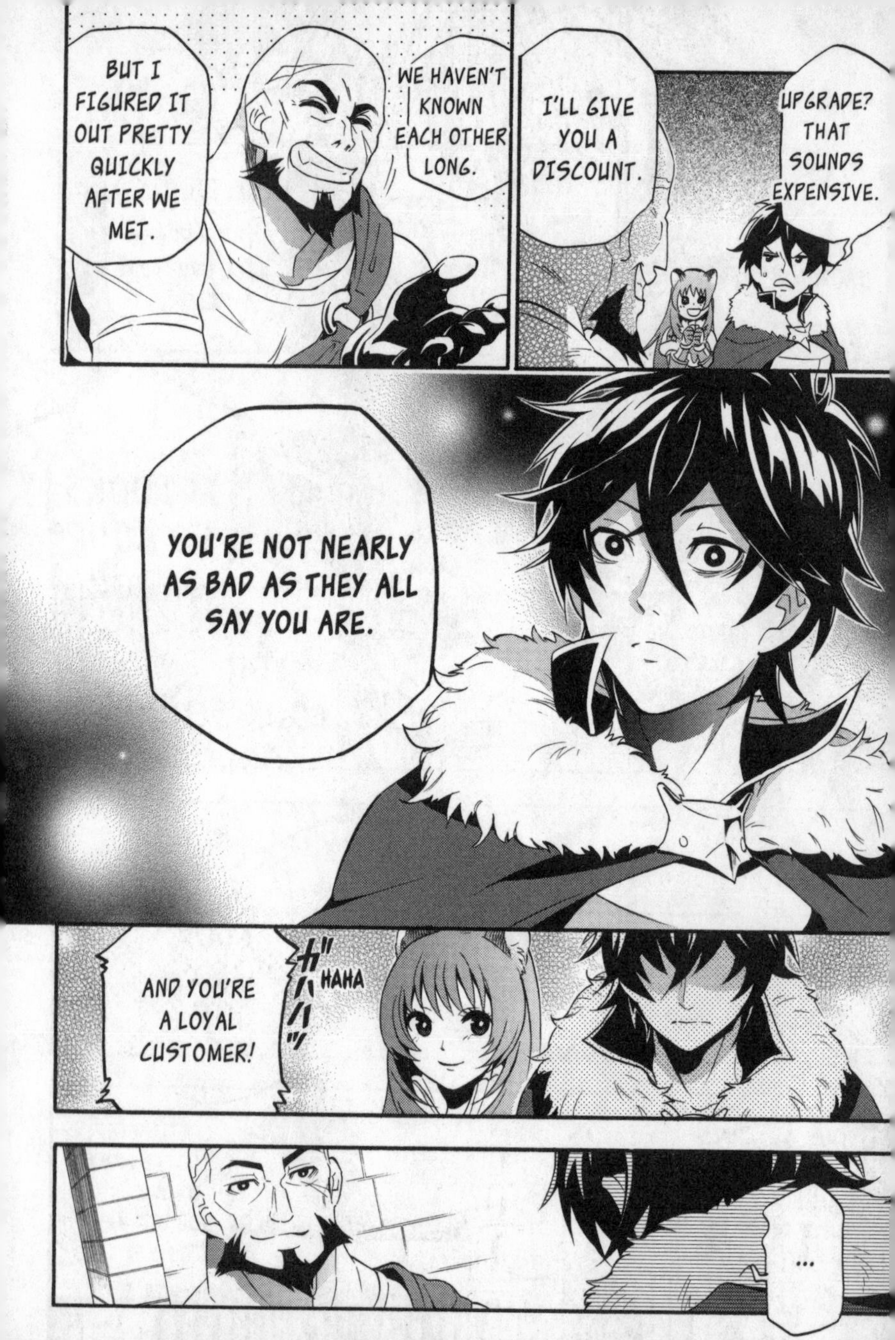
UPGRADE? THAT SOUNDS EXPENSIVE.
I'LL GIVE YOU A DISCOUNT.
WE HAVEN'T KNOWN EACH OTHER LONG.
BUT I FIGURED IT OUT PRETTY QUICKLY AFTER WE MET.
YOU'RE NOT NEARLY AS BAD AS THEY ALL SAY YOU ARE.
ガハハッ HAHA
AND YOU'RE A LOYAL CUSTOMER!
...

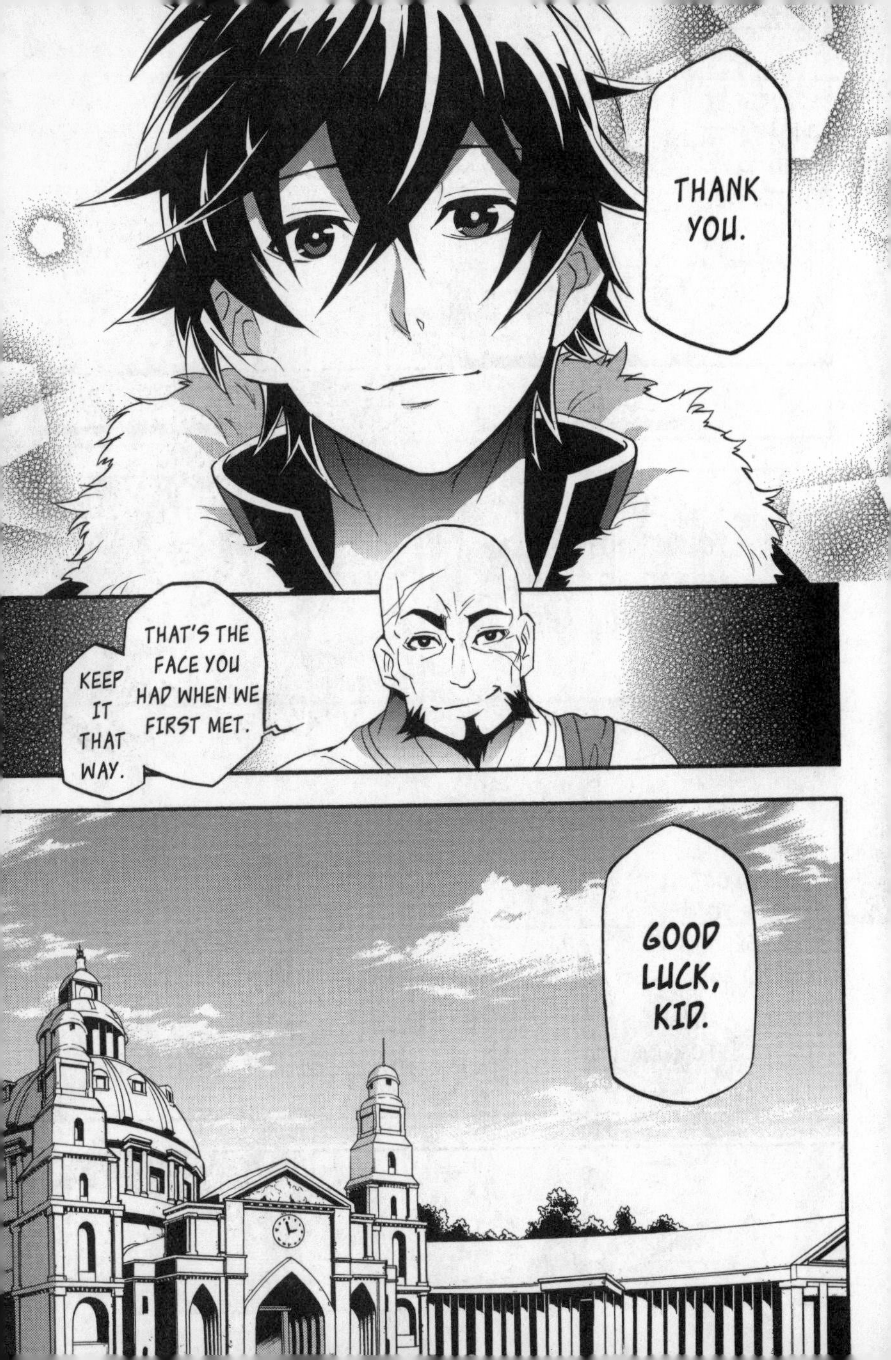
THANK YOU.
THAT'S THE FACE YOU HAD WHEN WE FIRST MET.
KEEP IT THAT WAY.
GOOD LUCK, KID.

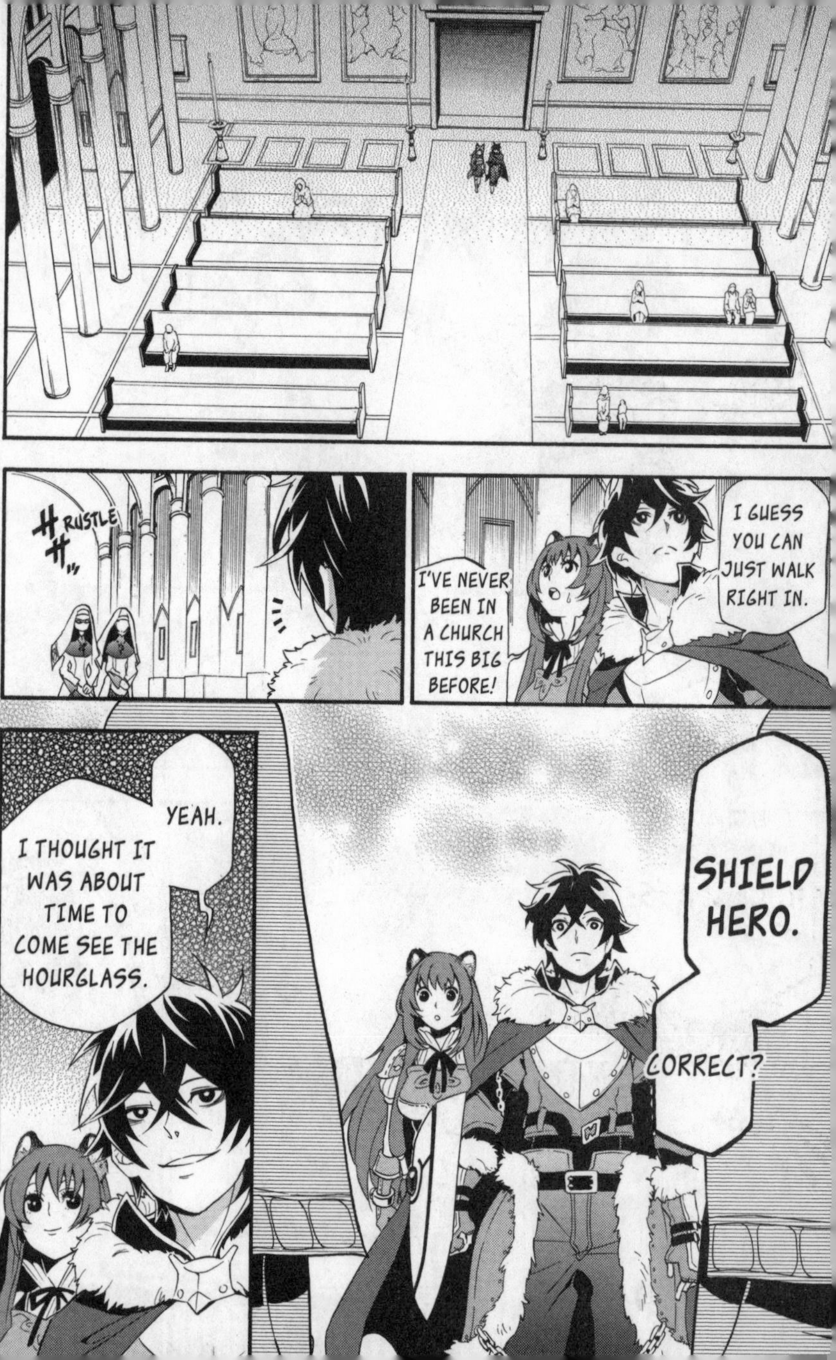

I GUESS YOU CAN JUST WALK RIGHT IN.
I'VE NEVER BEEN IN A CHURCH THIS BIG BEFORE!
RUSTLE
SHIELD HERO.
CORRECT?
YEAH.
I THOUGHT IT WAS ABOUT TIME TO COME SEE THE HOURGLASS.

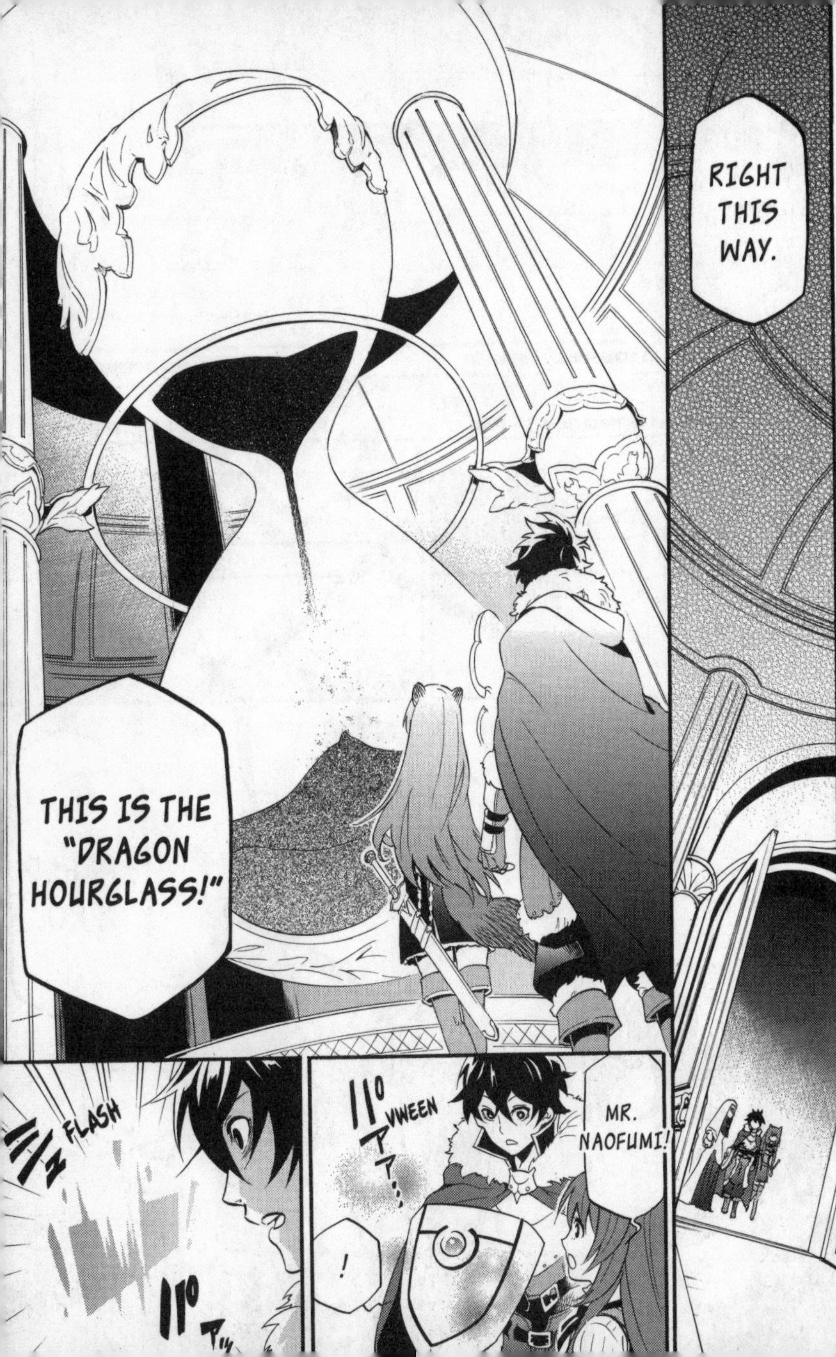
RIGHT THIS WAY.
THIS IS THE "DRAGON HOURGLASS!"
MR. NAOFUMI!
VWEEN
!
FLASH

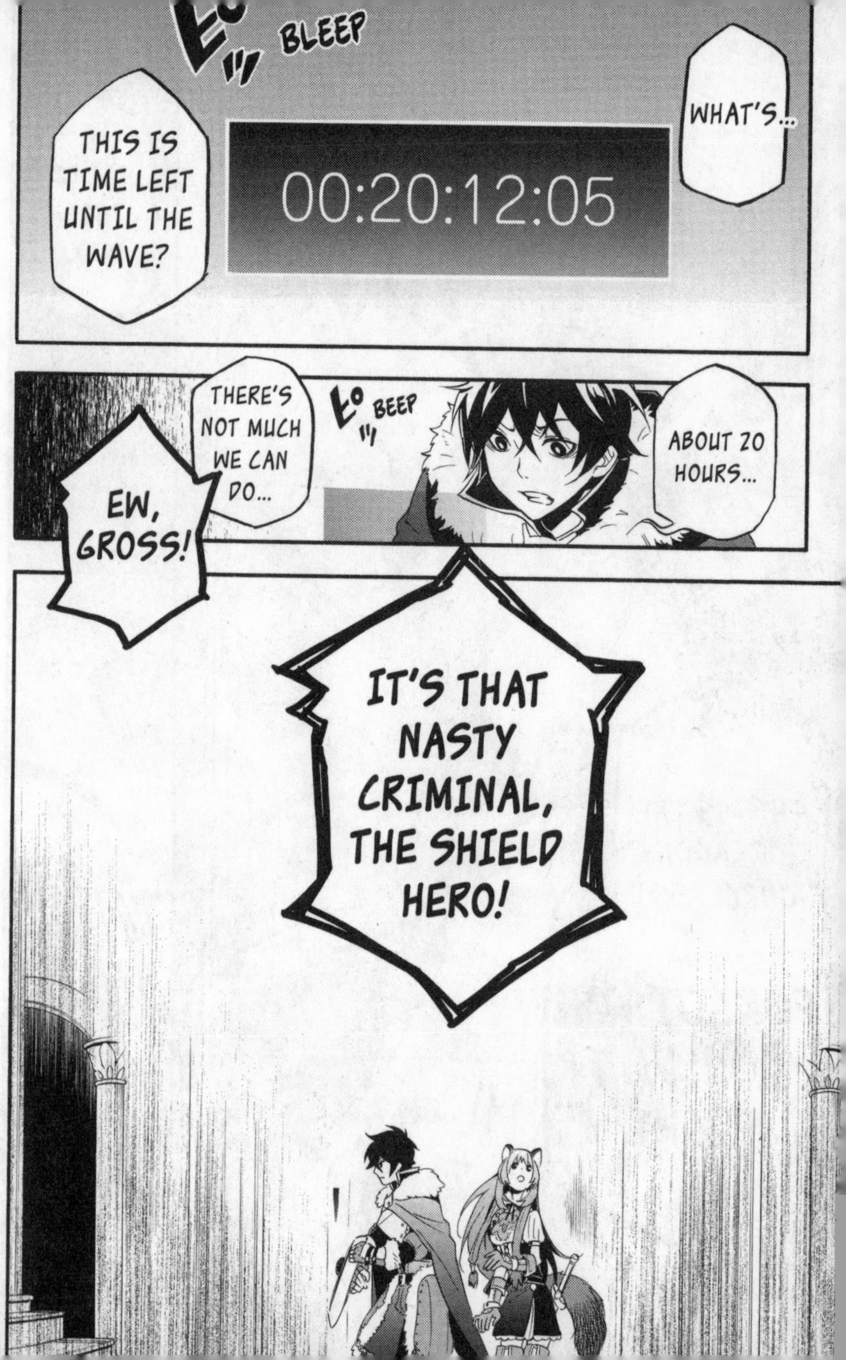
BLEEP
WHAT'S...
THIS IS TIME LEFT UNTIL THE WAVE?
00:20:12:05
ABOUT 20 HOURS...
BEEP
THERE'S NOT MUCH WE CAN DO...
EW, GROSS!
IT'S THAT NASTY CRIMINAL, THE SHIELD HERO!

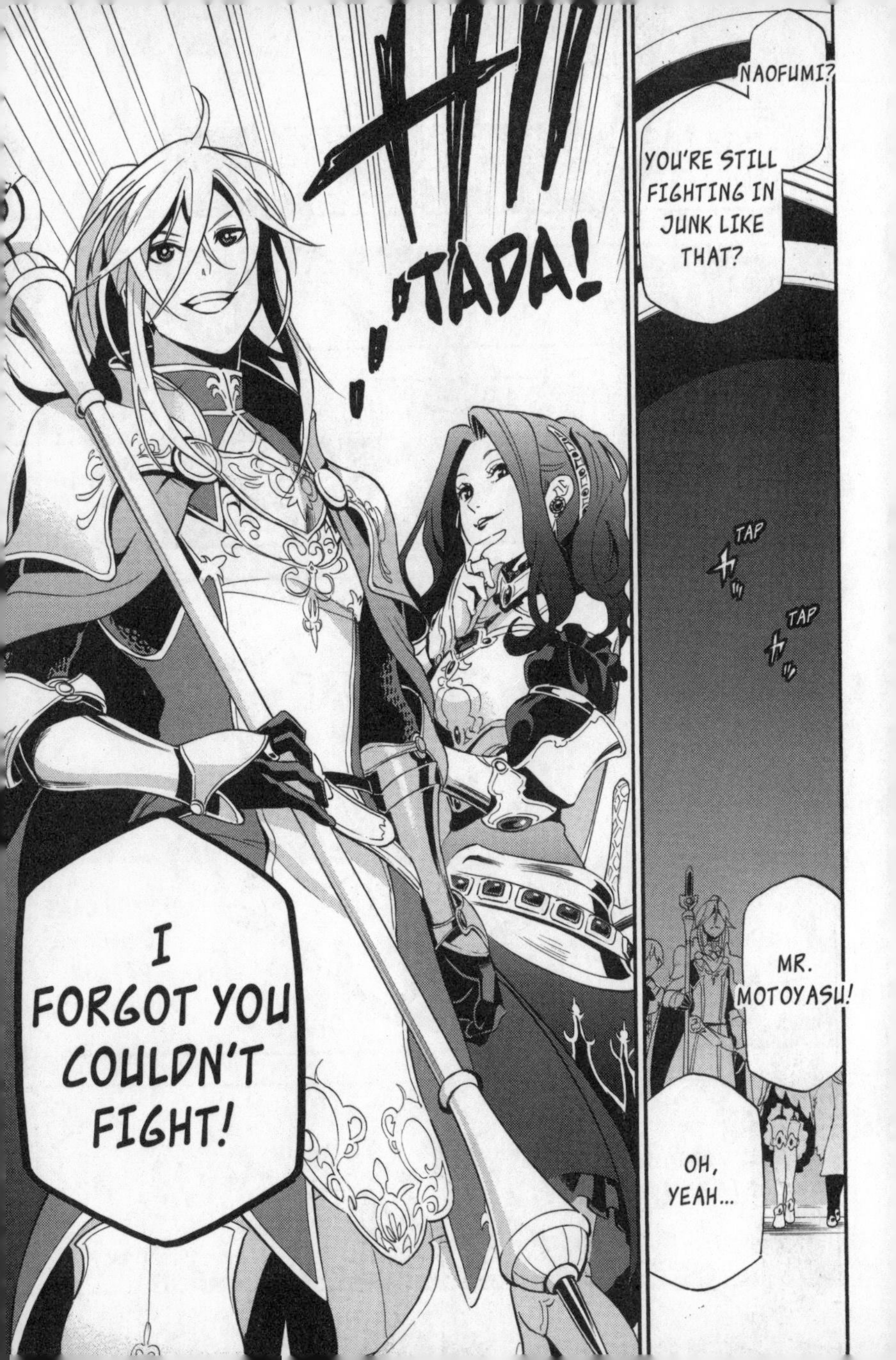
NAOFUMI?
YOU'RE STILL FIGHTING IN JUNK LIKE THAT?
TAP
TAP
MR. MOTOYASU!
OH, YEAH...
TADA!
I FORGOT YOU COULDN'T FIGHT!

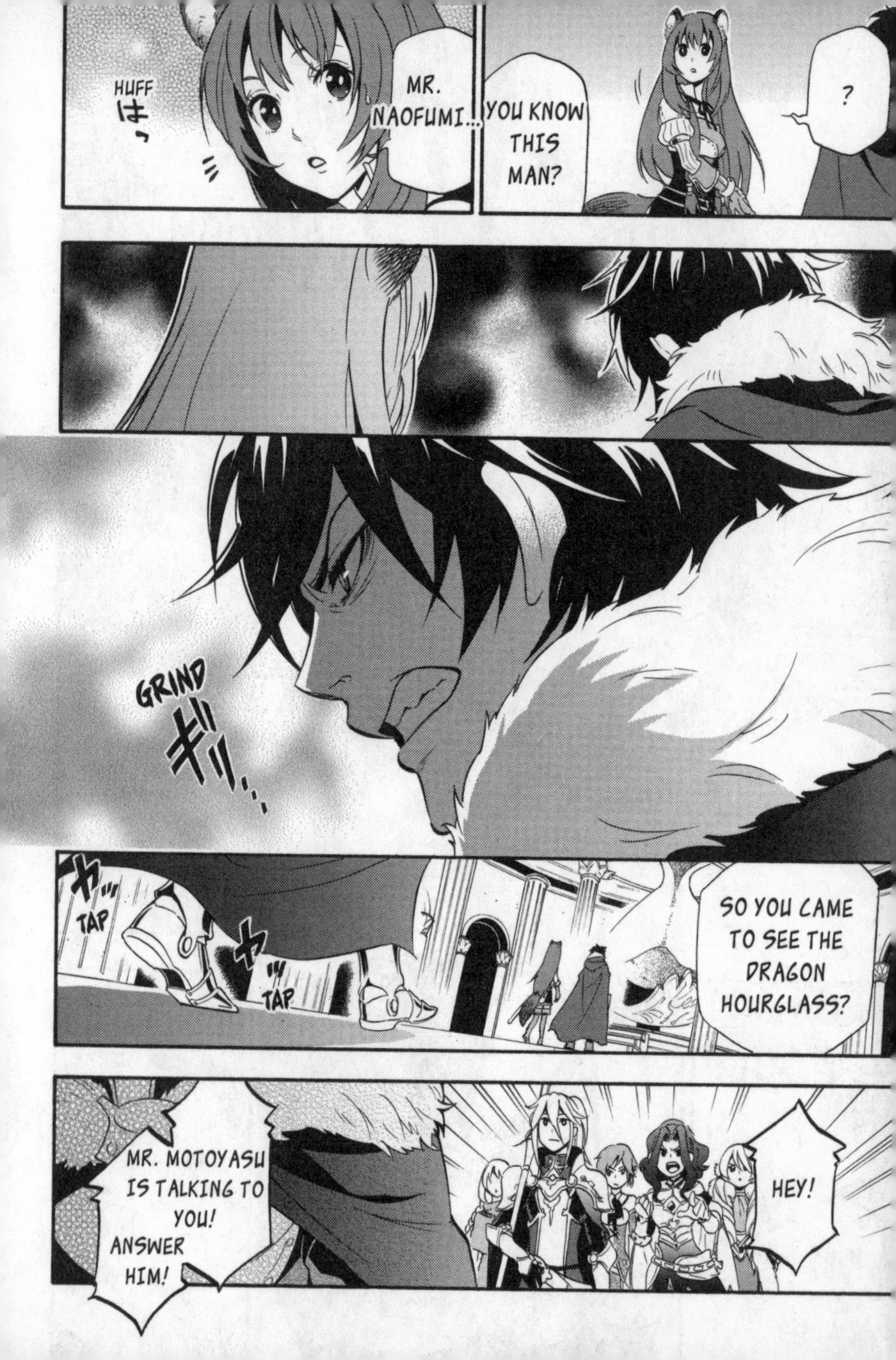
?
YOU KNOW THIS MAN?
MR. NAOFUMI...
HUFF
はっ
GRIND
ギリ...
SO YOU CAME TO SEE THE DRAGON HOURGLASS?
TAP
カッ
TAP
カッ
HEY!
MR. MOTOYASU IS TALKING TO YOU! ANSWER HIM!

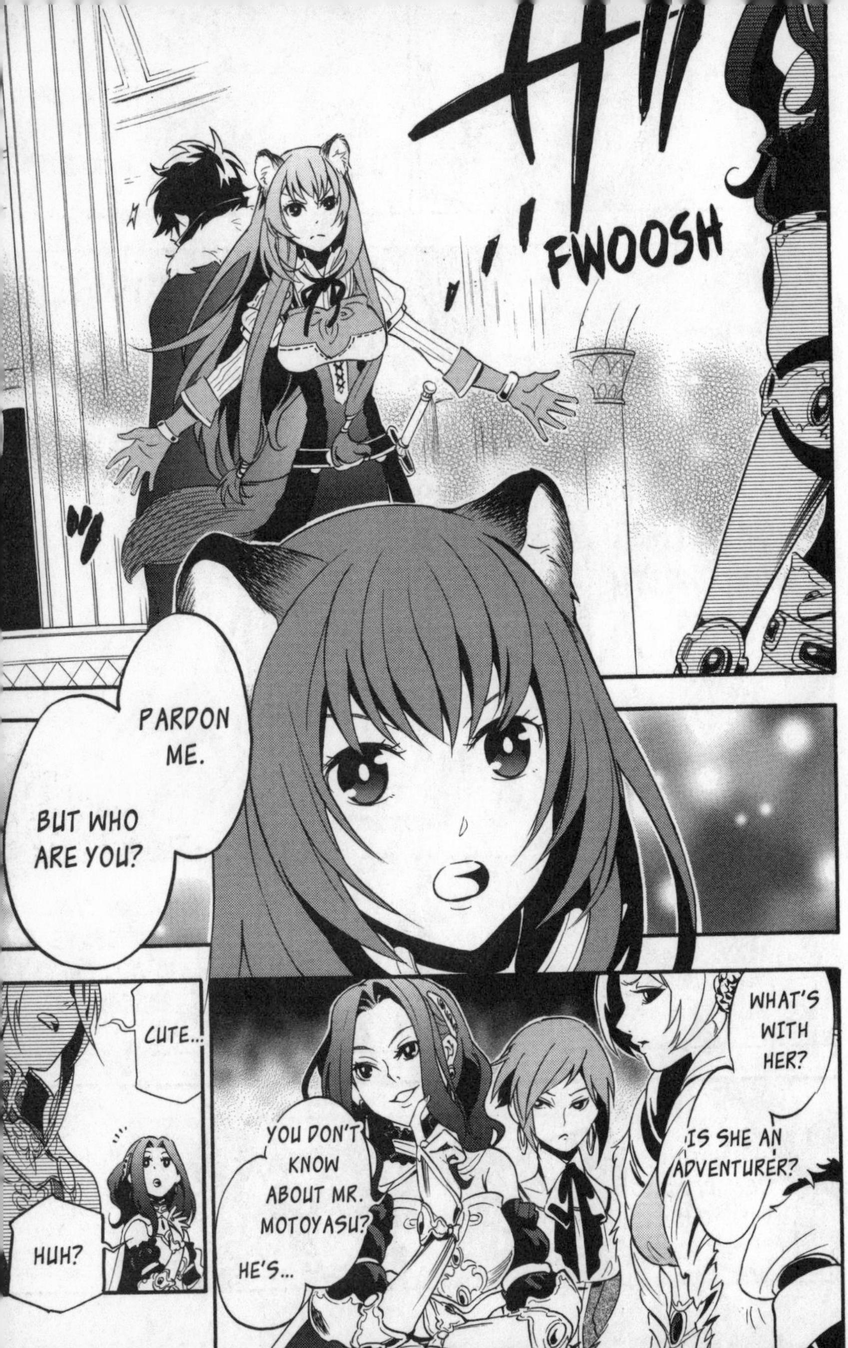
FWOOSH
PARDON ME.
BUT WHO ARE YOU?
WHAT'S WITH HER?
IS SHE AN ADVENTURER?
YOU DON'T KNOW ABOUT MR. MOTOYASU?
HE'S...
CUTE...
HUH?

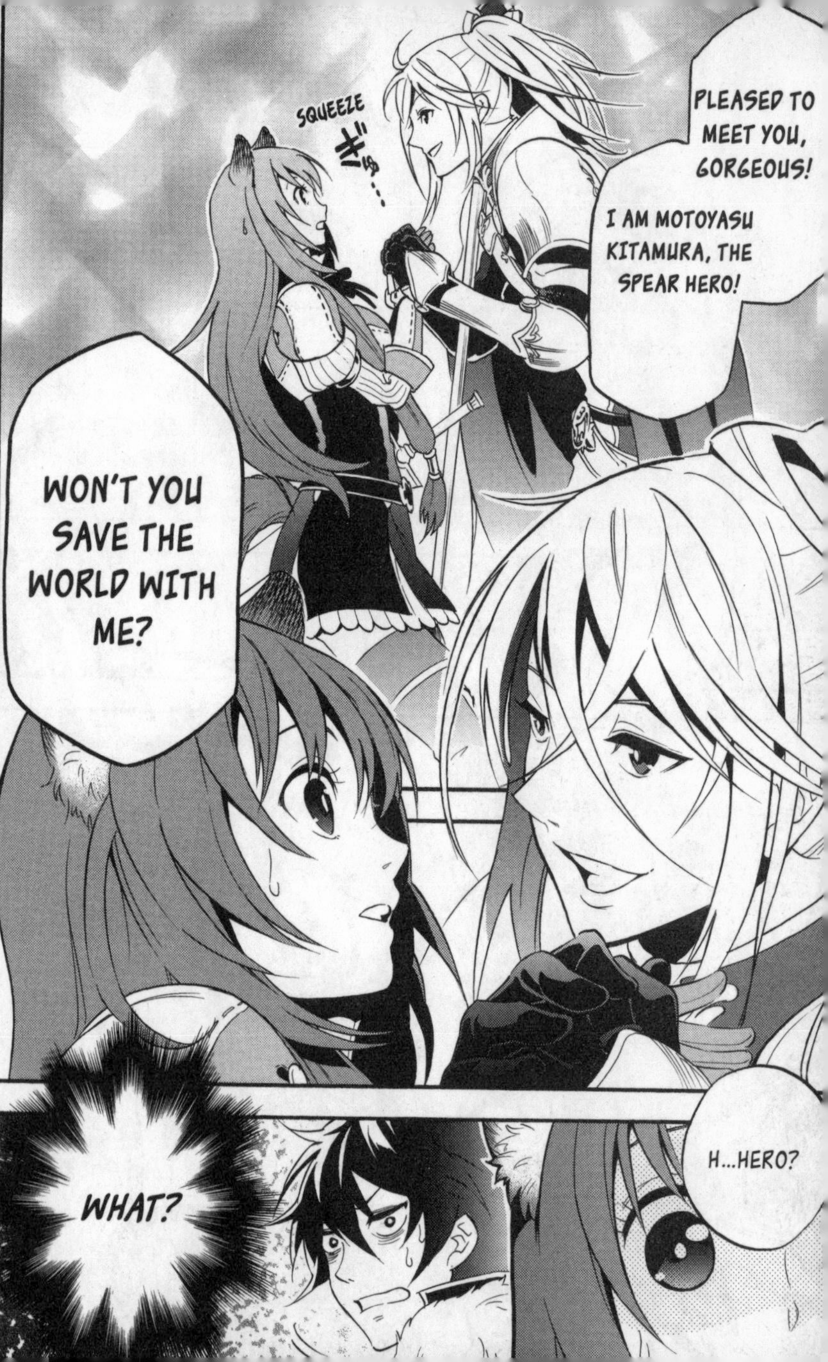
PLEASED TO MEET YOU, GORGEOUS!
I AM MOTOYASU KITAMURA, THE SPEAR HERO!
SQUEEZE
WON'T YOU SAVE THE WORLD WITH ME?
H...HERO?
WHAT?

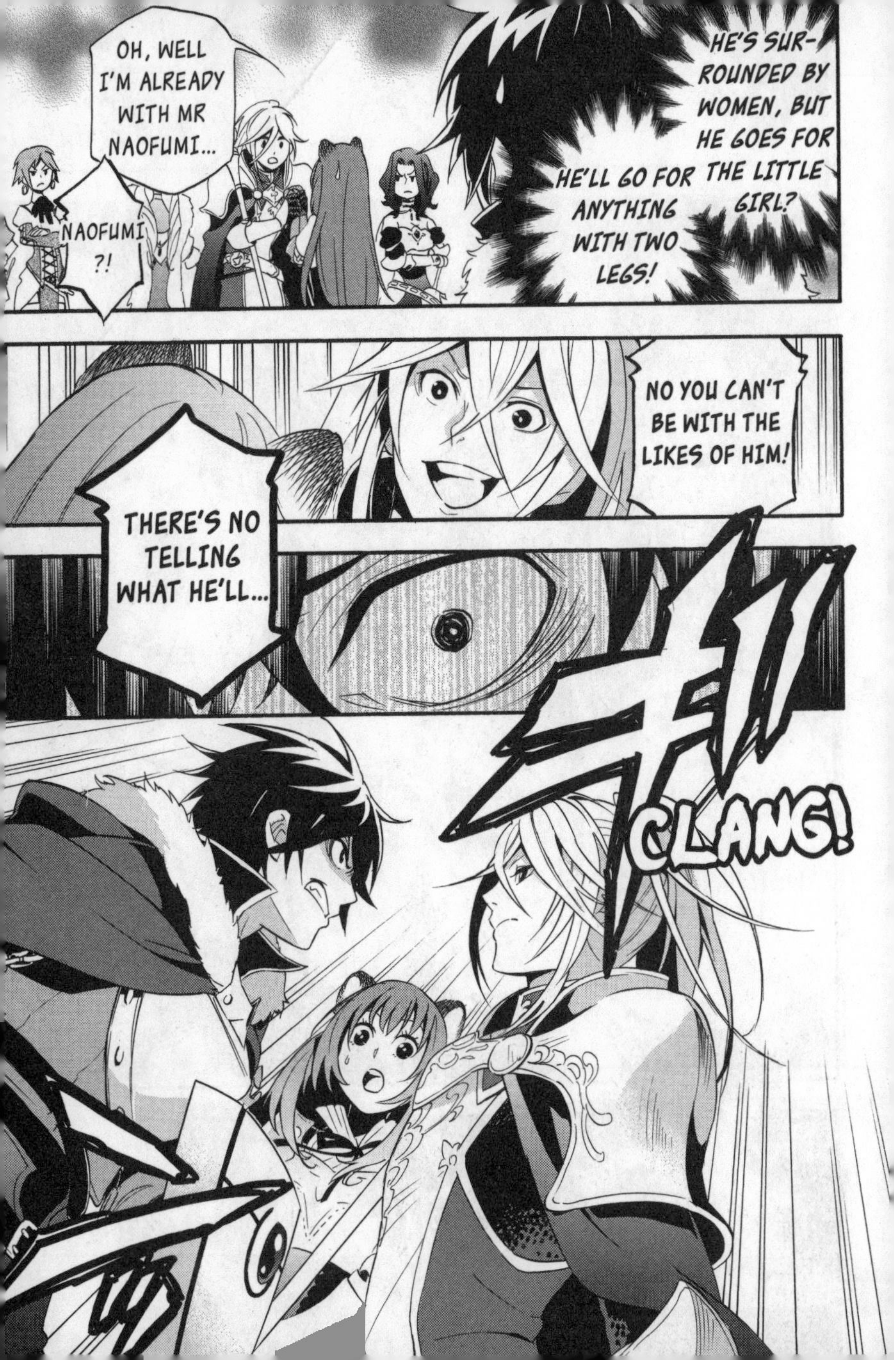
HE'S SURROUNDED BY WOMEN, BUT HE GOES FOR THE LITTLE GIRL?
HE'LL GO FOR ANYTHING WITH TWO LEGS!
OH, WELL I'M ALREADY WITH MR NAOFUMI...
NAOFUMI ?!
NO YOU CAN'T BE WITH THE LIKES OF HIM!
THERE'S NO TELLING WHAT HE'LL...
CLANG!

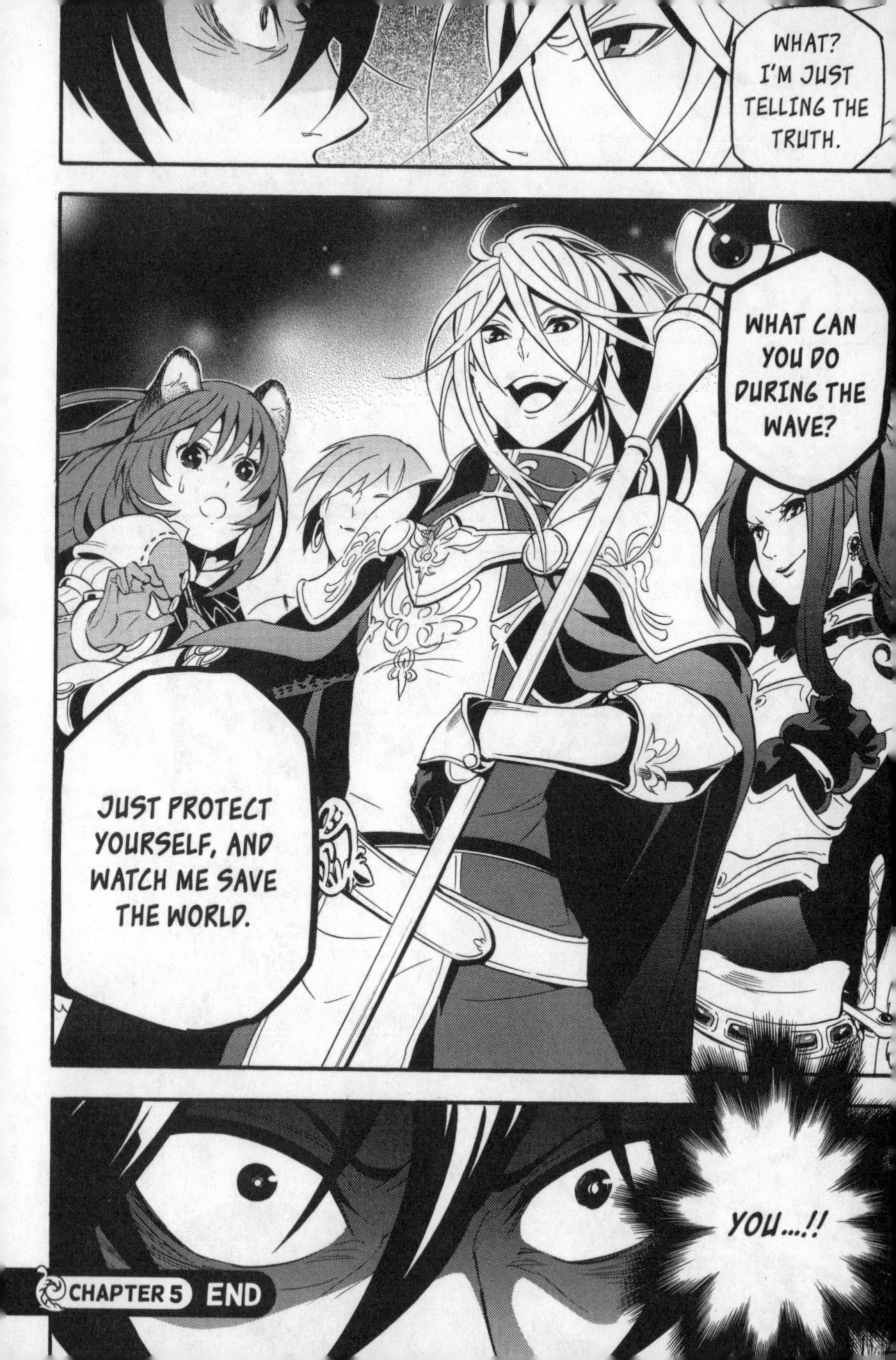

WHAT? I'M JUST TELLING THE TRUTH.
WHAT CAN YOU DO DURING THE WAVE?
JUST PROTECT YOURSELF, AND WATCH ME SAVE THE WORLD.
YOU...!!
CHAPTER 5 END

THE RISING OF 2 THE SHIELD HERO

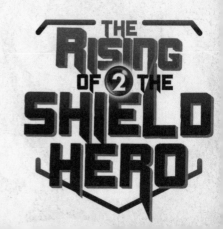

CHAPTER 6 THE WAVE OF DESTRUCTION

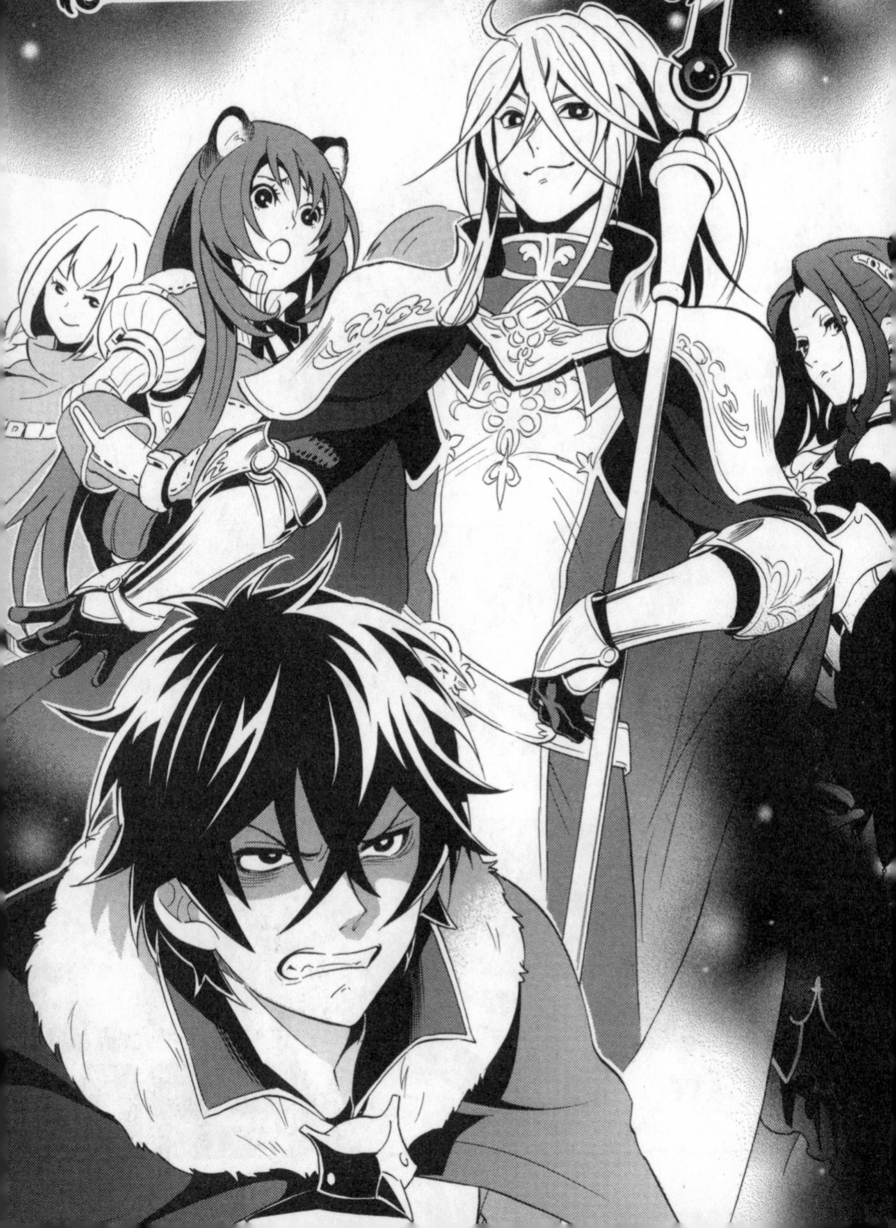

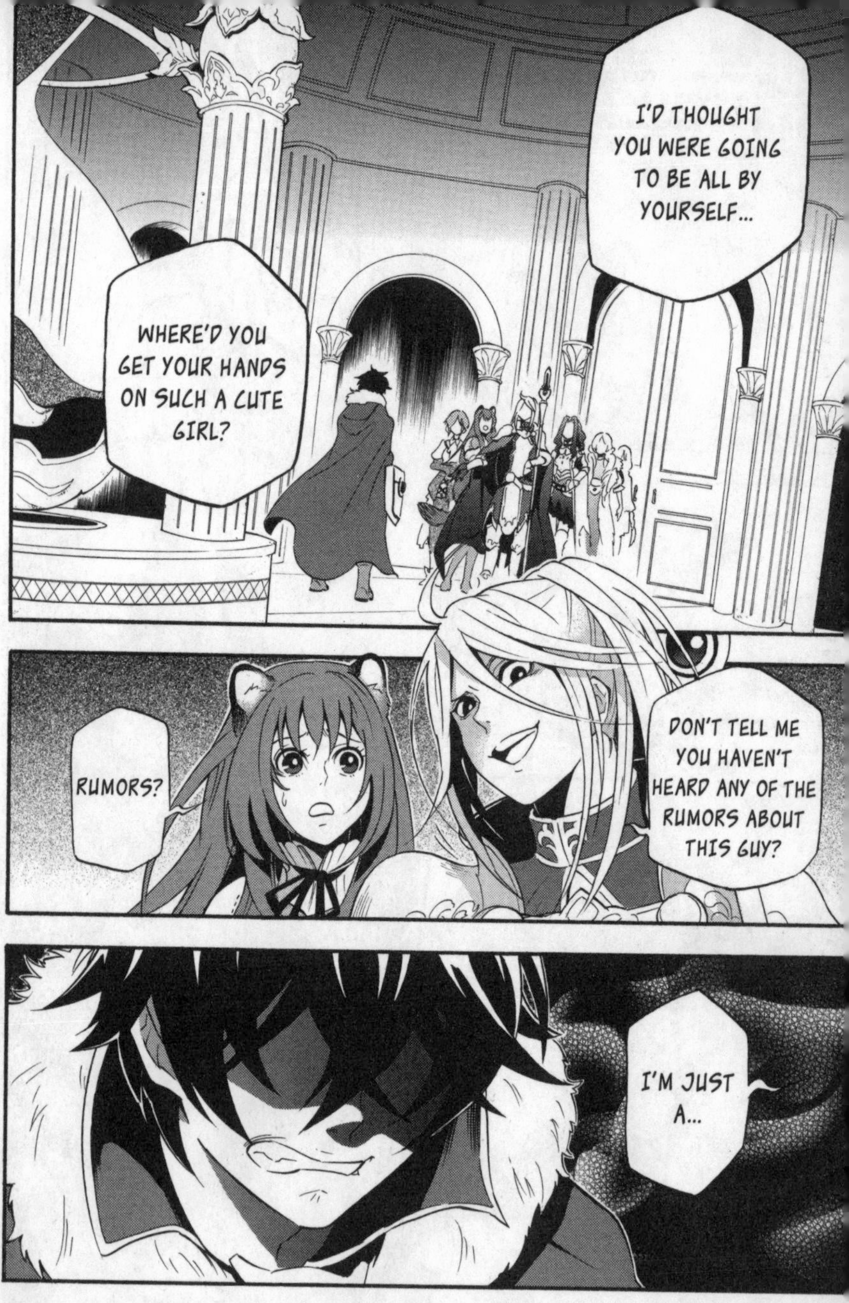
I'D THOUGHT YOU WERE GOING TO BE ALL BY YOURSELF...
WHERE'D YOU GET YOUR HANDS ON SUCH A CUTE GIRL?
DON'T TELL ME YOU HAVEN'T HEARD ANY OF THE RUMORS ABOUT THIS GUY?
RUMORS?
I'M JUST A...

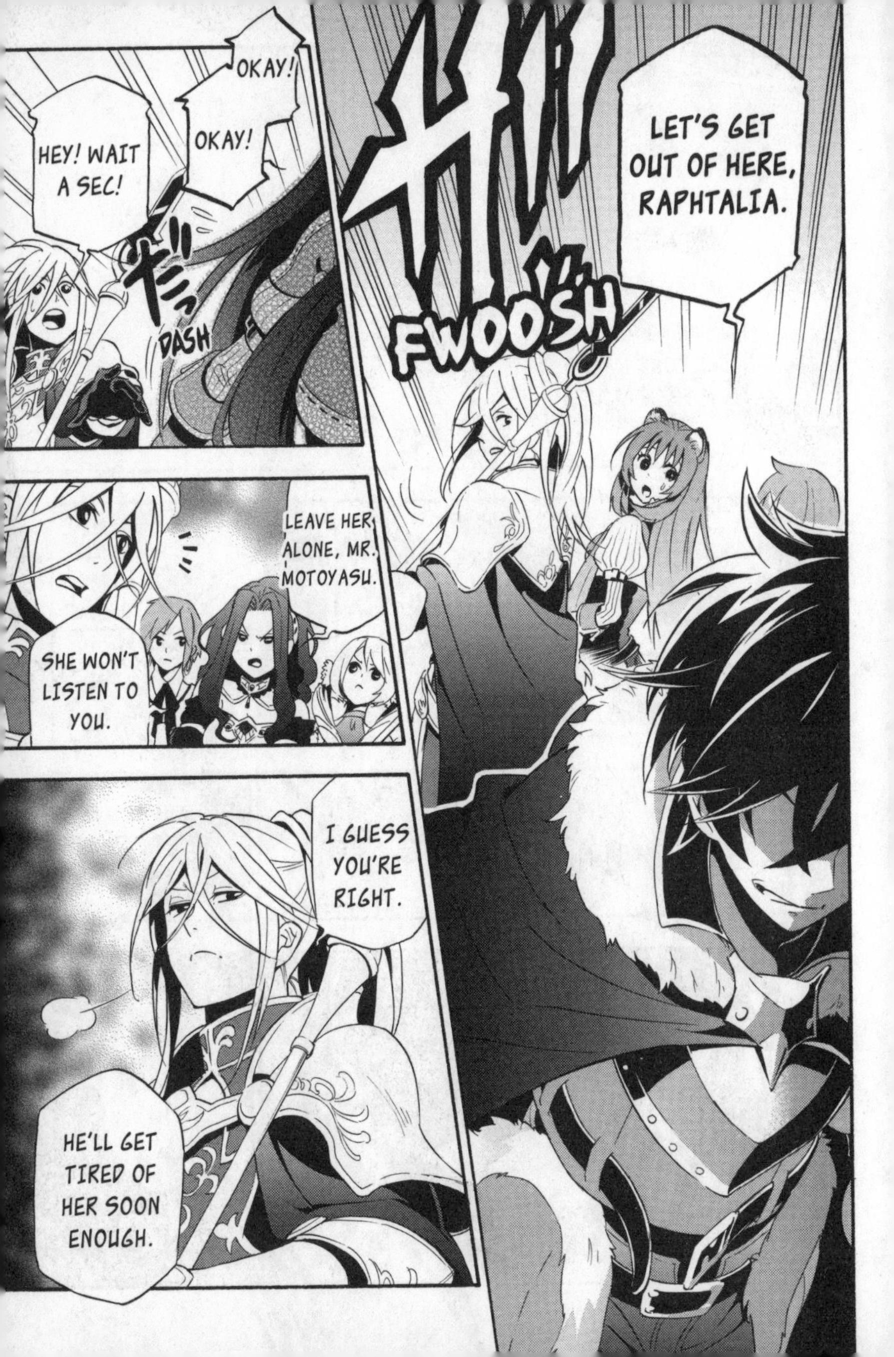
LET'S GET OUT OF HERE, RAPHTALIA.
FWOOSH
OKAY!
OKAY!
HEY! WAIT A SEC!
DASH
LEAVE HER ALONE, MR. MOTOYASU.
SHE WON'T LISTEN TO YOU.
I GUESS YOU'RE RIGHT.
HE'LL GET TIRED OF HER SOON ENOUGH.

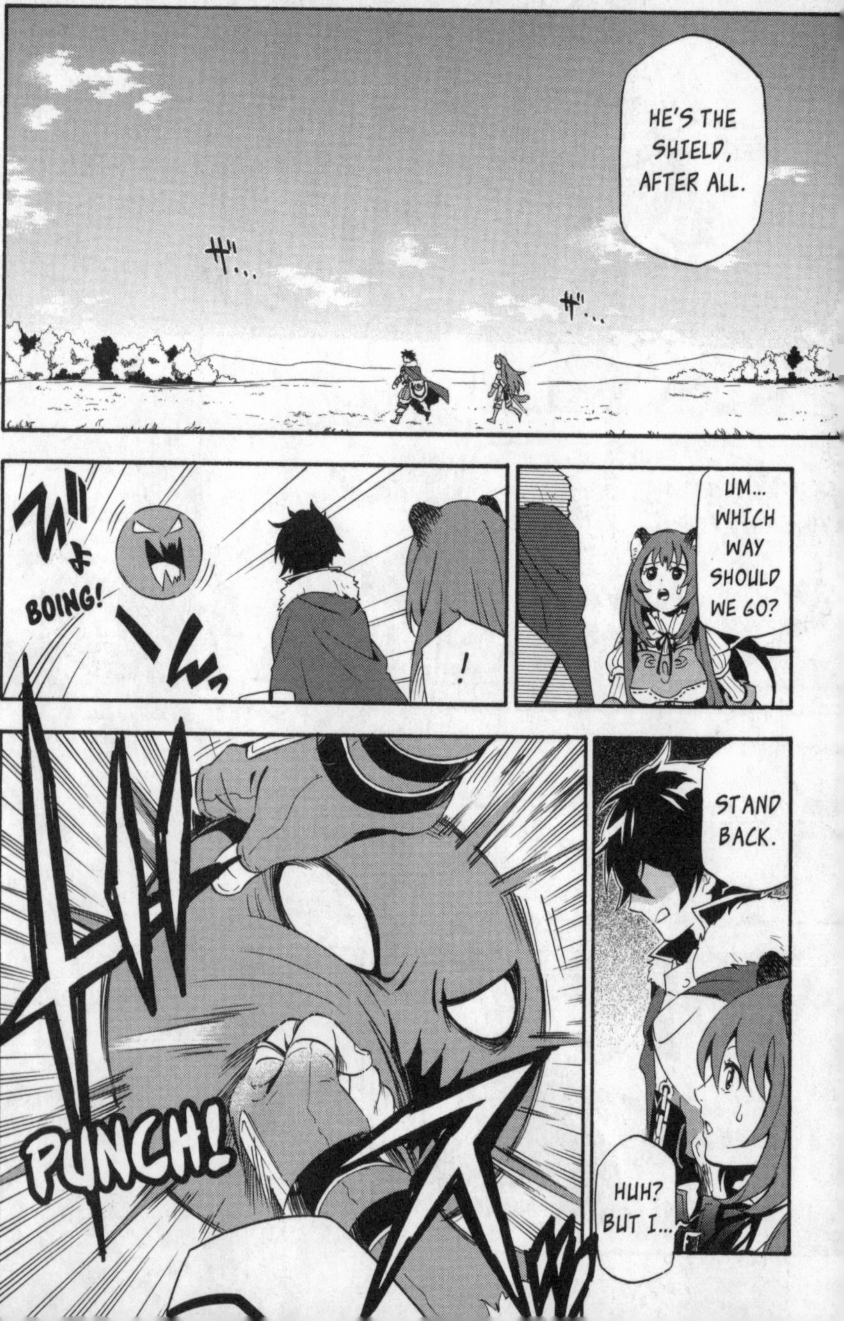
HE'S THE SHIELD, AFTER ALL.
UM... WHICH WAY SHOULD WE GO?
BOING!
!
STAND BACK.
HUH? BUT I...
PUNCH!

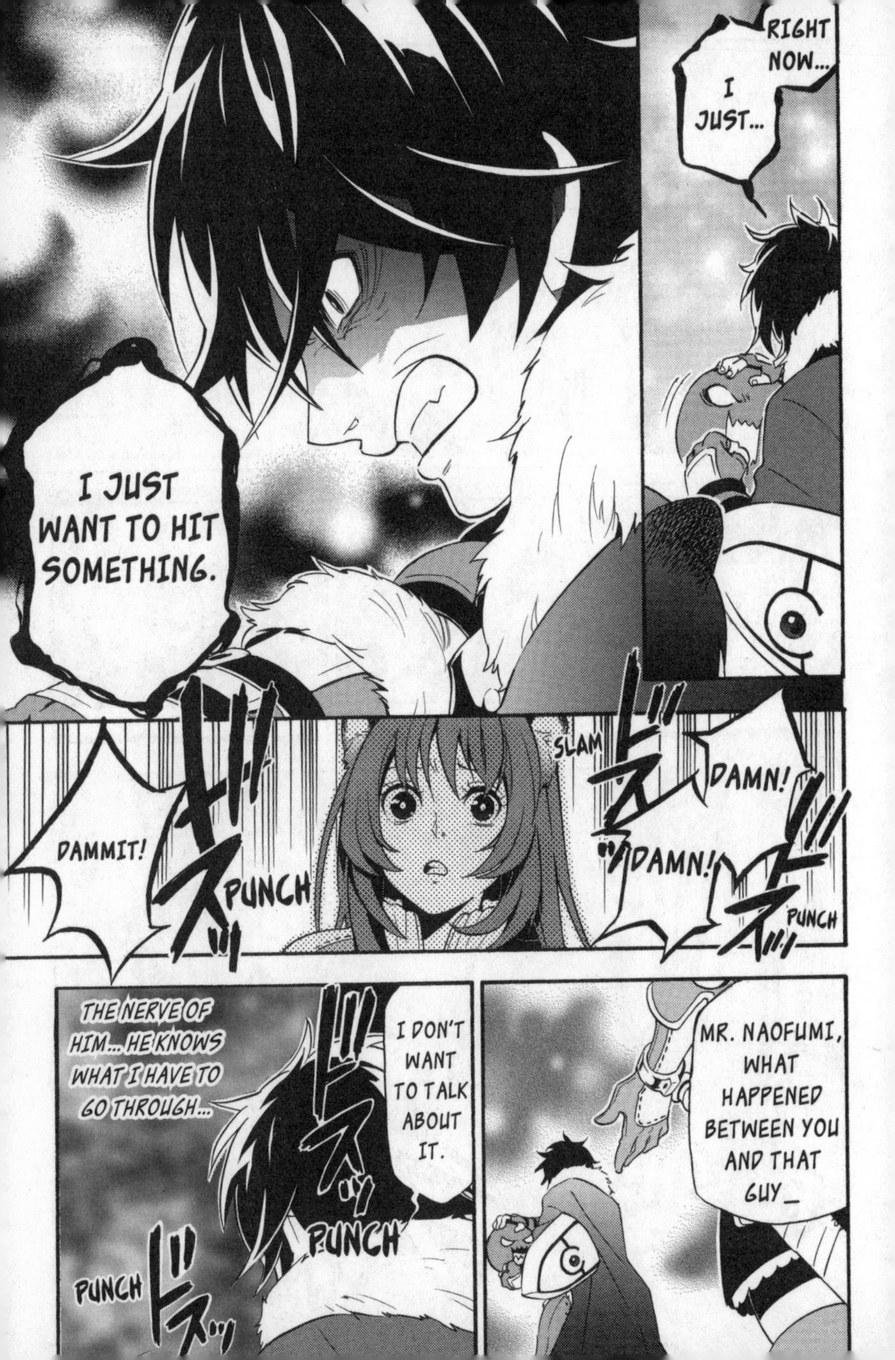
RIGHT NOW... I JUST...
I JUST WANT TO HIT SOMETHING.
DAMN!
DAMN!
PUNCH
SLAM
PUNCH
DAMMIT!
MR. NAOFUMI, WHAT HAPPENED BETWEEN YOU AND THAT GUY_
I DON'T WANT TO TALK ABOUT IT.
THE NERVE OF HIM... HE KNOWS WHAT I HAVE TO GO THROUGH...
PUNCH
PUNCH

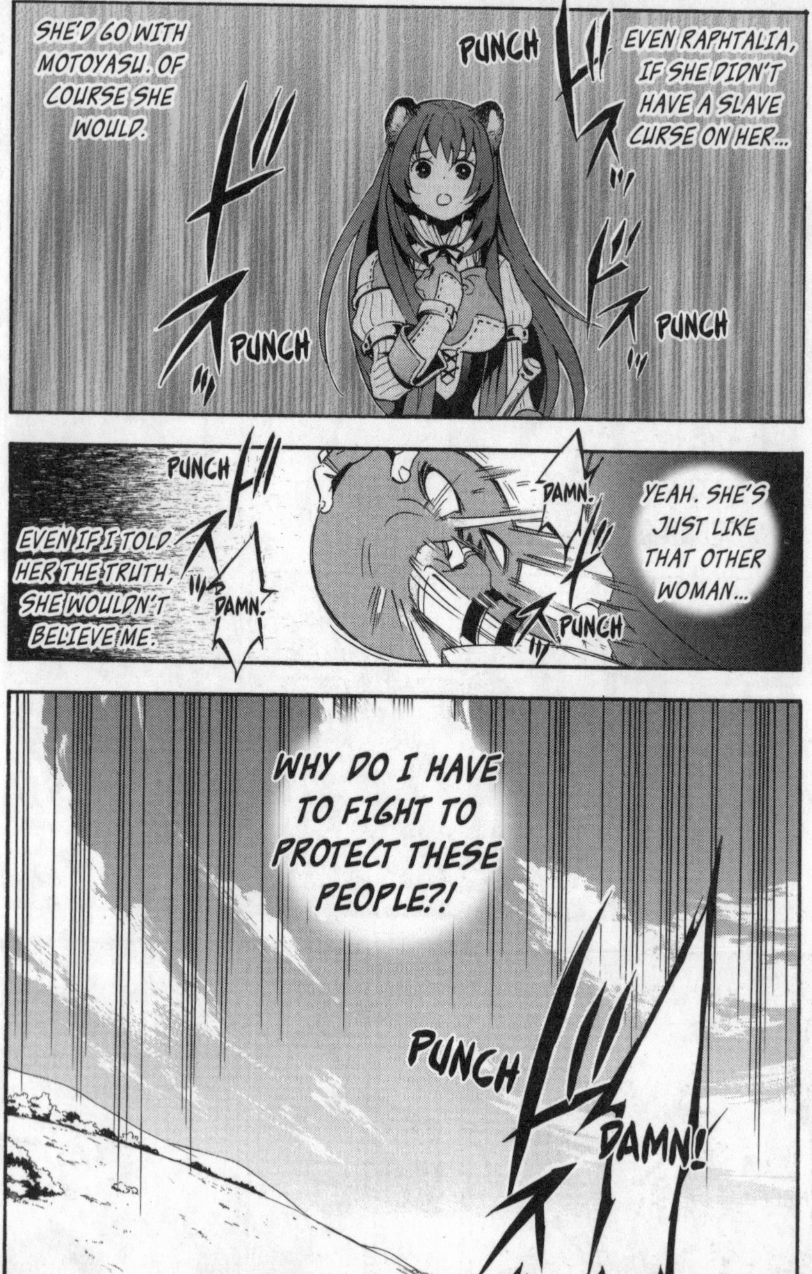
EVEN RAPHTALIA, IF SHE DIDN'T HAVE A SLAVE CURSE ON HER...
PUNCH
SHE'D GO WITH MOTOYASU. OF COURSE SHE WOULD.
PUNCH
PUNCH
YEAH. SHE'S JUST LIKE THAT OTHER WOMAN...
DAMN.
PUNCH
PUNCH
EVEN IF I TOLD HER THE TRUTH, SHE WOULDN'T BELIEVE ME.
DAMN.
WHY DO I HAVE TO FIGHT TO PROTECT THESE PEOPLE?!
PUNCH
DAMN!

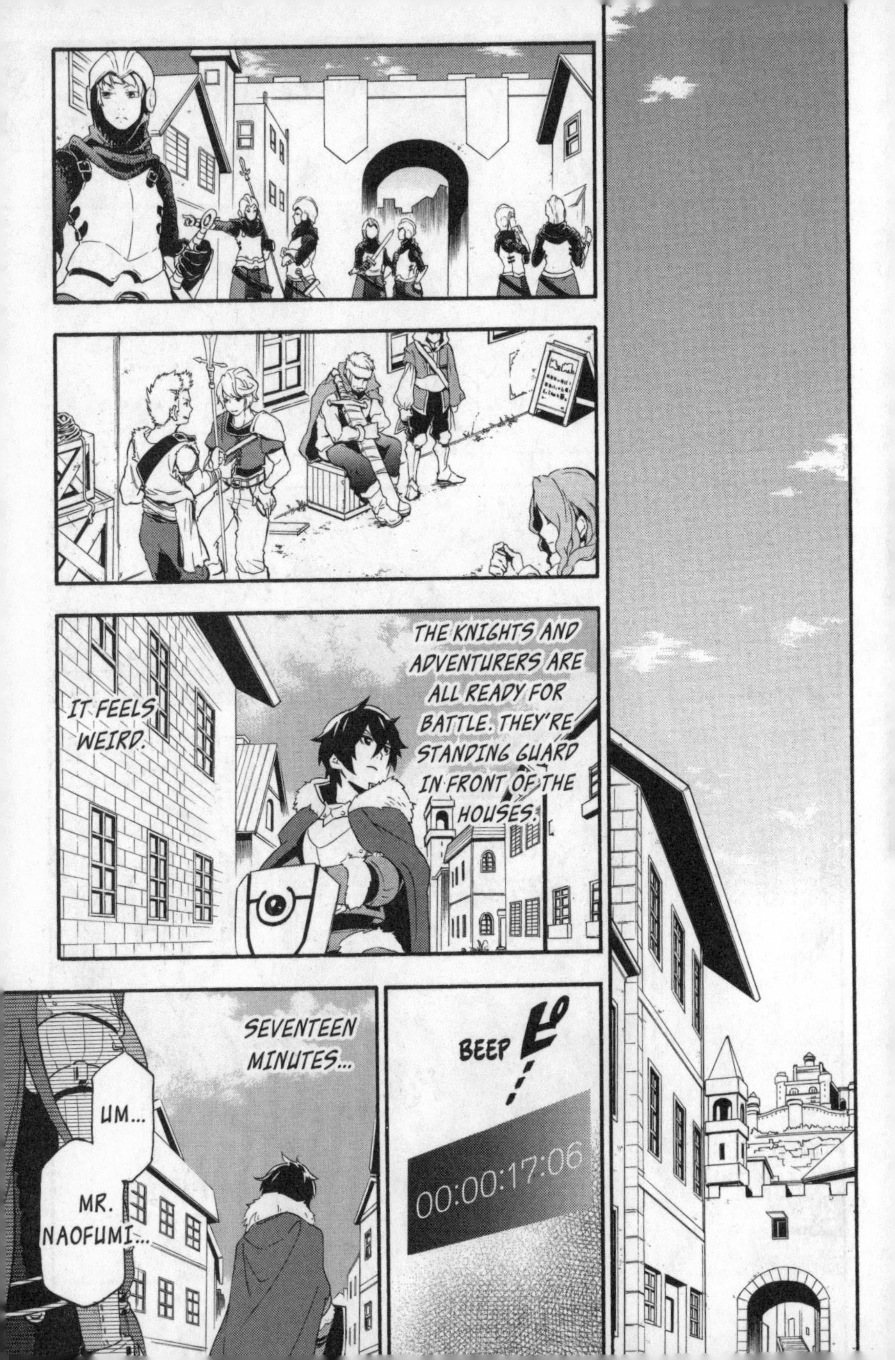
THE KNIGHTS AND ADVENTURERS ARE ALL READY FOR BATTLE. THEY'RE STANDING GUARD IN FRONT OF THE HOUSES.
IT FEELS WEIRD.
BEEP
ピ
00:00:17:06
SEVENTEEN MINUTES...
UM...
MR. NAOFUMI...

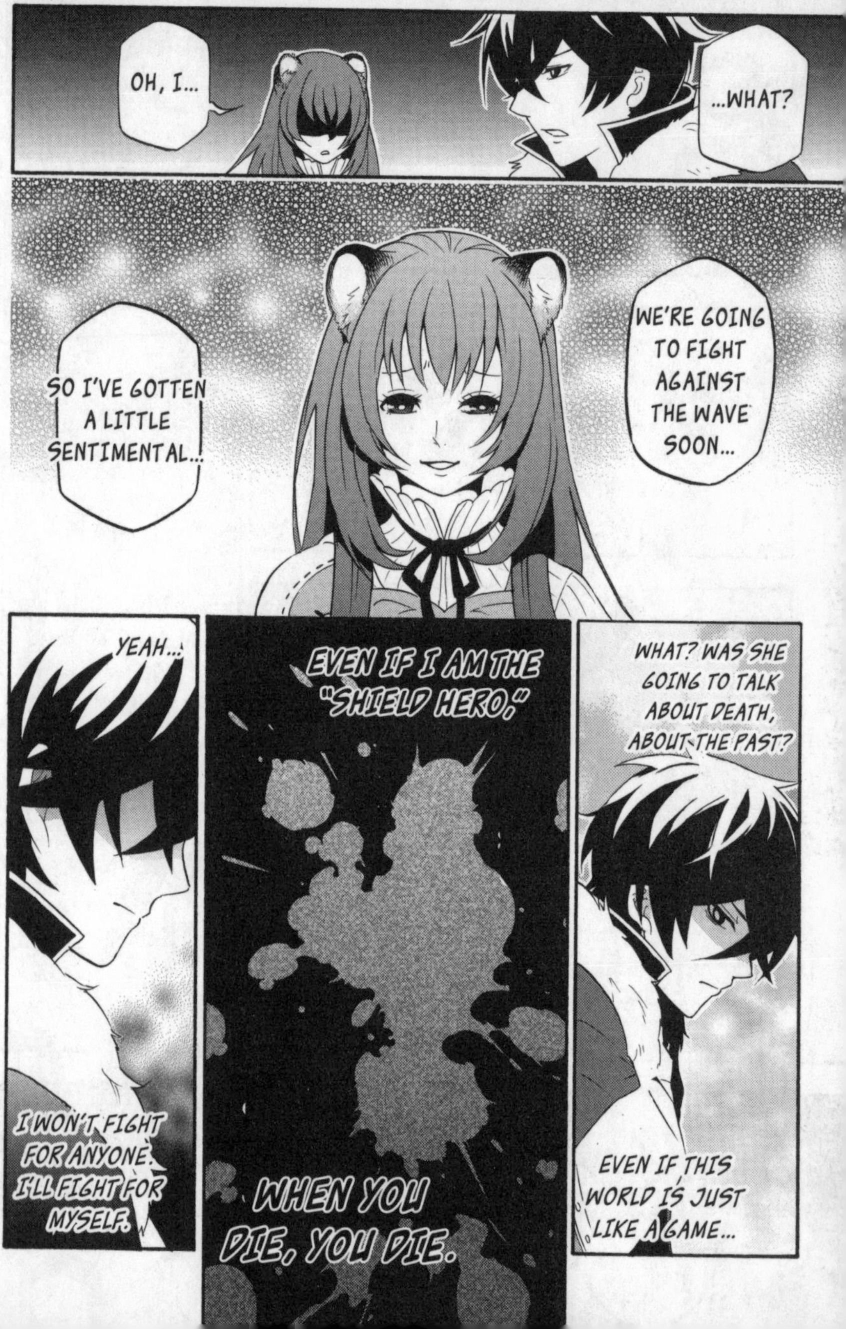
...WHAT?
OH, I...
WE'RE GOING TO FIGHT AGAINST THE WAVE SOON...
SO I'VE GOTTEN A LITTLE SENTIMENTAL...
WHAT? WAS SHE GOING TO TALK ABOUT DEATH, ABOUT THE PAST?
EVEN IF THIS WORLD IS JUST LIKE A GAME...
EVEN IF I AM THE "SHIELD HERO,"
WHEN YOU DIE, YOU DIE.
YEAH...
I WON'T FIGHT FOR ANYONE. I'LL FIGHT FOR MYSELF.

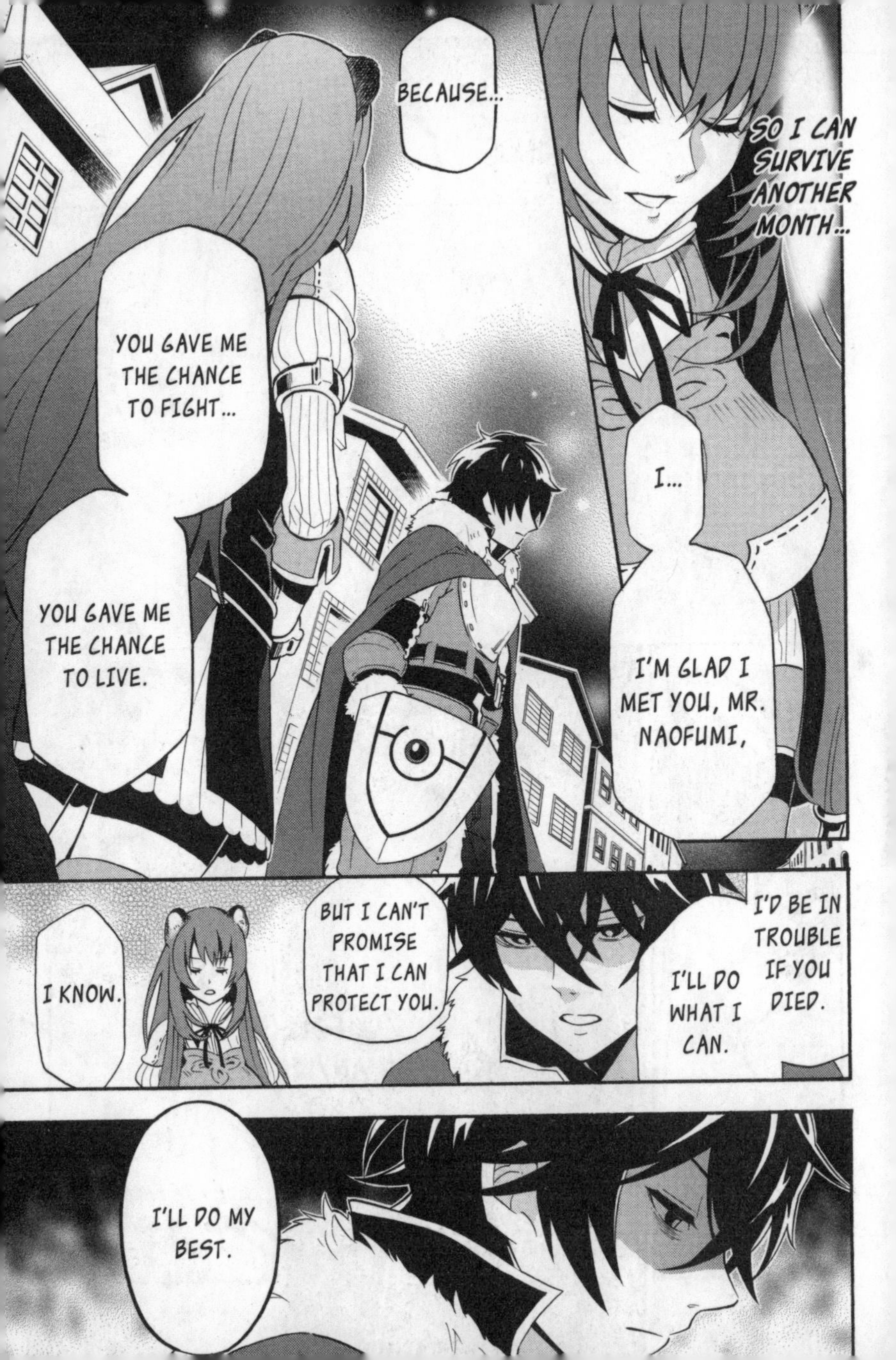
SO I CAN SURVIVE ANOTHER MONTH...
I...
I'M GLAD I MET YOU, MR. NAOFUMI,
BECAUSE...
YOU GAVE ME THE CHANCE TO FIGHT...
YOU GAVE ME THE CHANCE TO LIVE.
I'D BE IN TROUBLE IF YOU DIED.
I'LL DO WHAT I CAN.
BUT I CAN'T PROMISE THAT I CAN PROTECT YOU.
I KNOW.
I'LL DO MY BEST.

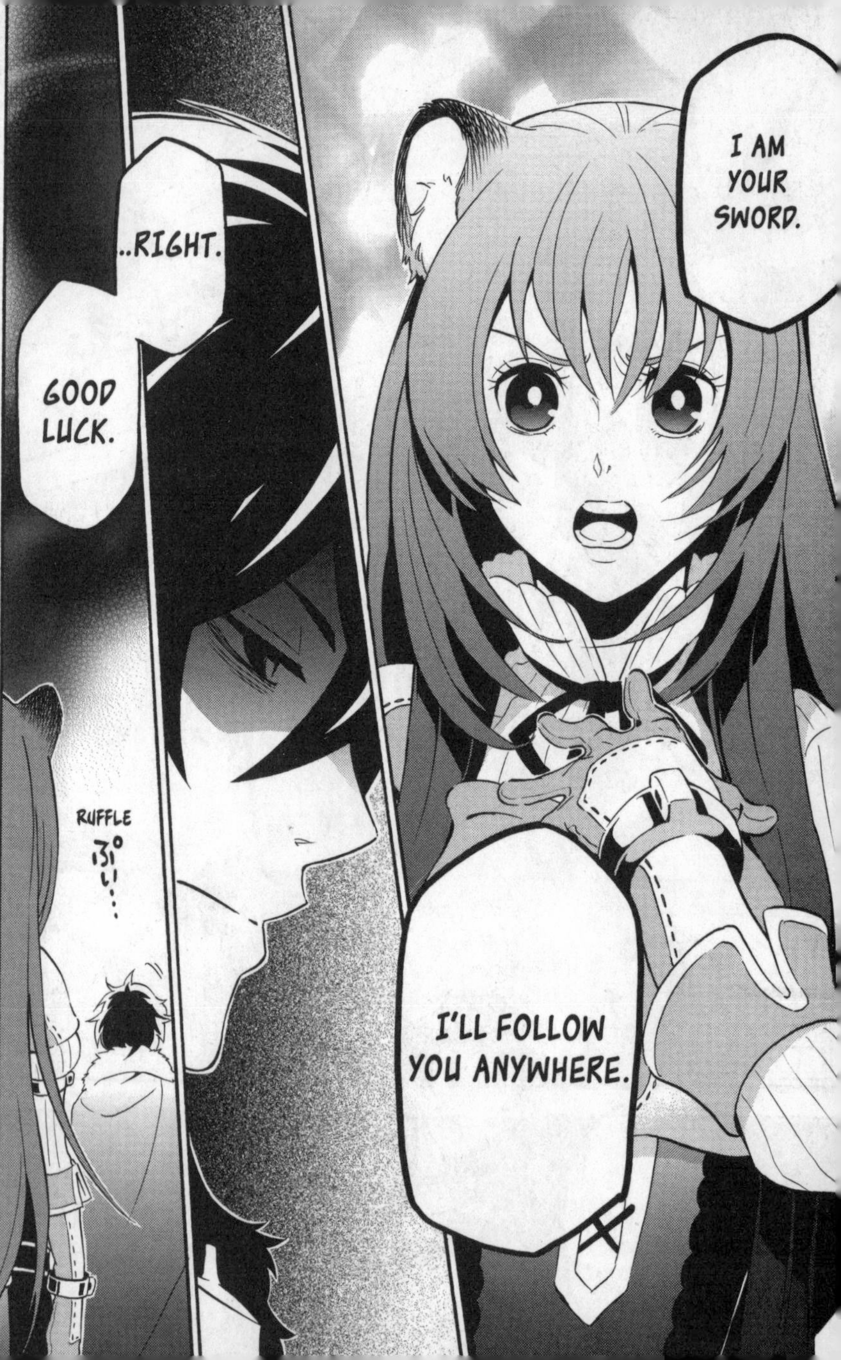
I AM YOUR SWORD.
I'LL FOLLOW YOU ANYWHERE.
..RIGHT.
GOOD LUCK.
RUFFLE

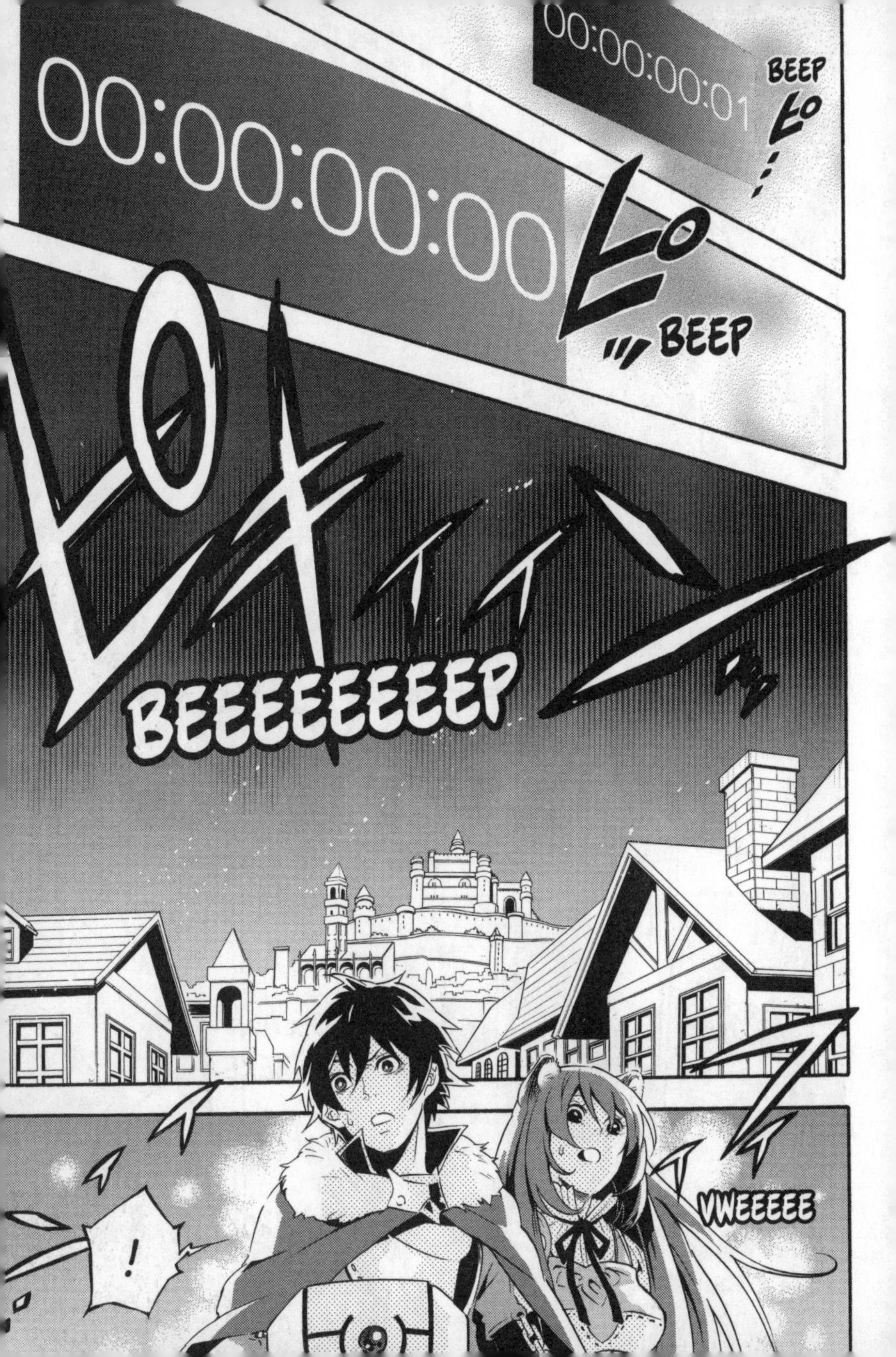

00:00:00:01
BEEP
ピ…
00:00:00:00
ピ
BEEP
BEEEEEEEEEP
VWEEEEE
!

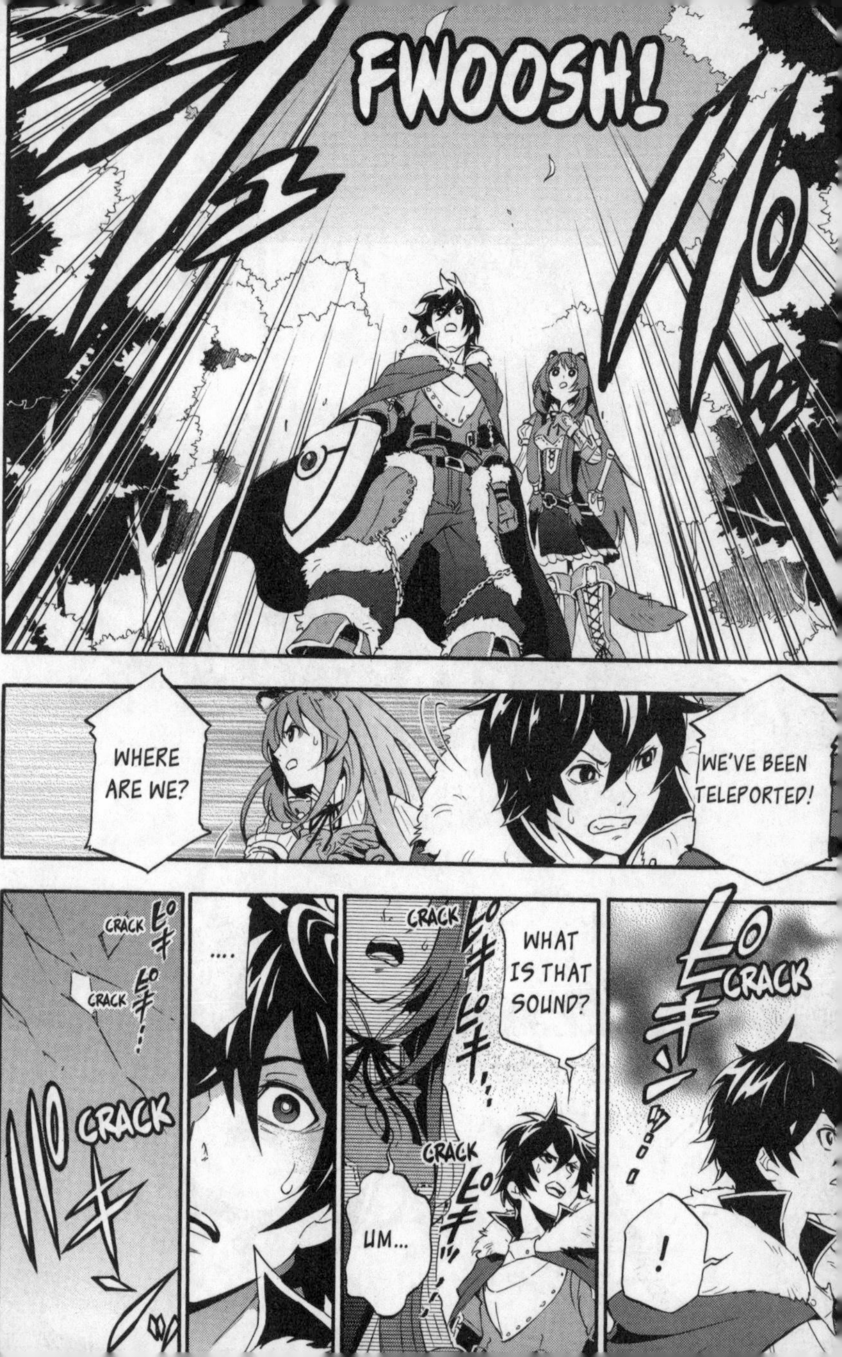
FWOOSH!
WE'VE BEEN TELEPORTED!
WHERE ARE WE?
CRACK
!
WHAT IS THAT SOUND?
CRACK
CRACK
UM...
....
CRACK
CRACK
CRACK

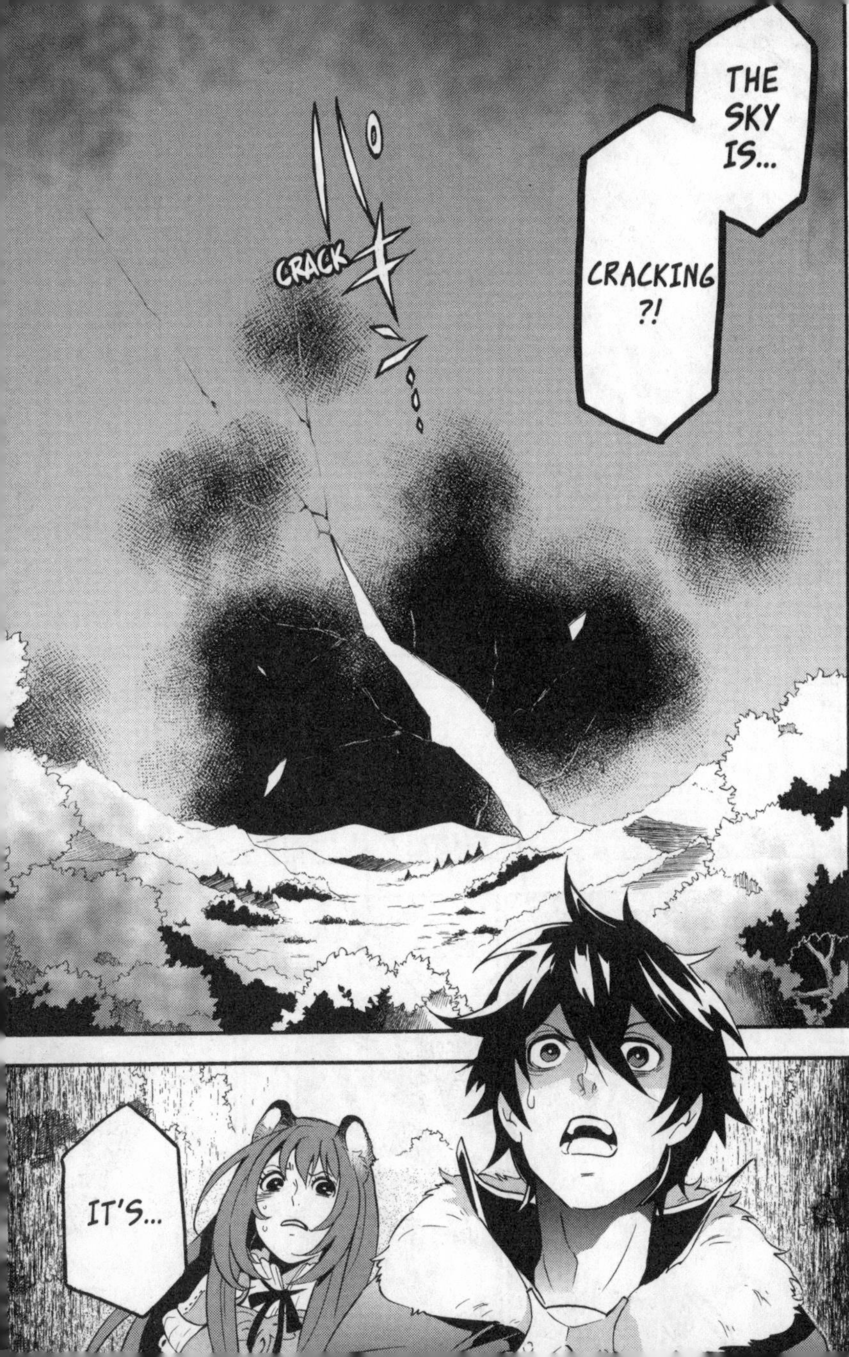
THE SKY IS...
CRACKING ?!
CRACK
IT'S...

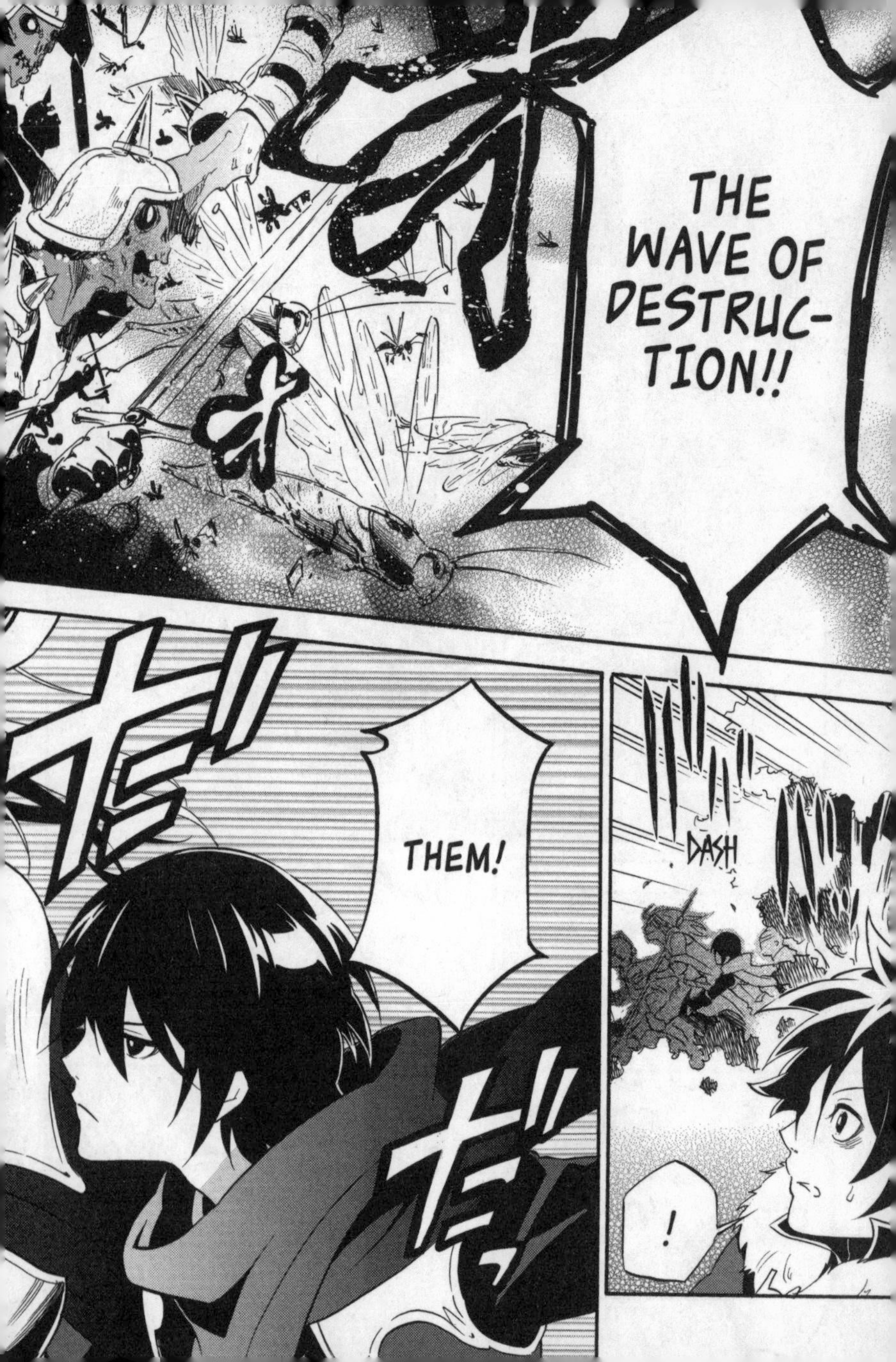
THE WAVE OF DESTRUC-TION!!
DASH
!
THEM!

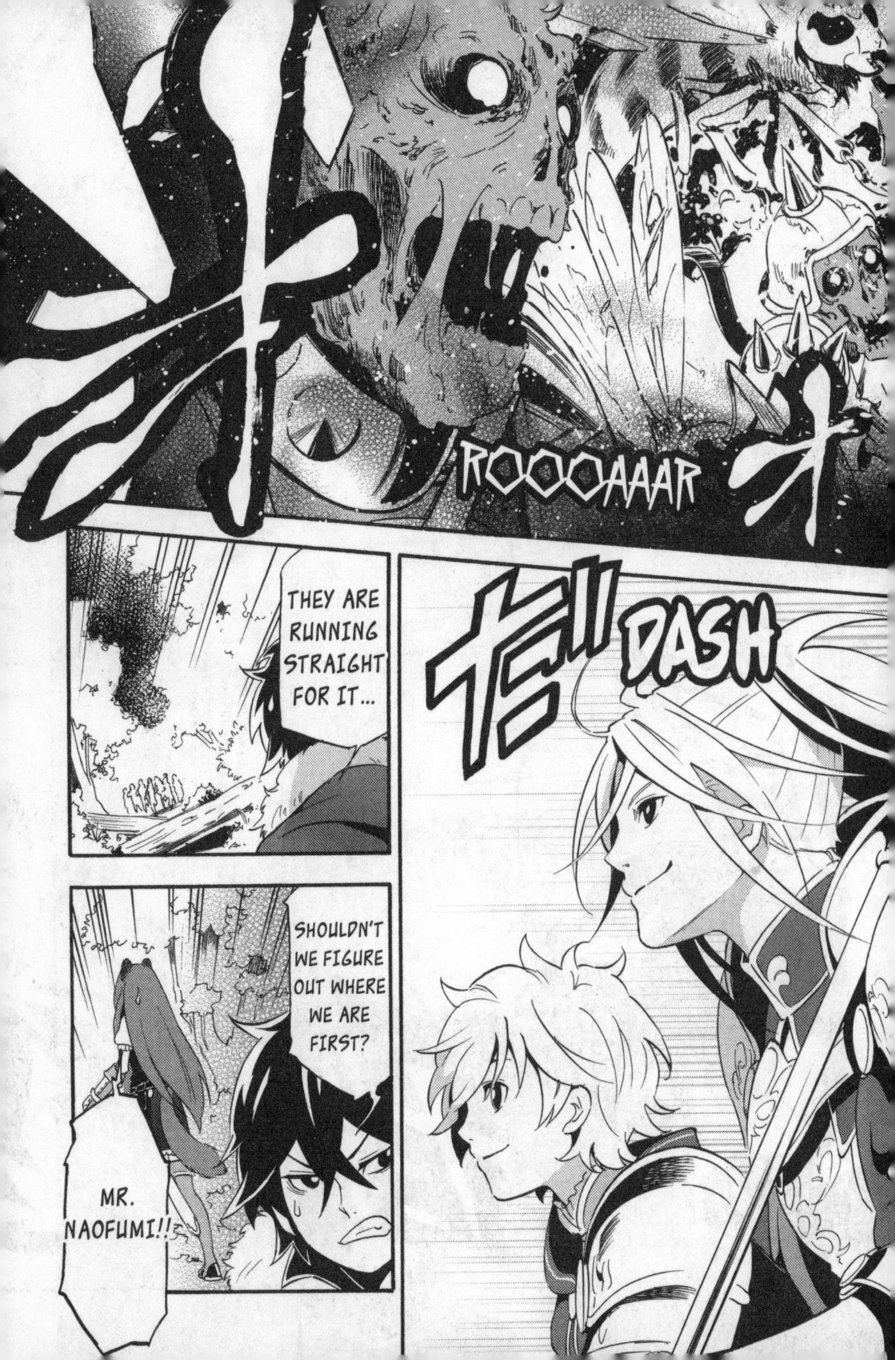
ROOOAAAR
DASH
THEY ARE RUNNING STRAIGHT FOR IT...
SHOULDN'T WE FIGURE OUT WHERE WE ARE FIRST?
MR. NAOFUMI!!

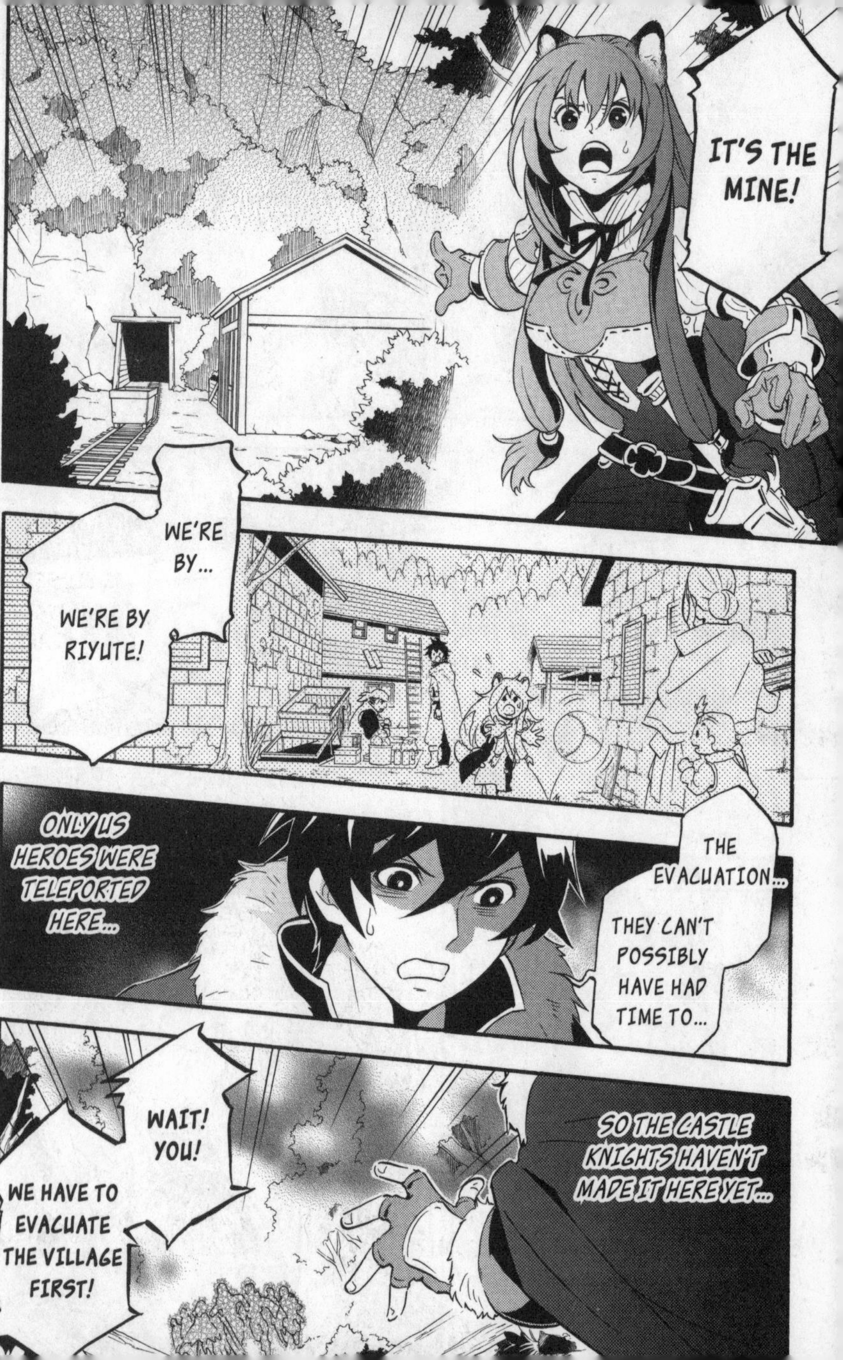
IT'S THE MINE!
WE'RE BY...
WE'RE BY RIYUTE!
THE EVACUATION...
THEY CAN'T POSSIBLY HAVE HAD TIME TO...
ONLY US HEROES WERE TELEPORTED HERE...
SO THE CASTLE KNIGHTS HAVEN'T MADE IT HERE YET...
WAIT! YOU!
WE HAVE TO EVACUATE THE VILLAGE FIRST!

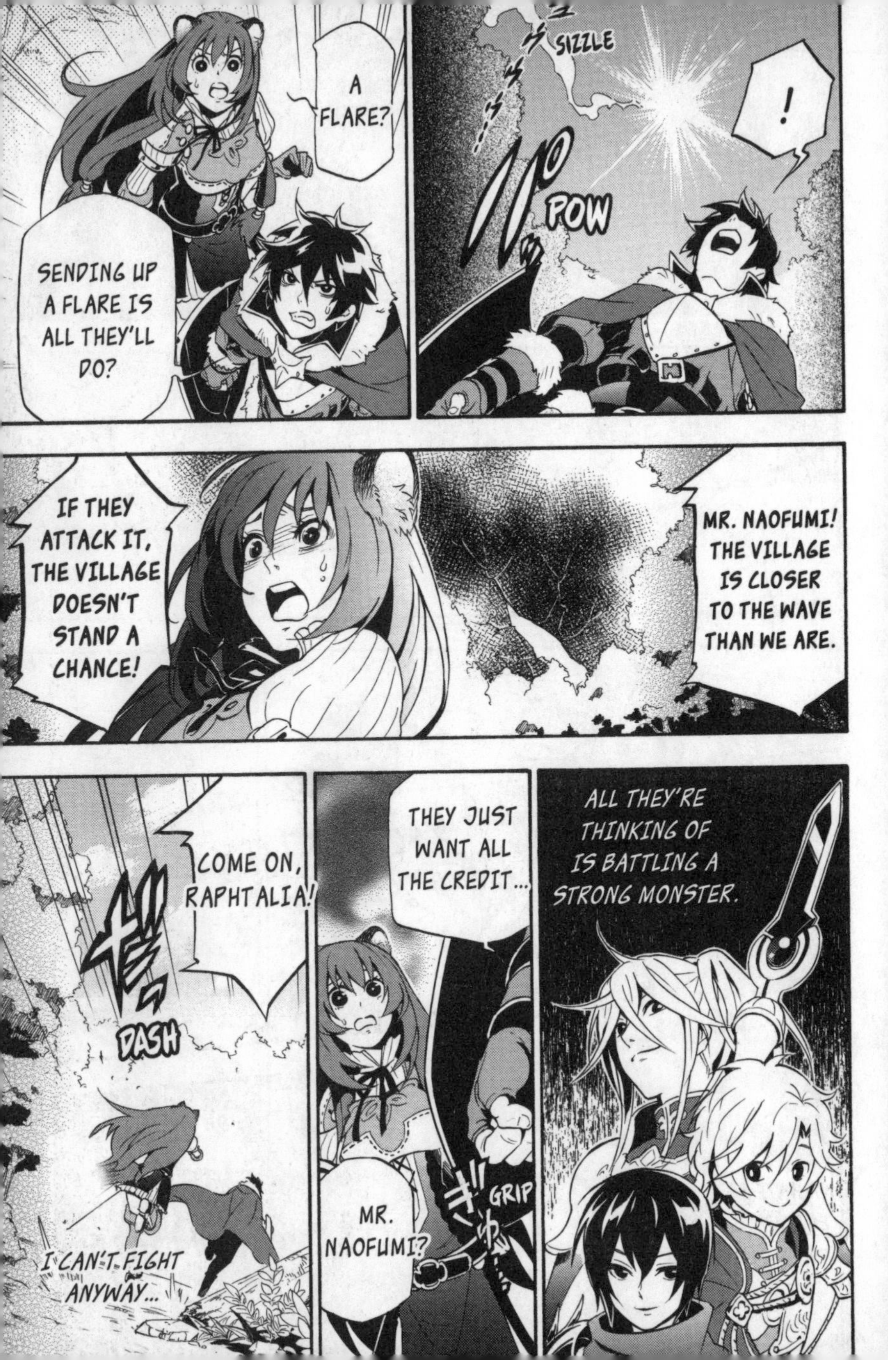
SIZZLE
POW
!
A FLARE?
SENDING UP A FLARE IS ALL THEY'LL DO?
MR. NAOFUMI! THE VILLAGE IS CLOSER TO THE WAVE THAN WE ARE.
IF THEY ATTACK IT, THE VILLAGE DOESN'T STAND A CHANCE!
ALL THEY'RE THINKING OF IS BATTLING A STRONG MONSTER.
THEY JUST WANT ALL THE CREDIT...
GRIP
MR. NAOFUMI?
COME ON, RAPHTALIA!
DASH
I CAN'T FIGHT ANYWAY...

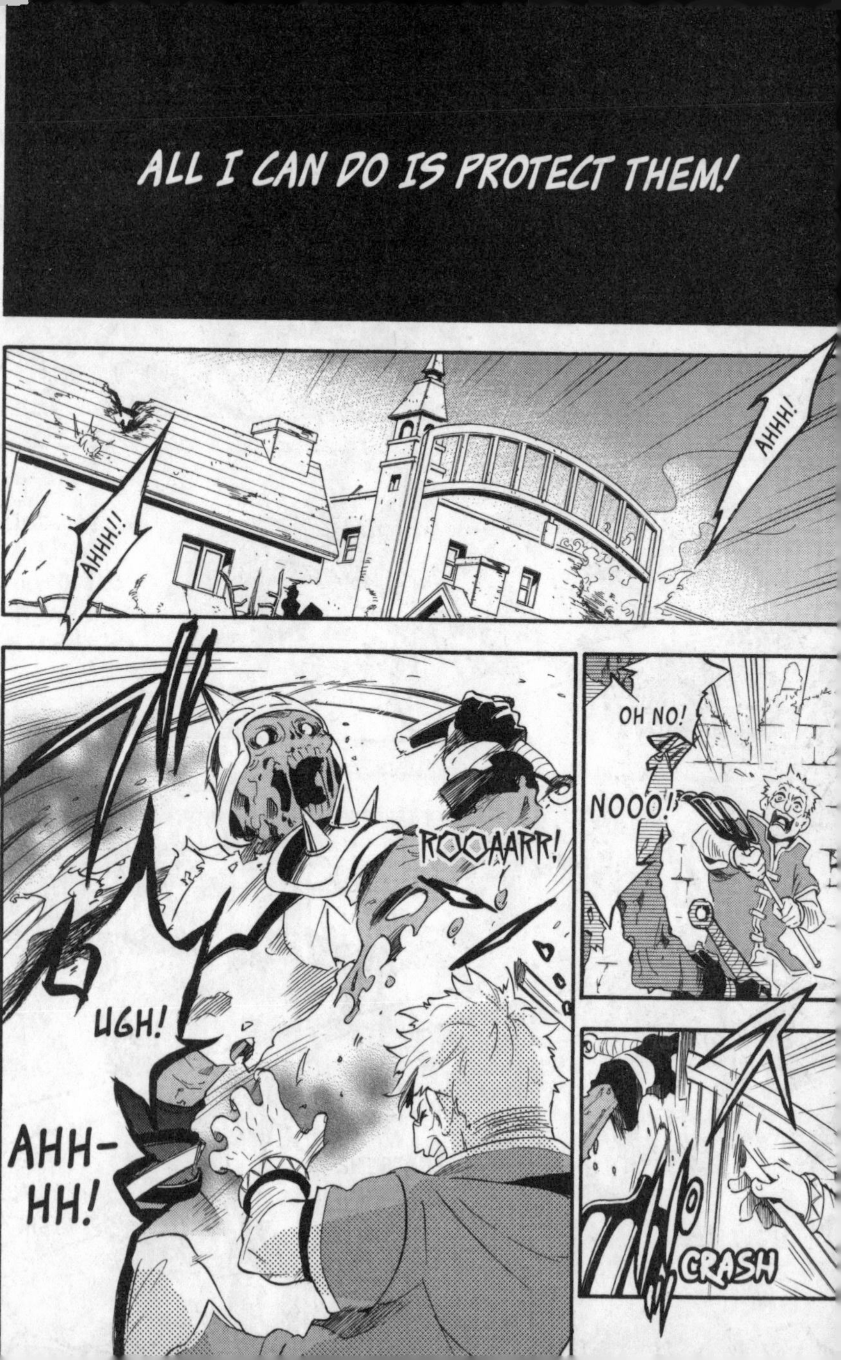
ALL I CAN DO IS PROTECT THEM!
AHHH!
AHHH!!
OH NO!
NOOO!
CRASH
ROOAARR!
UGH!
AHH-
HH!

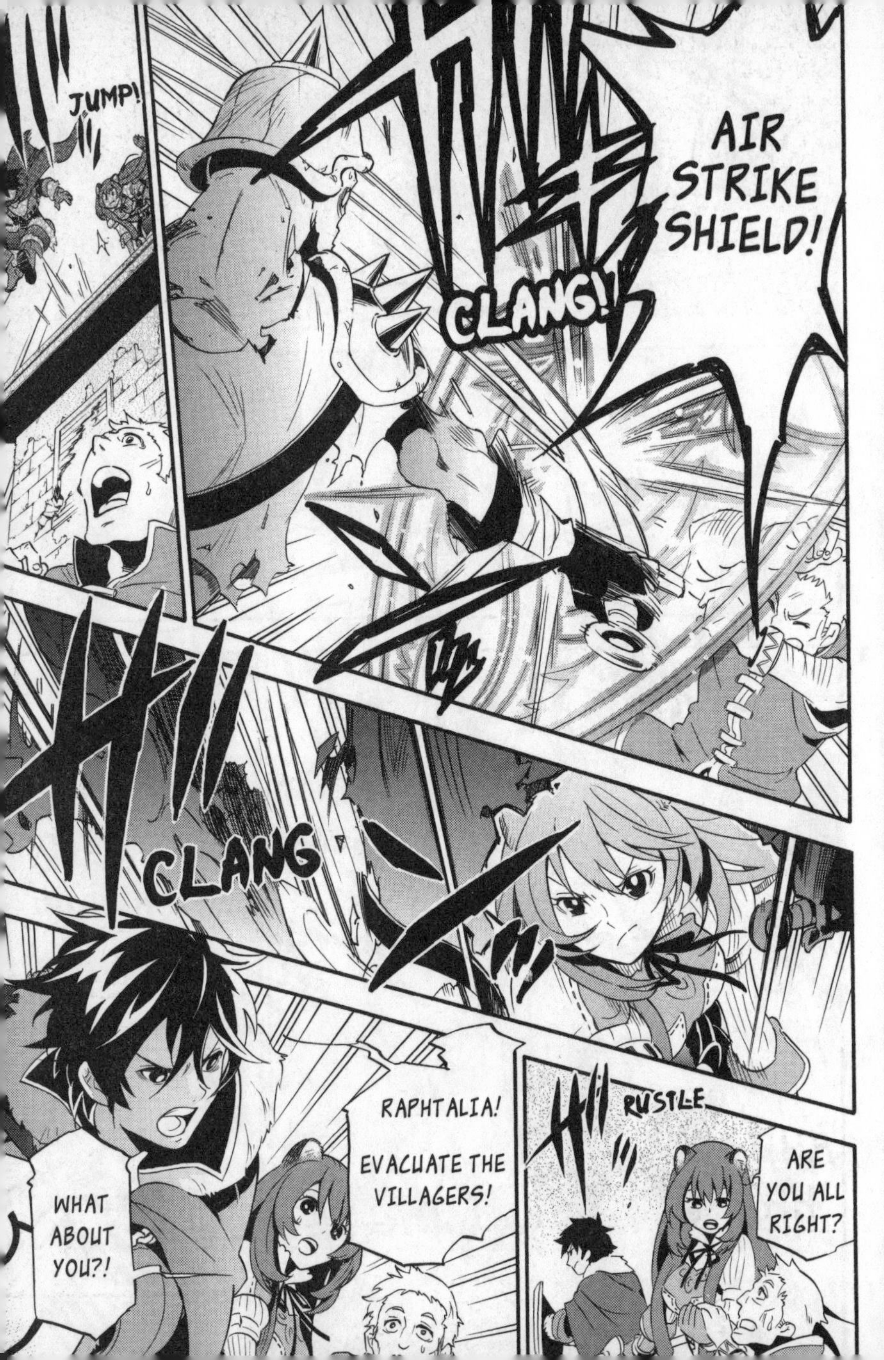
AIR STRIKE SHIELD!
CLANG!
JUMP!
CLANG
RUSTLE
ARE YOU ALL RIGHT?
RAPHTALIA!
EVACUATE THE VILLAGERS!
WHAT ABOUT YOU?!

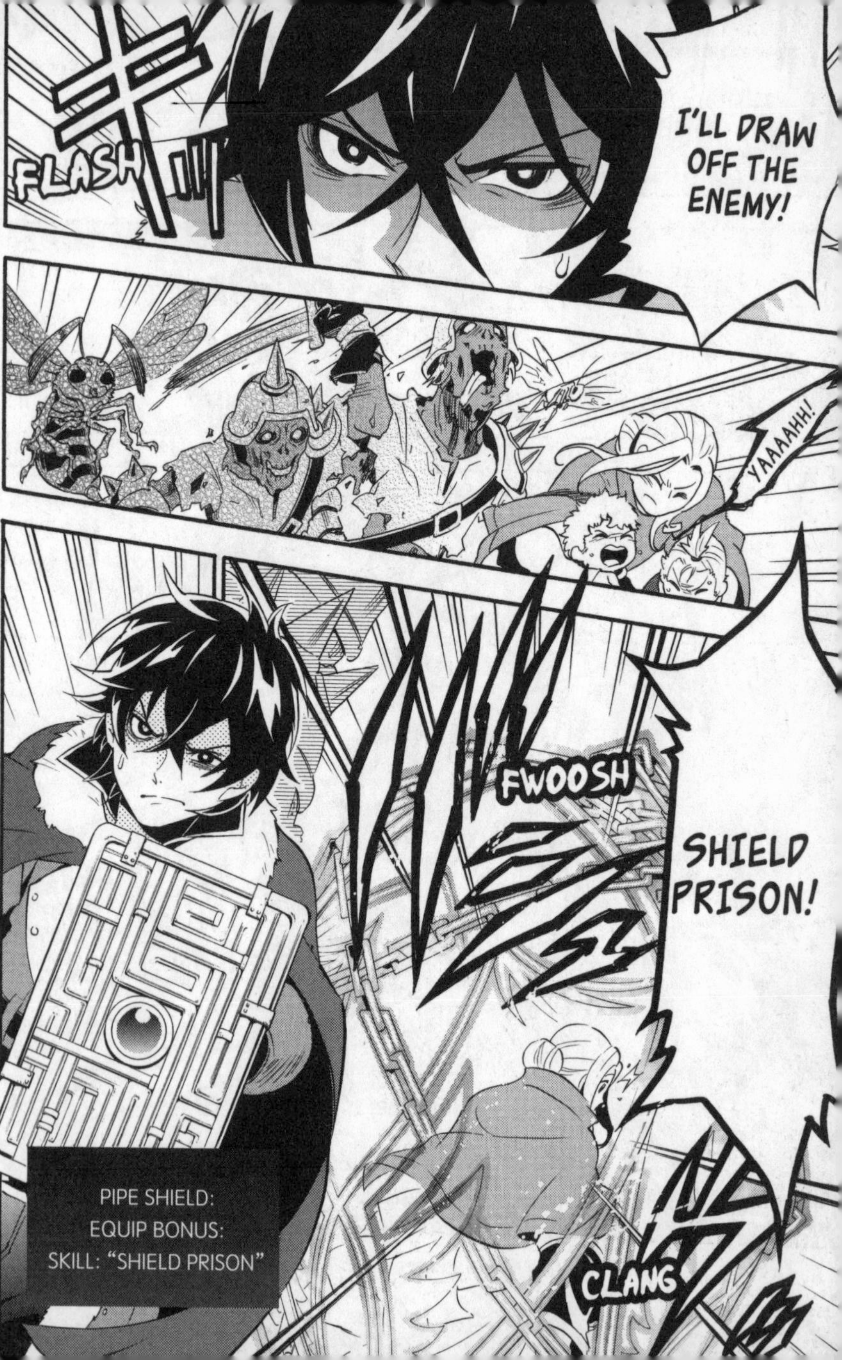
I'LL DRAW OFF THE ENEMY!
FLASH
YAAAAHH!
FWOOSH
SHIELD PRISON!
PIPE SHIELD:
EQUIP BONUS:
SKILL: "SHIELD PRISON"
CLANG

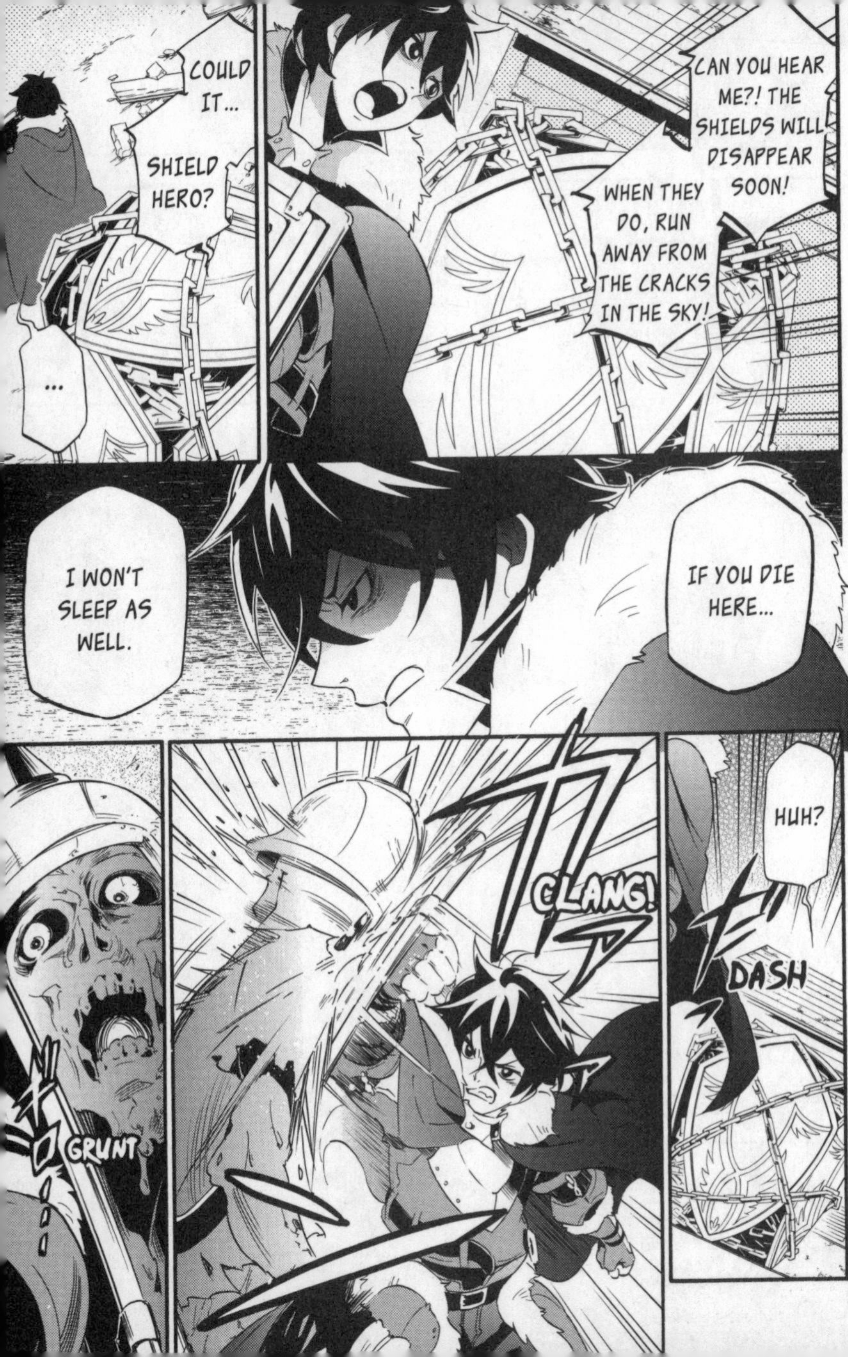
CAN YOU HEAR ME?! THE SHIELDS WILL DISAPPEAR SOON!
WHEN THEY DO, RUN AWAY FROM THE CRACKS IN THE SKY!
COULD IT...
SHIELD HERO?
...
IF YOU DIE HERE...
I WON'T SLEEP AS WELL.
HUH?
DASH
CLANG!
GRUNT

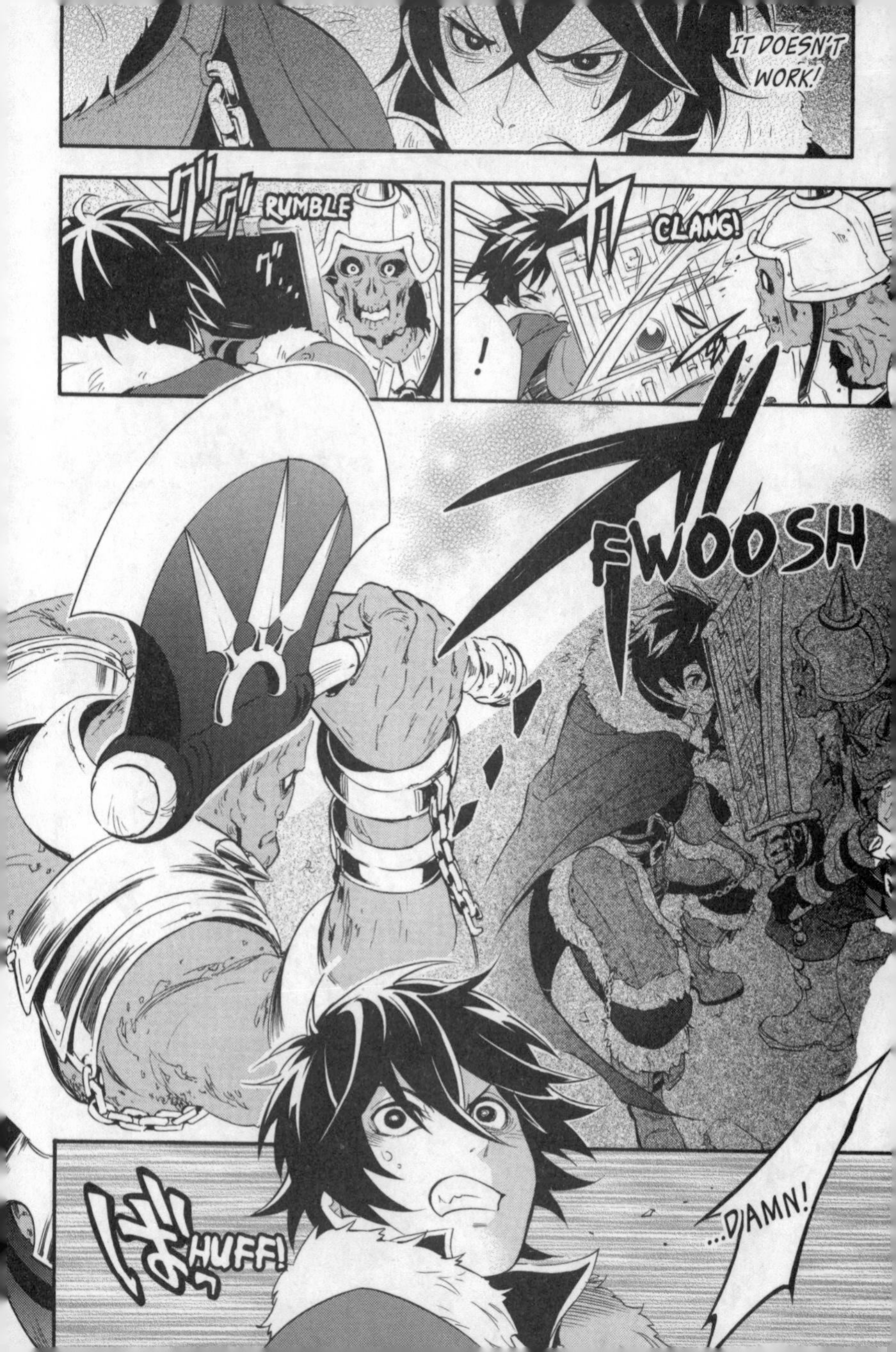
IT DOESN'T WORK!
CLANG!
!
RUMBLE
FWOOSH
...DAMN!
HUFF!

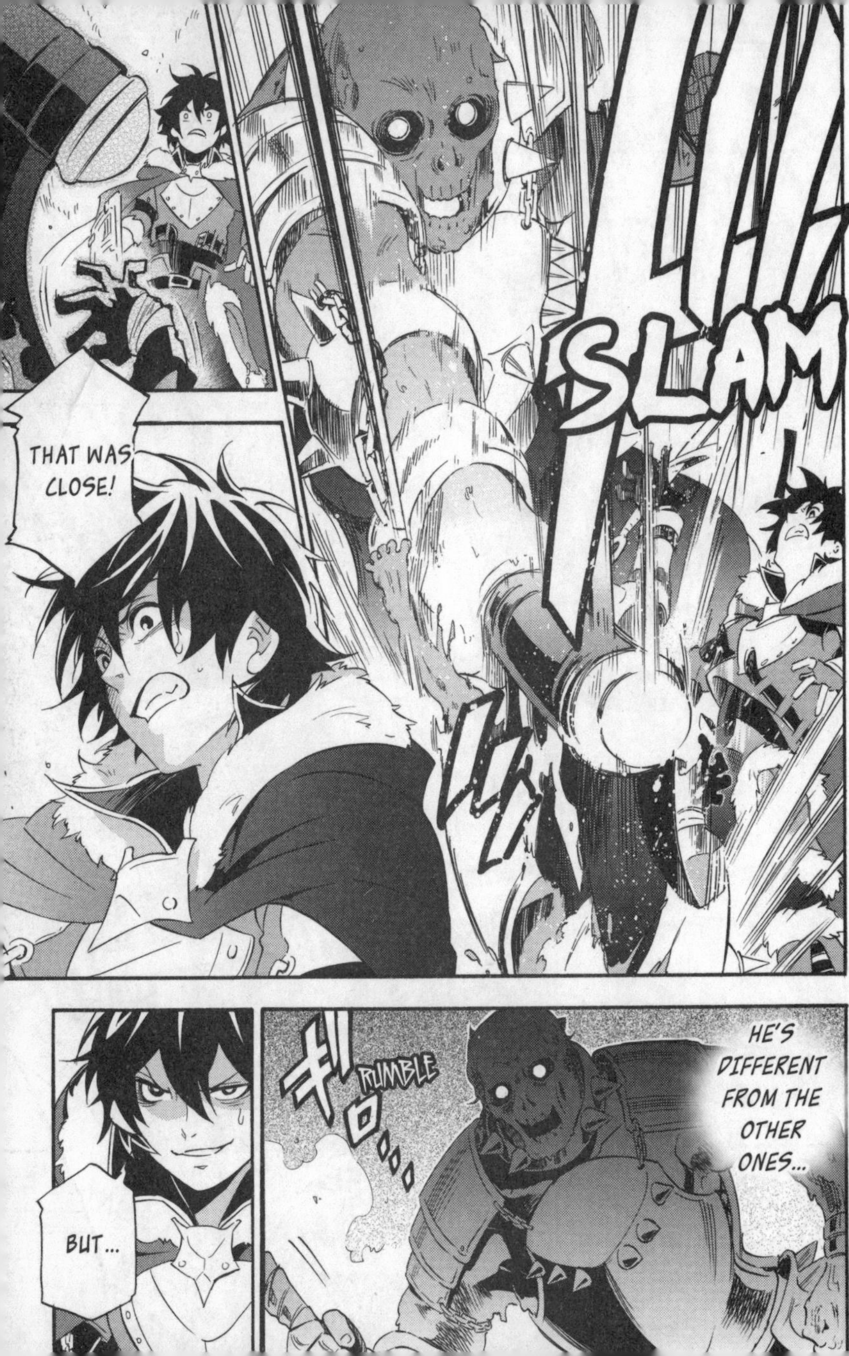
SLAM
THAT WAS CLOSE!
HE'S DIFFERENT FROM THE OTHER ONES...
RUMBLE
BUT...

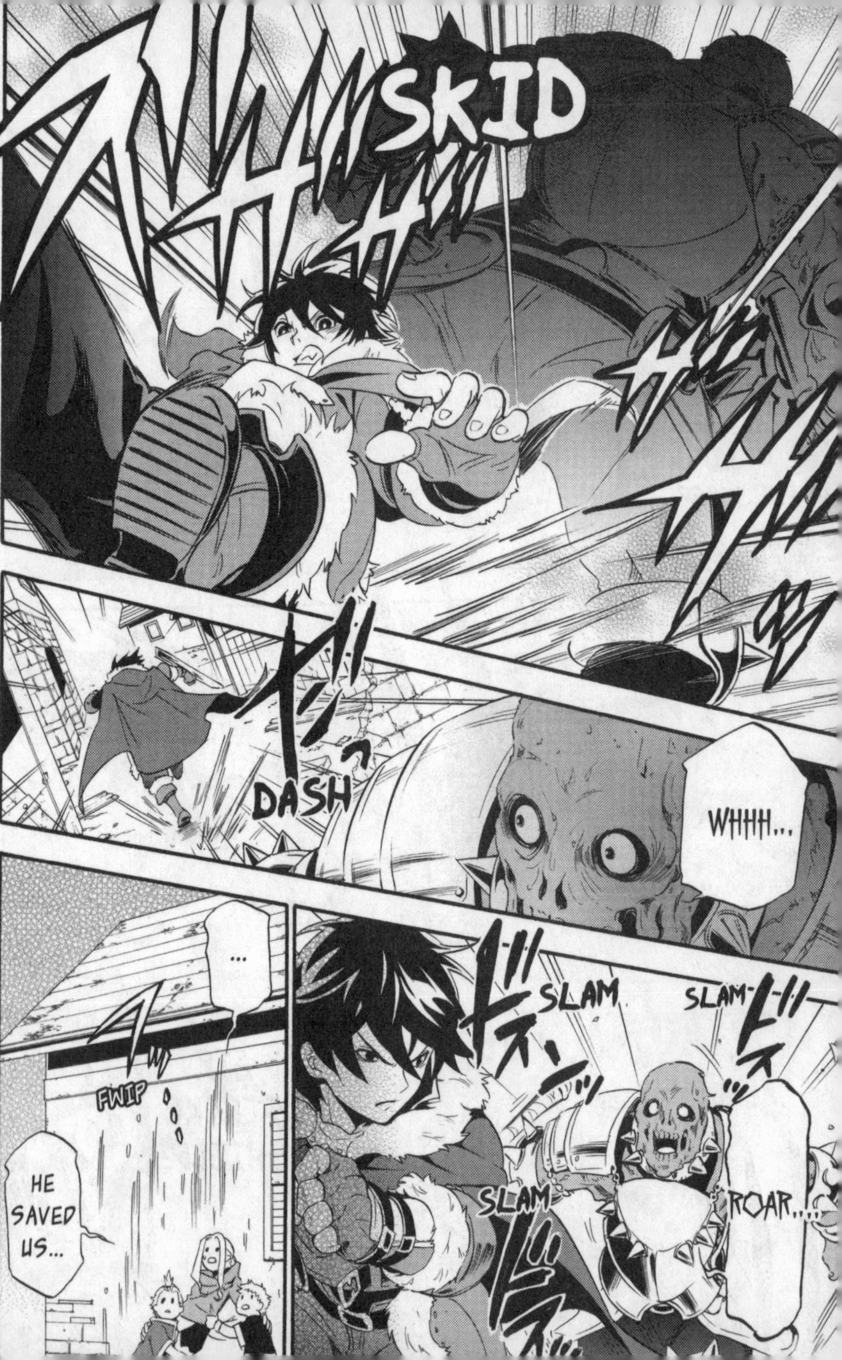
SKID
WHHH...
DASH
SLAM
SLAM
ROAR...
SLAM
...
FWIP
HE SAVED US...

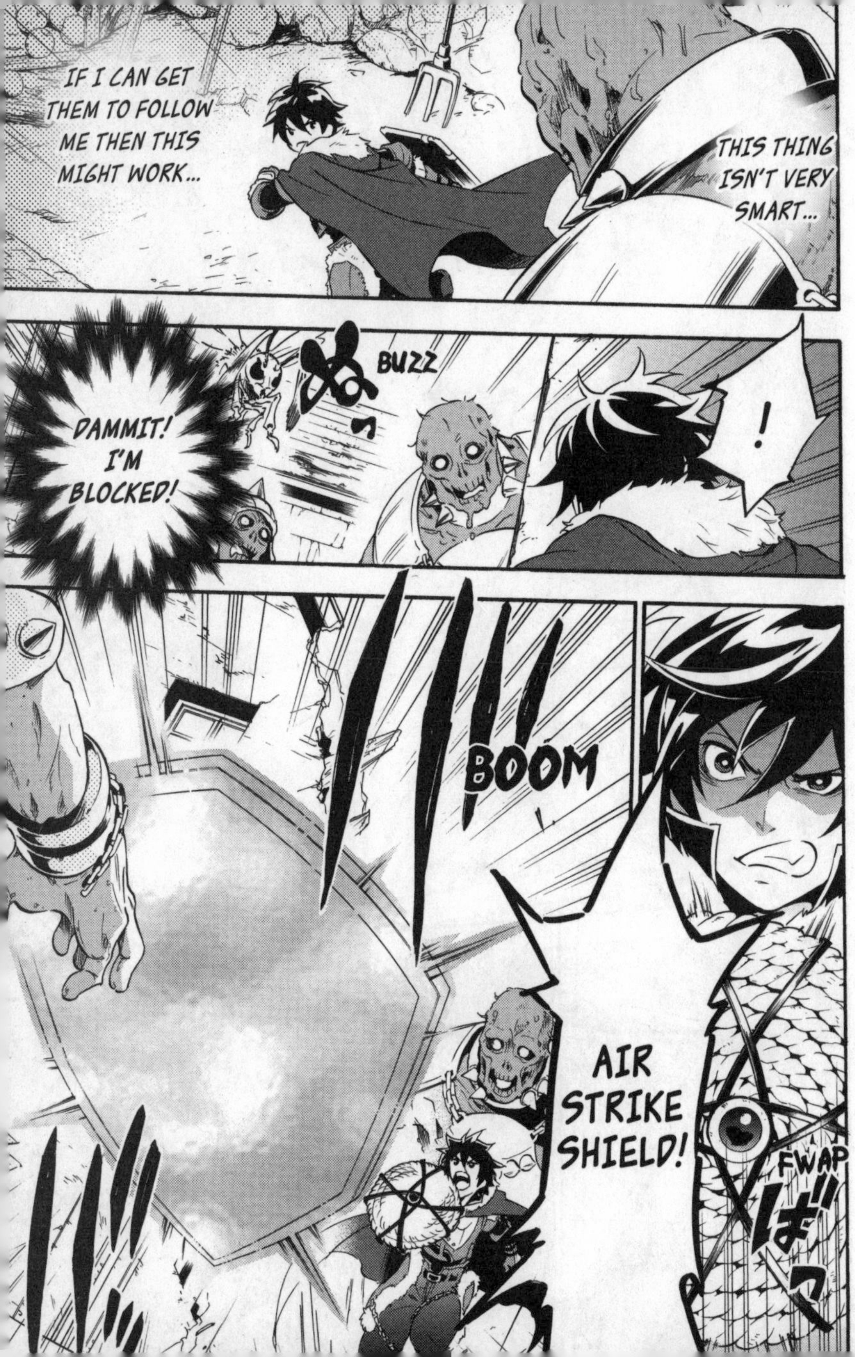
THIS THING ISN'T VERY SMART...
IF I CAN GET THEM TO FOLLOW ME THEN THIS MIGHT WORK...
!
BUZZ
DAMMIT! I'M BLOCKED!
AIR STRIKE SHIELD!
FWAP
ばっ
BOOM

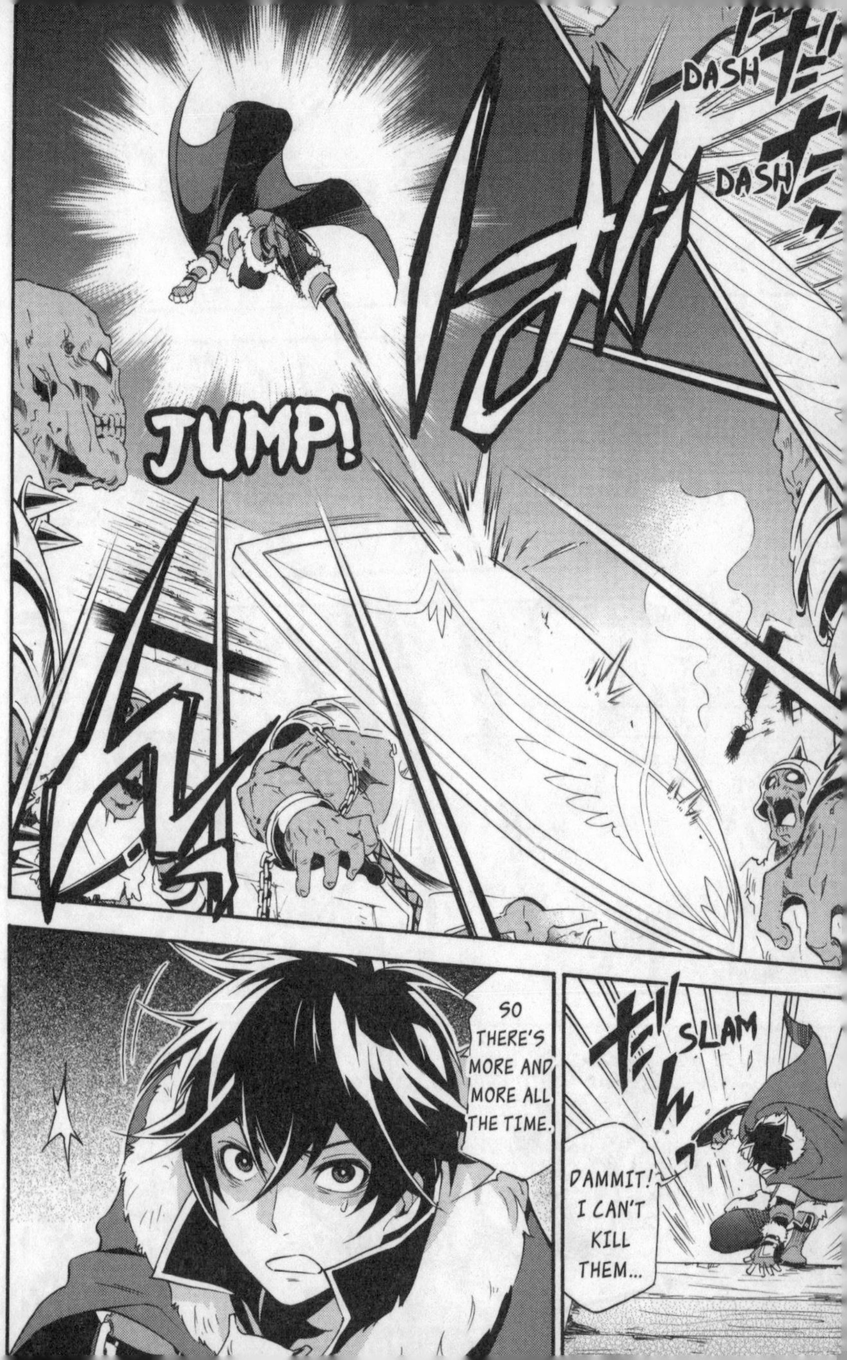
DASH
DASH
JUMP!
SLAM
DAMMIT! I CAN'T KILL THEM...
SO THERE'S MORE AND MORE ALL THE TIME.

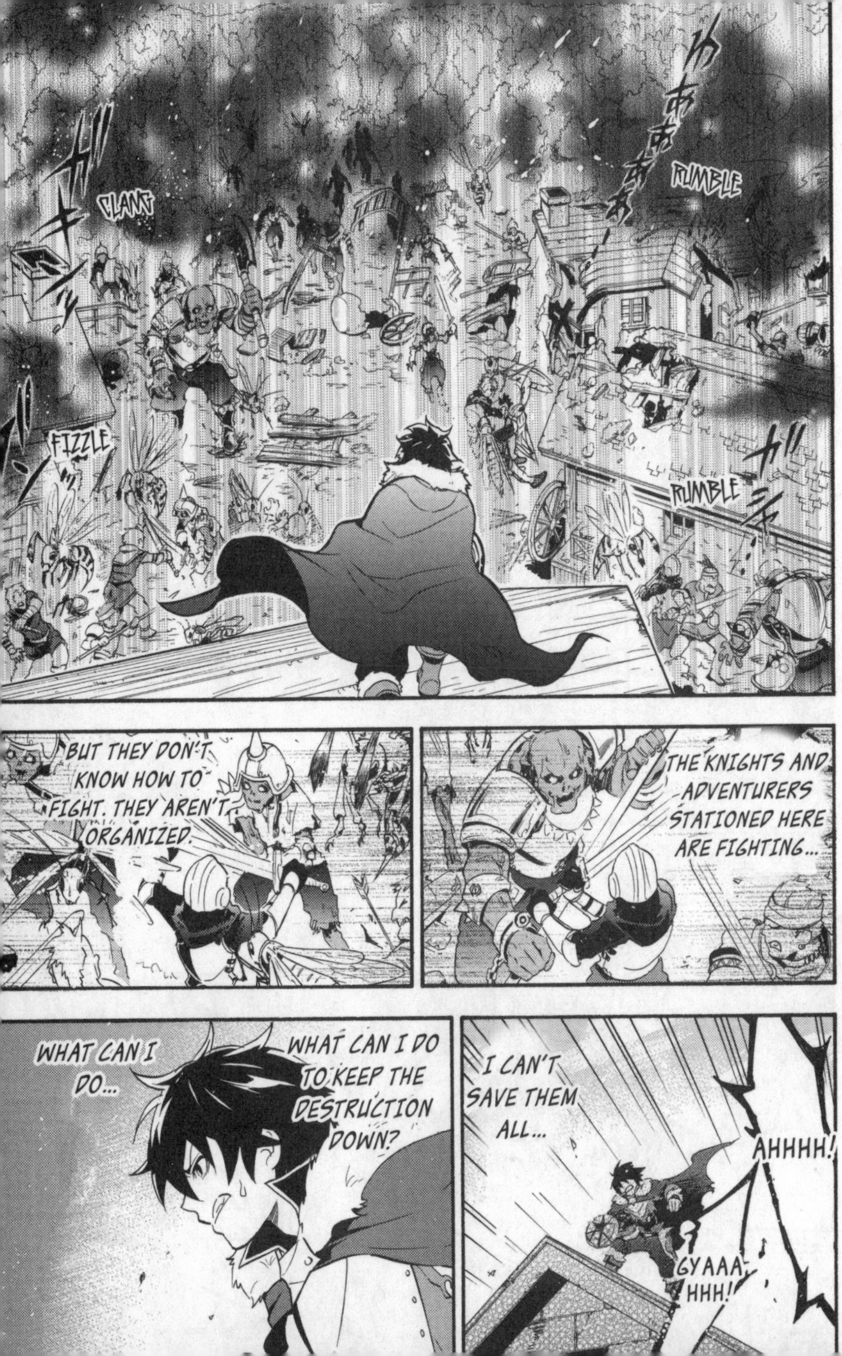
RUMBLE
RUMBLE
CLANG
FIZZLE
THE KNIGHTS AND ADVENTURERS STATIONED HERE ARE FIGHTING...
BUT THEY DON'T KNOW HOW TO FIGHT. THEY AREN'T ORGANIZED.
I CAN'T SAVE THEM ALL...
AHHHH!
GYAAAHHH!
WHAT CAN I DO TO KEEP THE DESTRUCTION DOWN?
WHAT CAN I DO...

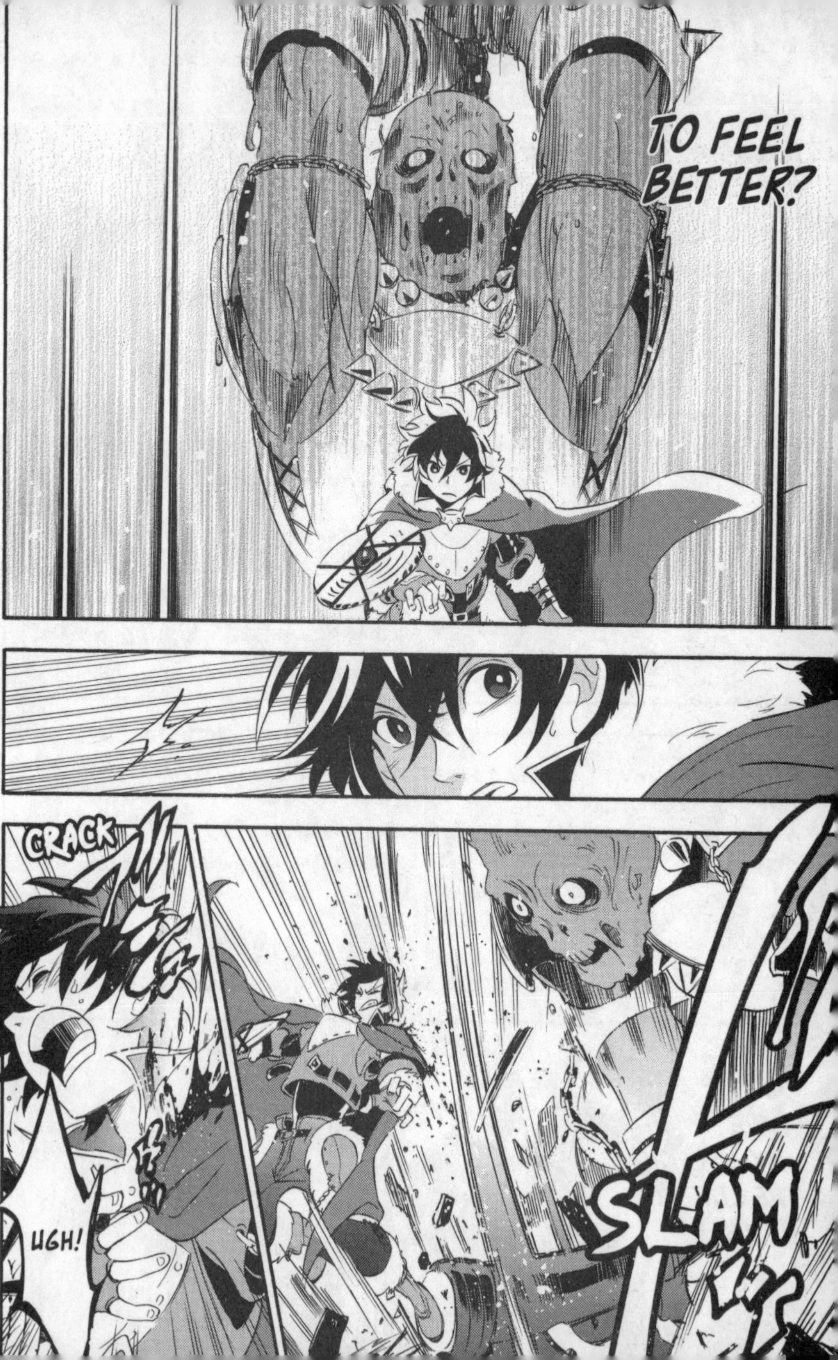
TO FEEL BETTER?
SLAM
CRACK
UGH!

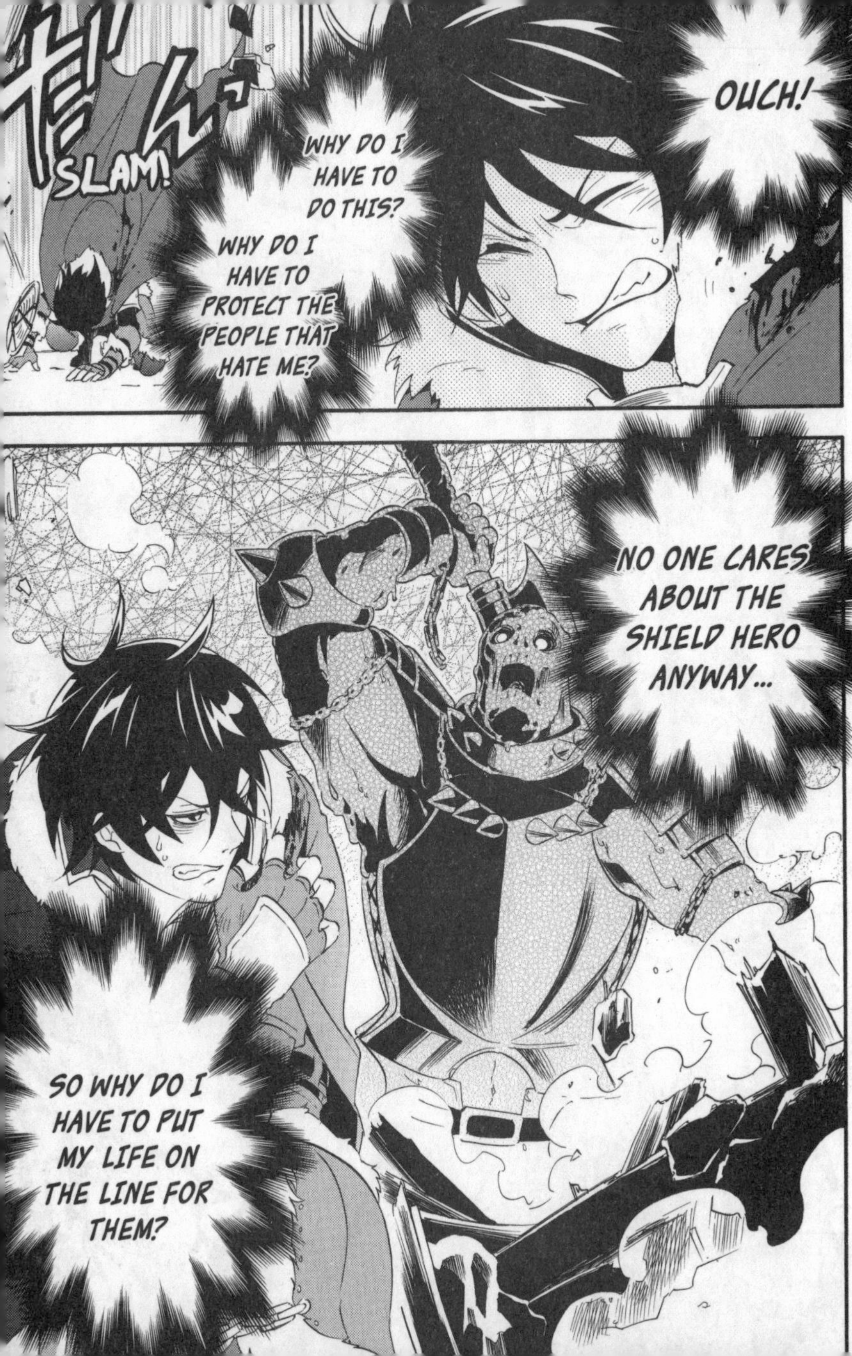
OUCH!
WHY DO I HAVE TO DO THIS?
WHY DO I HAVE TO PROTECT THE PEOPLE THAT HATE ME?
SLAM!
NO ONE CARES ABOUT THE SHIELD HERO ANYWAY...
SO WHY DO I HAVE TO PUT MY LIFE ON THE LINE FOR THEM?

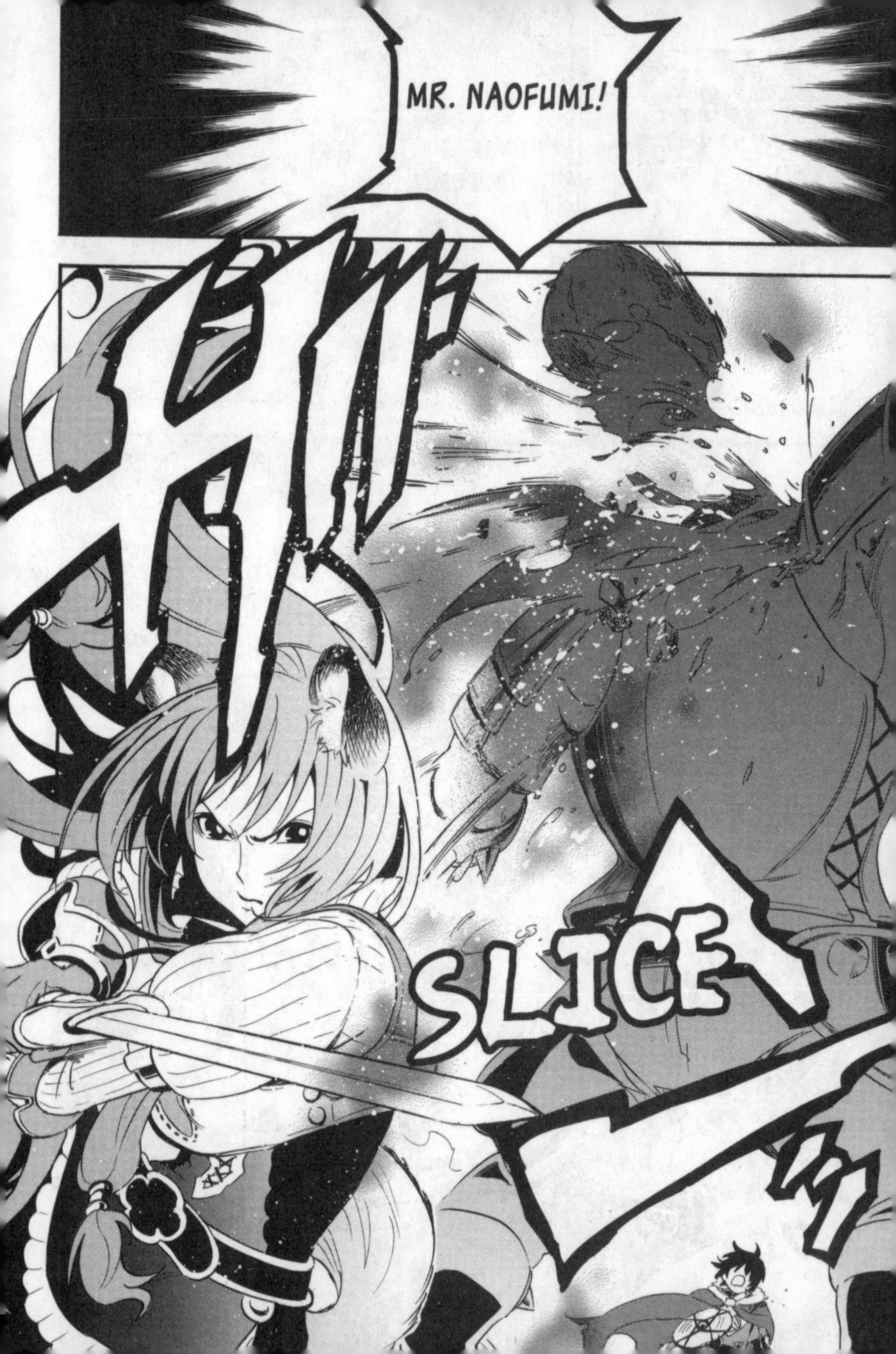
MR. NAOFUMI!
SLICE

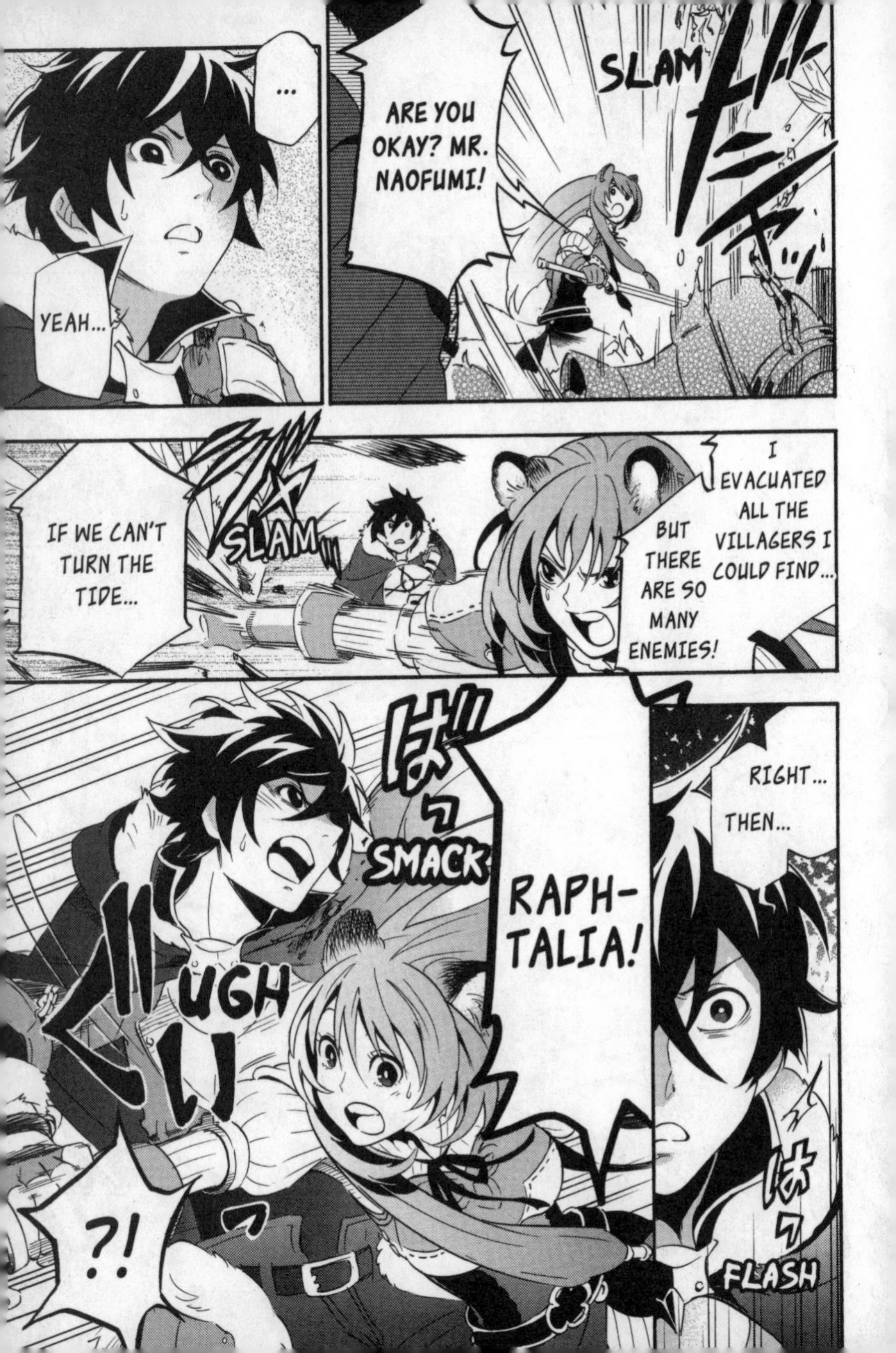
SLAM
ARE YOU OKAY? MR. NAOFUMI!
...
YEAH...
I EVACUATED ALL THE VILLAGERS I COULD FIND...
BUT THERE ARE SO MANY ENEMIES!
SLAM
IF WE CAN'T TURN THE TIDE...
RIGHT... THEN...
FLASH
RAPH-TALIA!
SMACK
UGH
?!

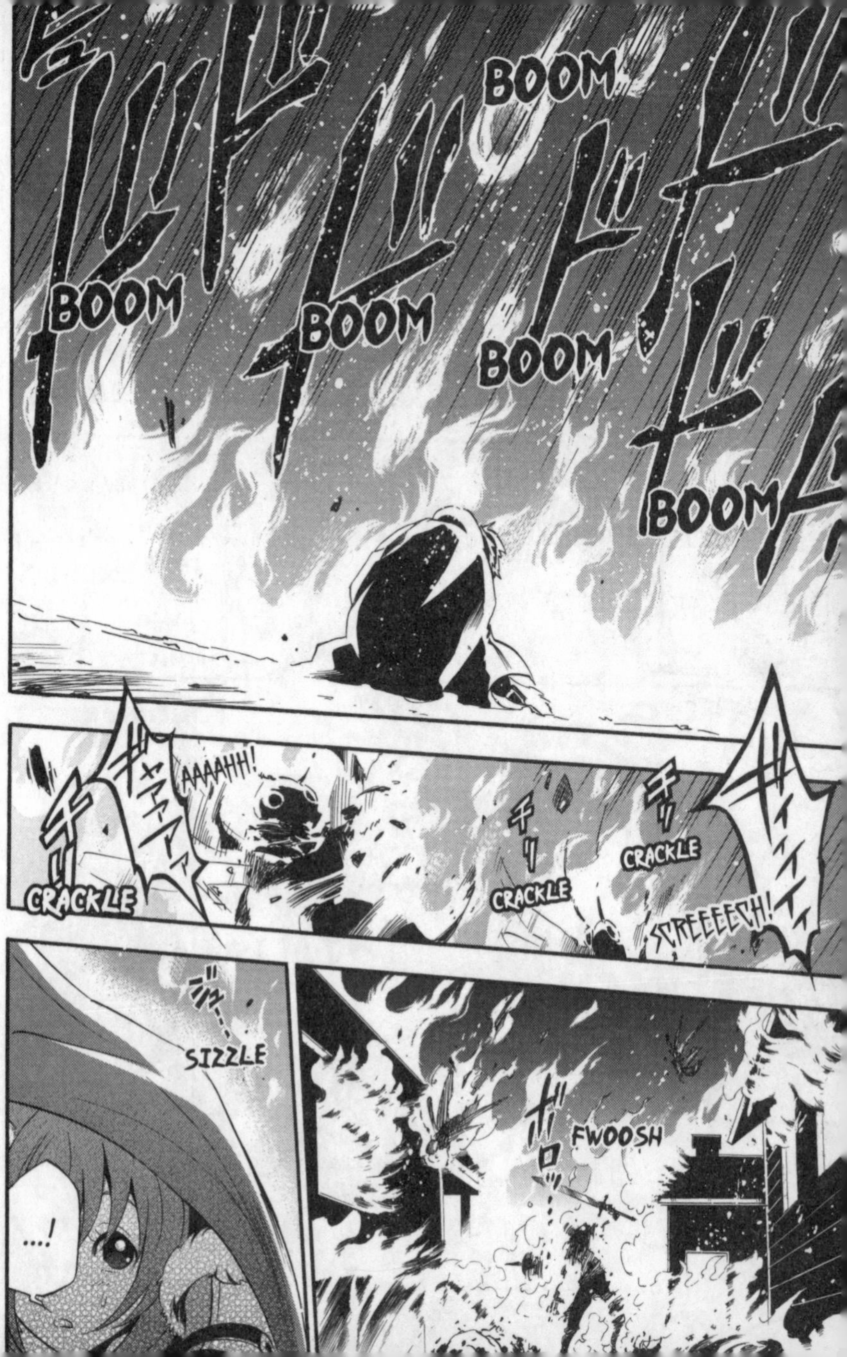
BOOM
BOOM
BOOM
BOOM
BOOM
SCREEEECH!
CRACKLE
CRACKLE
AAAAHH!
CRACKLE
FWOOSH
SIZZLE
....!

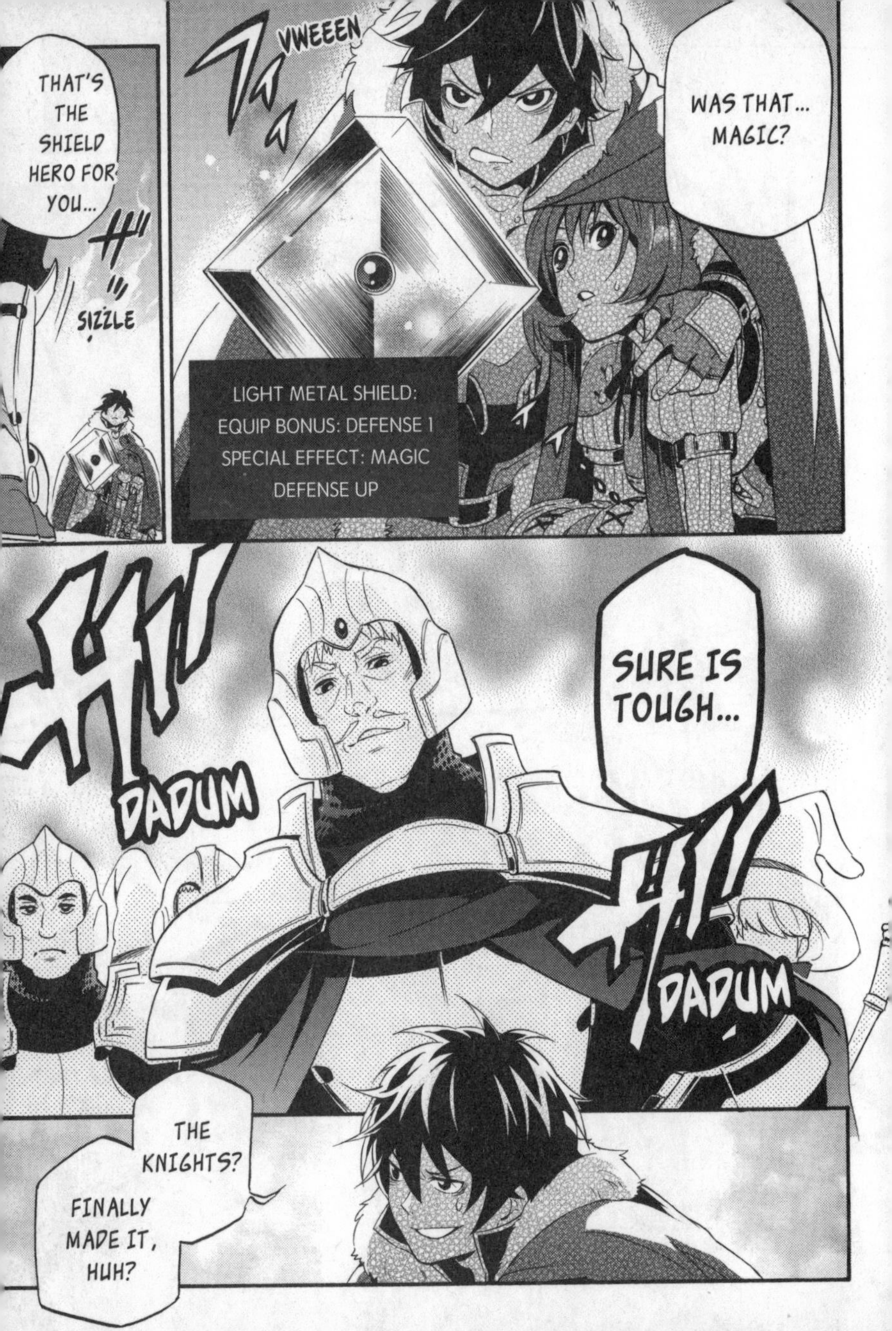

VWEEEN
WAS THAT... MAGIC?
LIGHT METAL SHIELD: EQUIP BONUS: DEFENSE 1 SPECIAL EFFECT: MAGIC DEFENSE UP
THAT'S THE SHIELD HERO FOR YOU...
SIZZLE
SURE IS TOUGH...
DADUM
DADUM
THE KNIGHTS?
FINALLY MADE IT, HUH?

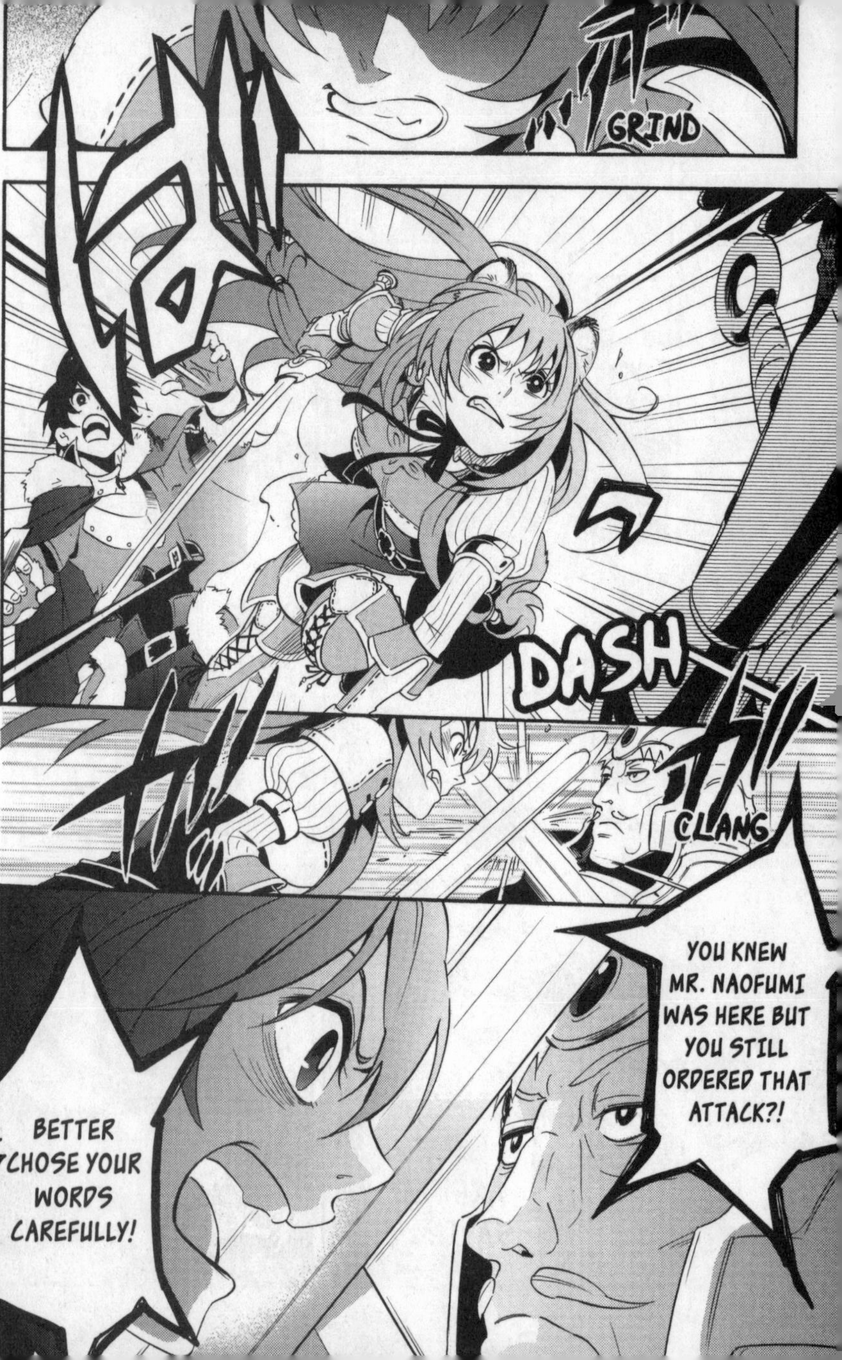
GRIND
DASH
CLANG
YOU KNEW MR. NAOFUMI WAS HERE BUT YOU STILL ORDERED THAT ATTACK?!
BETTER CHOSE YOUR WORDS CAREFULLY!

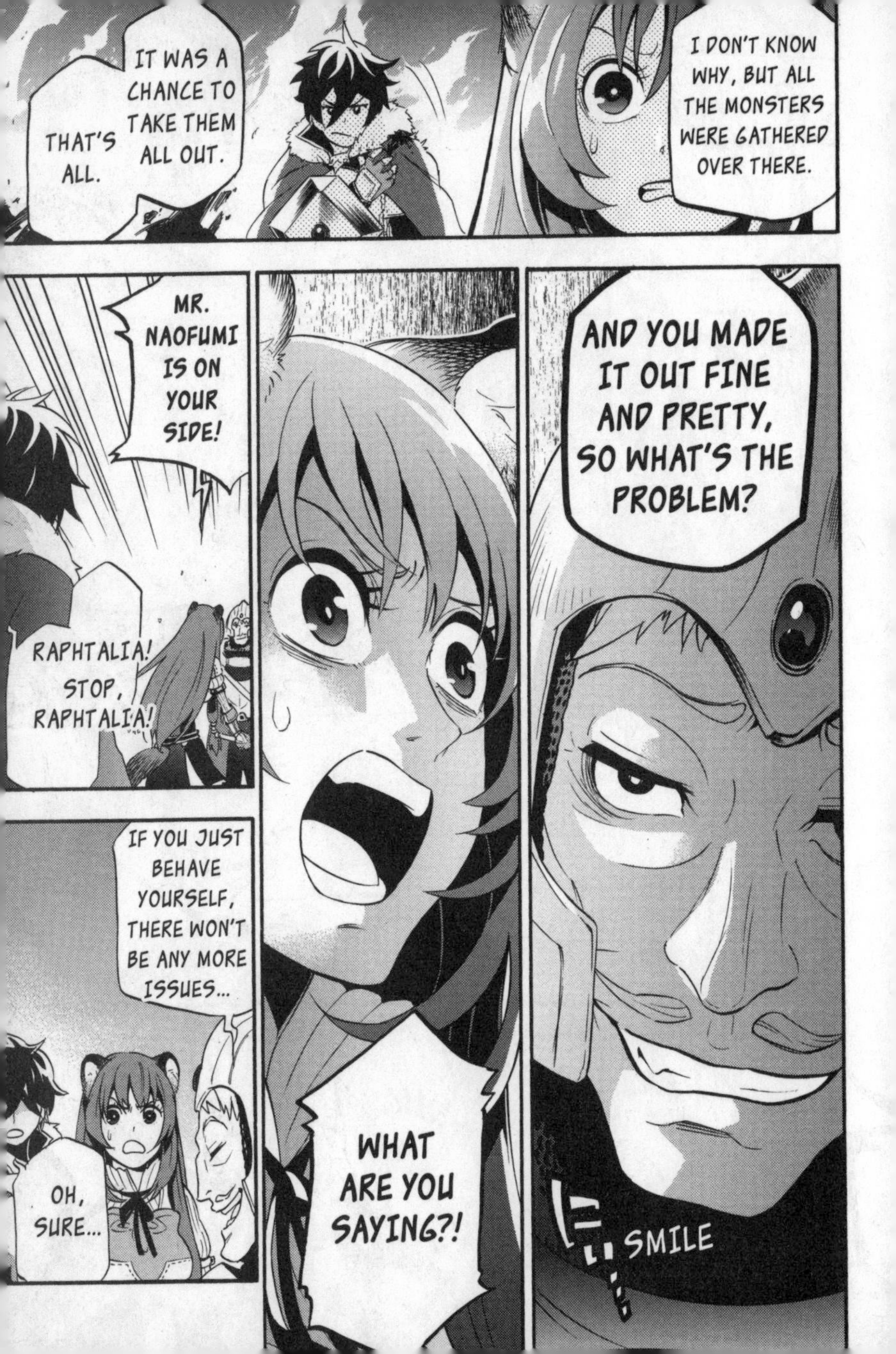
I DON'T KNOW WHY, BUT ALL THE MONSTERS WERE GATHERED OVER THERE.
IT WAS A CHANCE TO TAKE THEM ALL OUT.
THAT'S ALL.
AND YOU MADE IT OUT FINE AND PRETTY, SO WHAT'S THE PROBLEM?
SMILE
WHAT ARE YOU SAYING?!
MR. NAOFUMI IS ON YOUR SIDE!
RAPHTALIA! STOP, RAPHTALIA!
IF YOU JUST BEHAVE YOURSELF, THERE WON'T BE ANY MORE ISSUES...
OH, SURE...

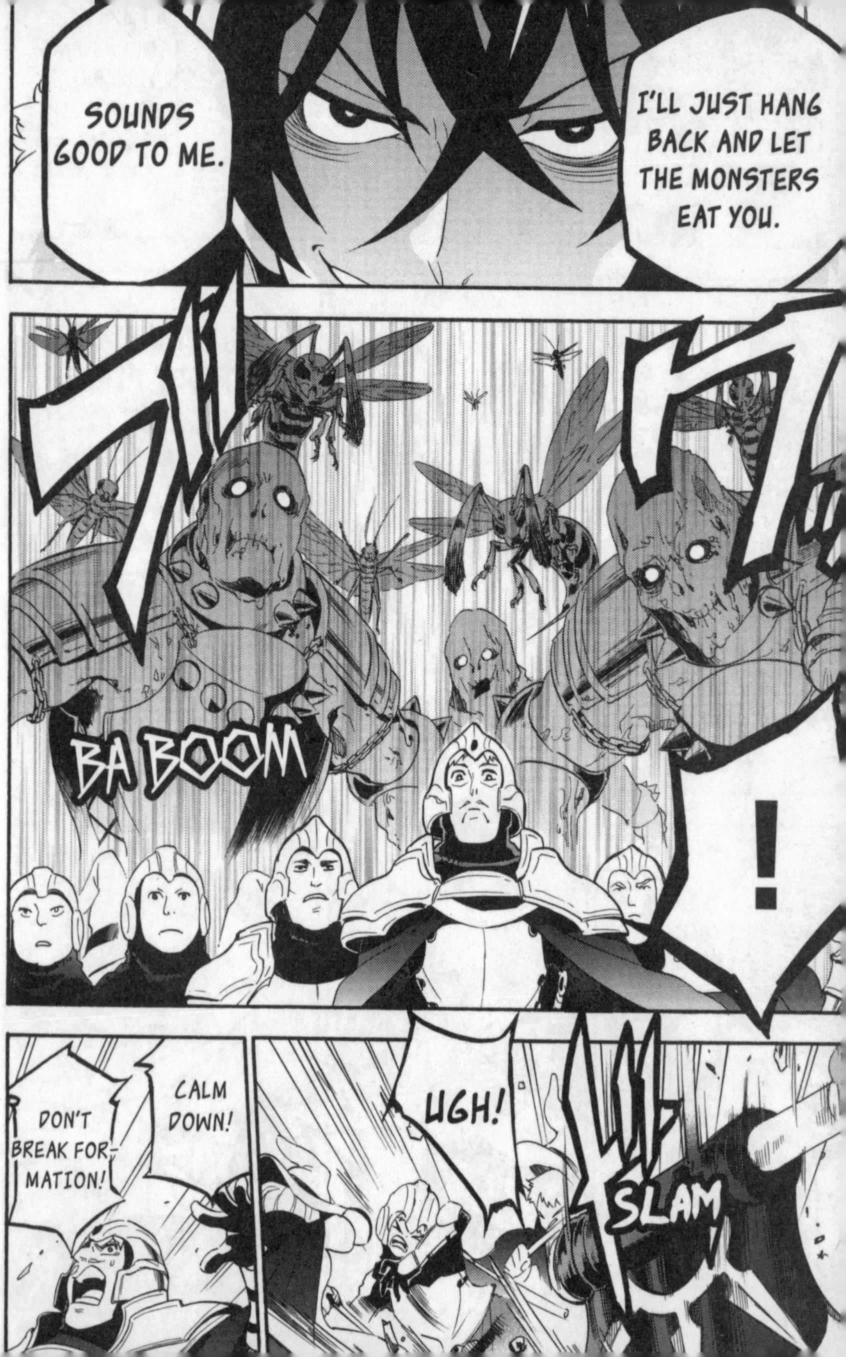
I'LL JUST HANG BACK AND LET THE MONSTERS EAT YOU.
SOUNDS GOOD TO ME.
!
BA BOOM
SLAM
UGH!
CALM DOWN!
DON'T BREAK FOR-MATION!

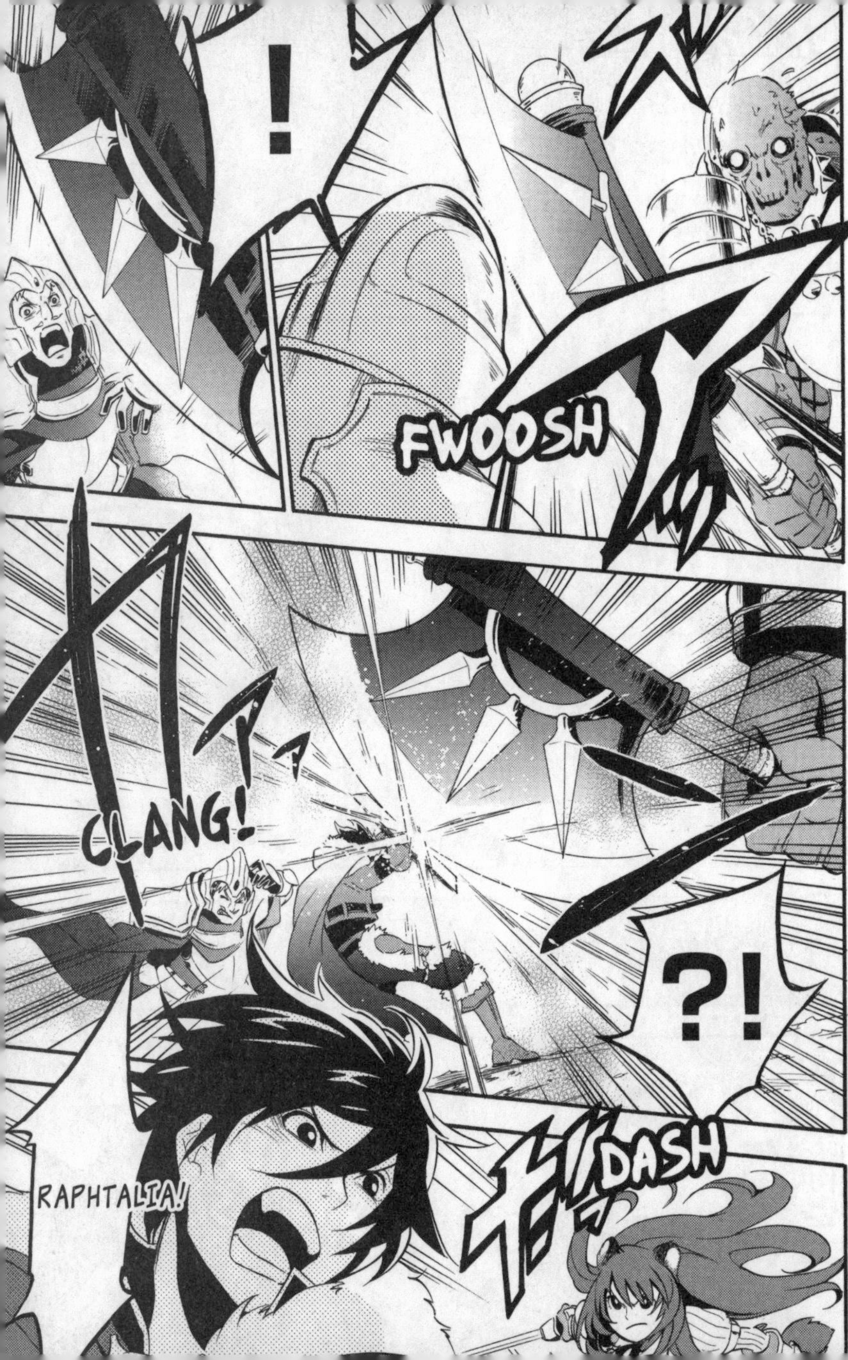
FWOOSH
!
?!
CLANG!
DASH
RAPHTALIA!

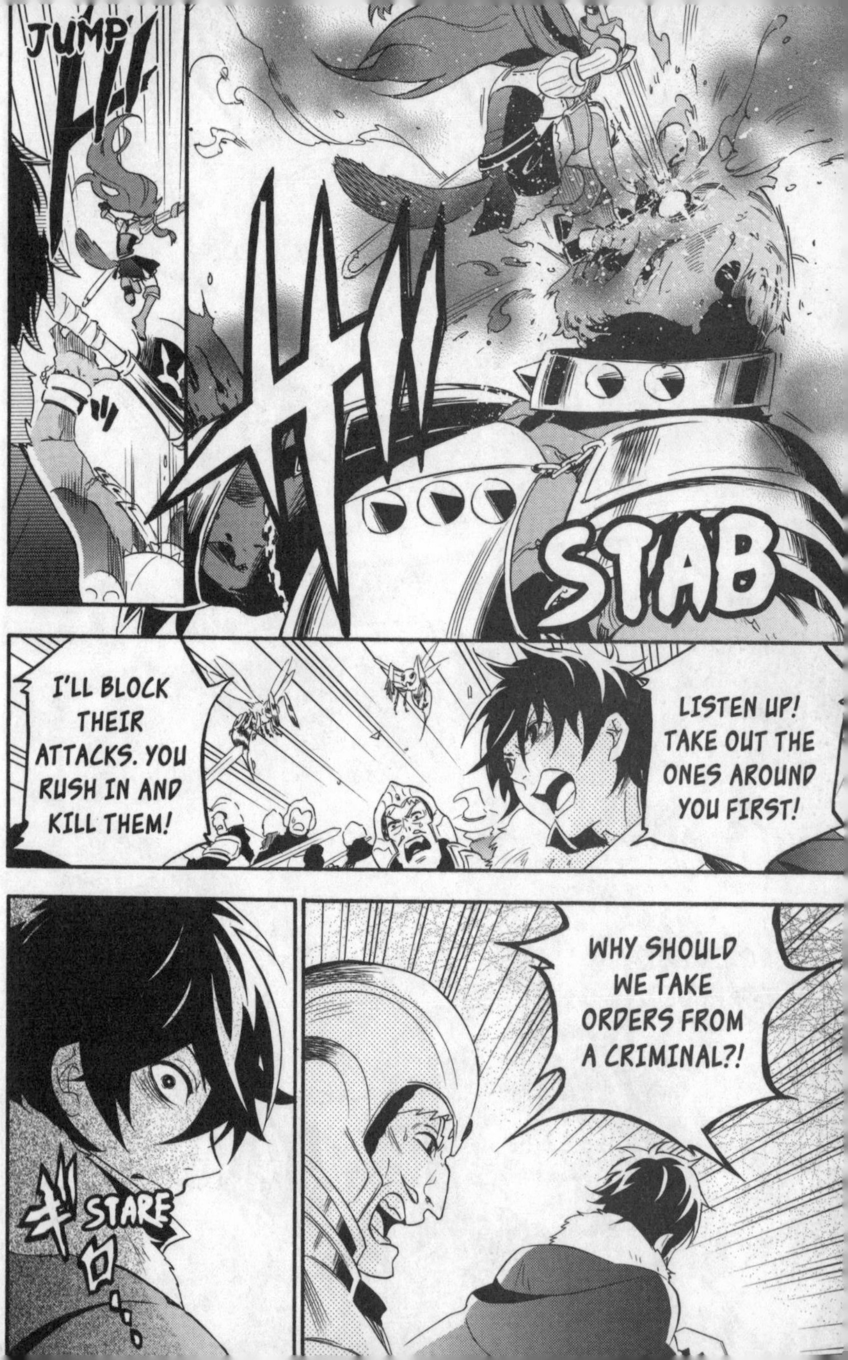
STAB
JUMP
LISTEN UP! TAKE OUT THE ONES AROUND YOU FIRST!
I'LL BLOCK THEIR ATTACKS. YOU RUSH IN AND KILL THEM!
WHY SHOULD WE TAKE ORDERS FROM A CRIMINAL?!
STARE

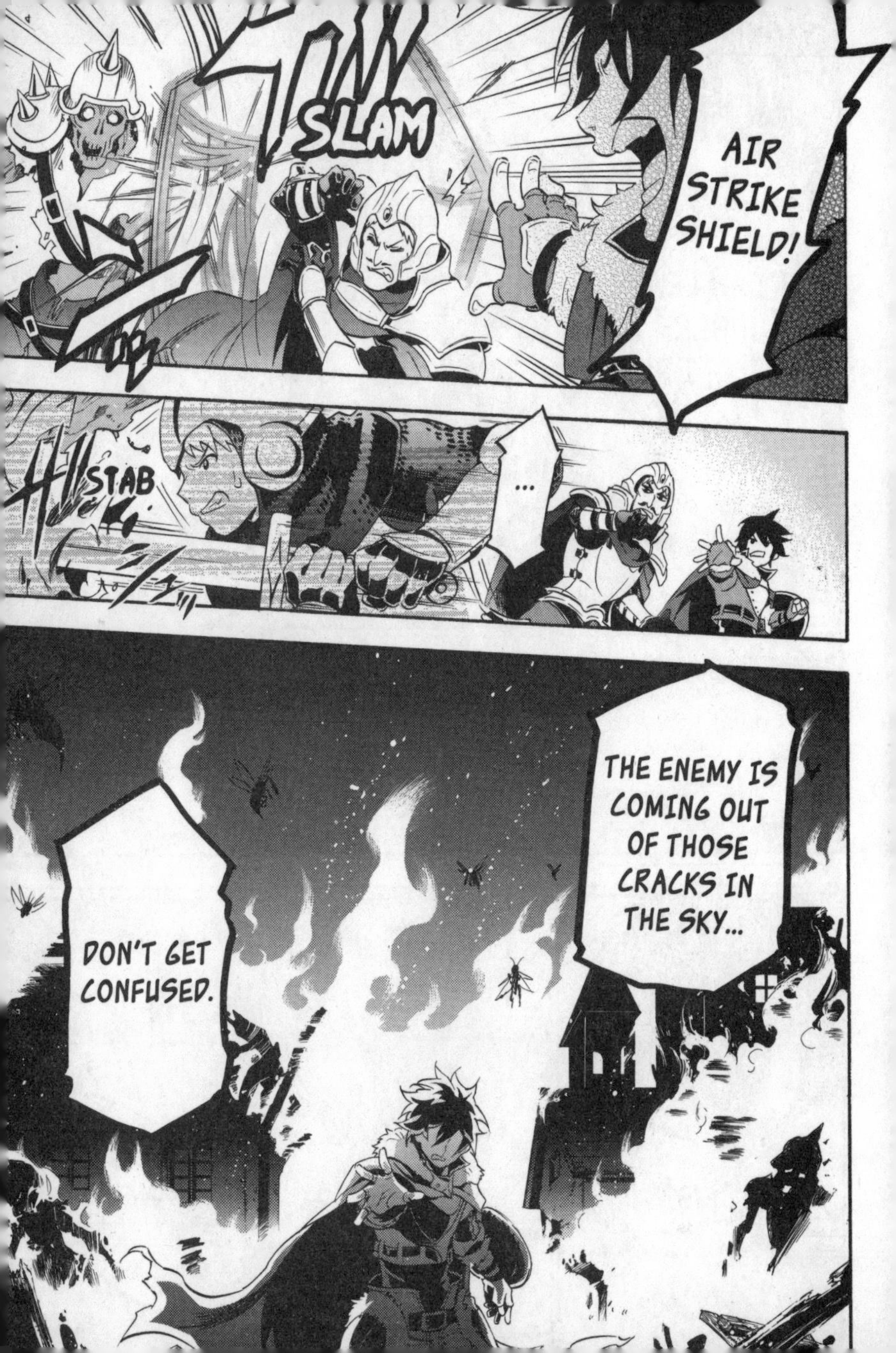
AIR STRIKE SHIELD!
SLAM
...
STAB
THE ENEMY IS COMING OUT OF THOSE CRACKS IN THE SKY...
DON'T GET CONFUSED.

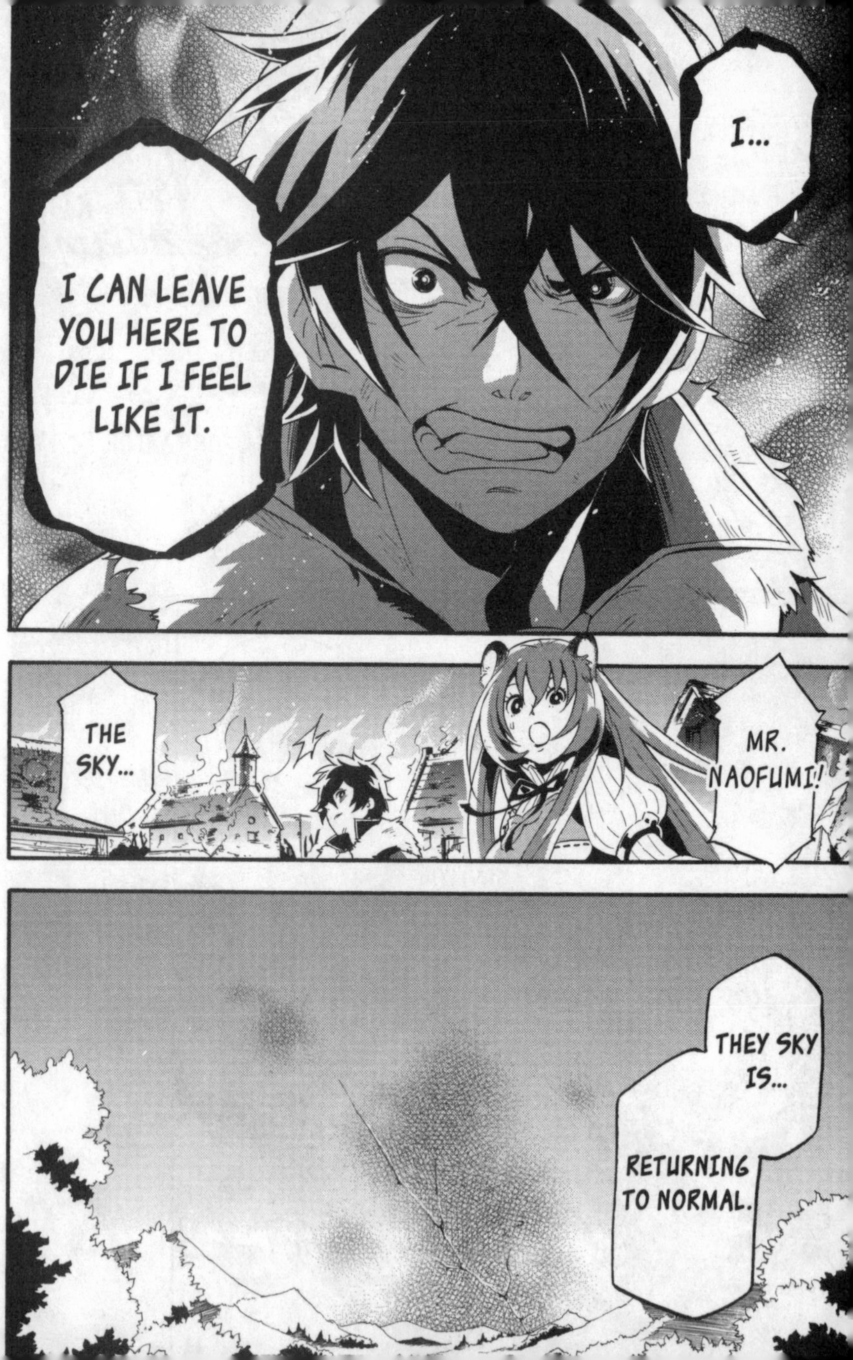
I...
I CAN LEAVE YOU HERE TO DIE IF I FEEL LIKE IT.
MR. NAOFUMI!
THE SKY...
THEY SKY IS...
RETURNING TO NORMAL.

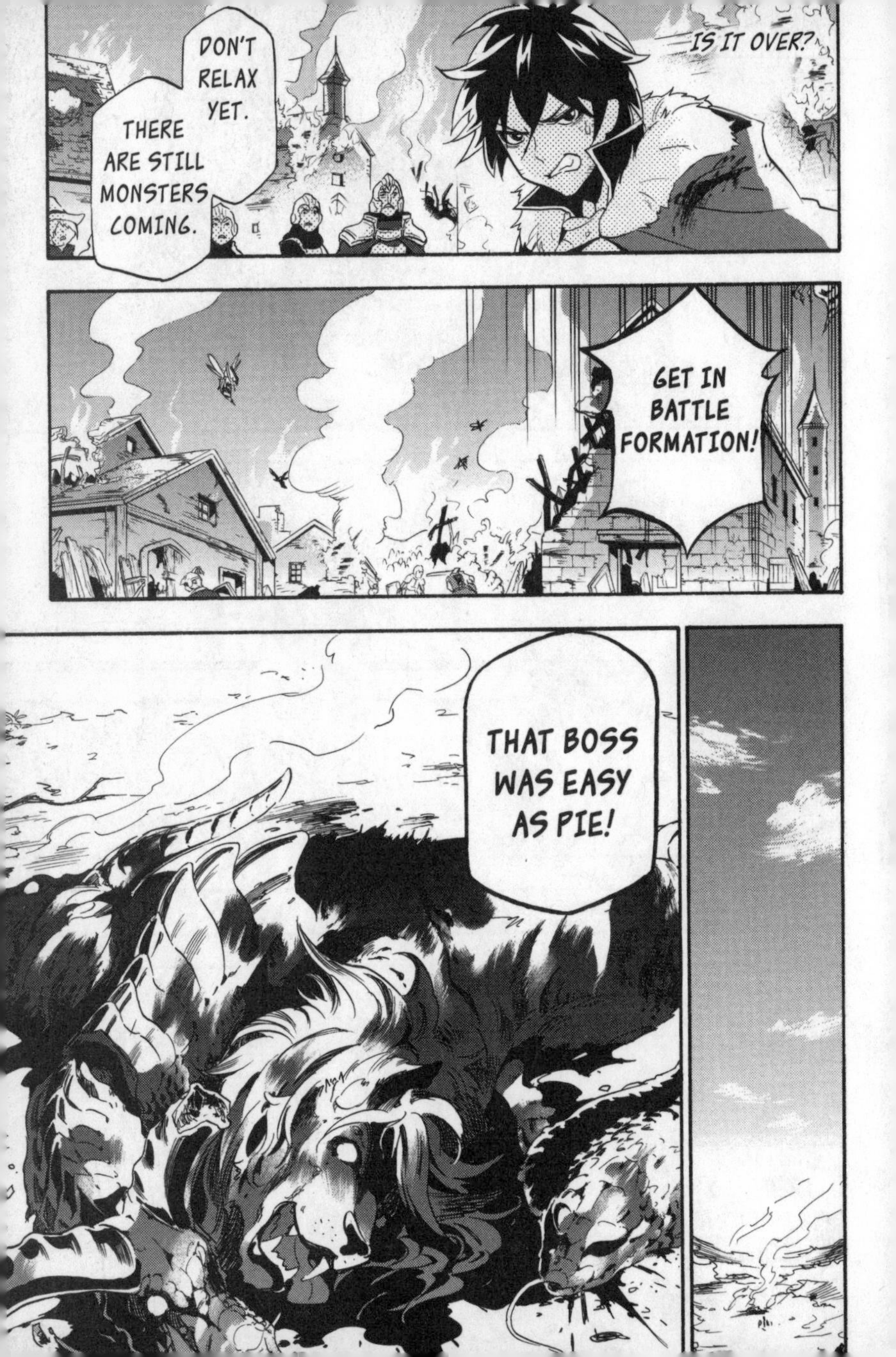
IS IT OVER?
DON'T RELAX YET.
THERE ARE STILL MONSTERS COMING.
GET IN BATTLE FORMATION!
THAT BOSS WAS EASY AS PIE!

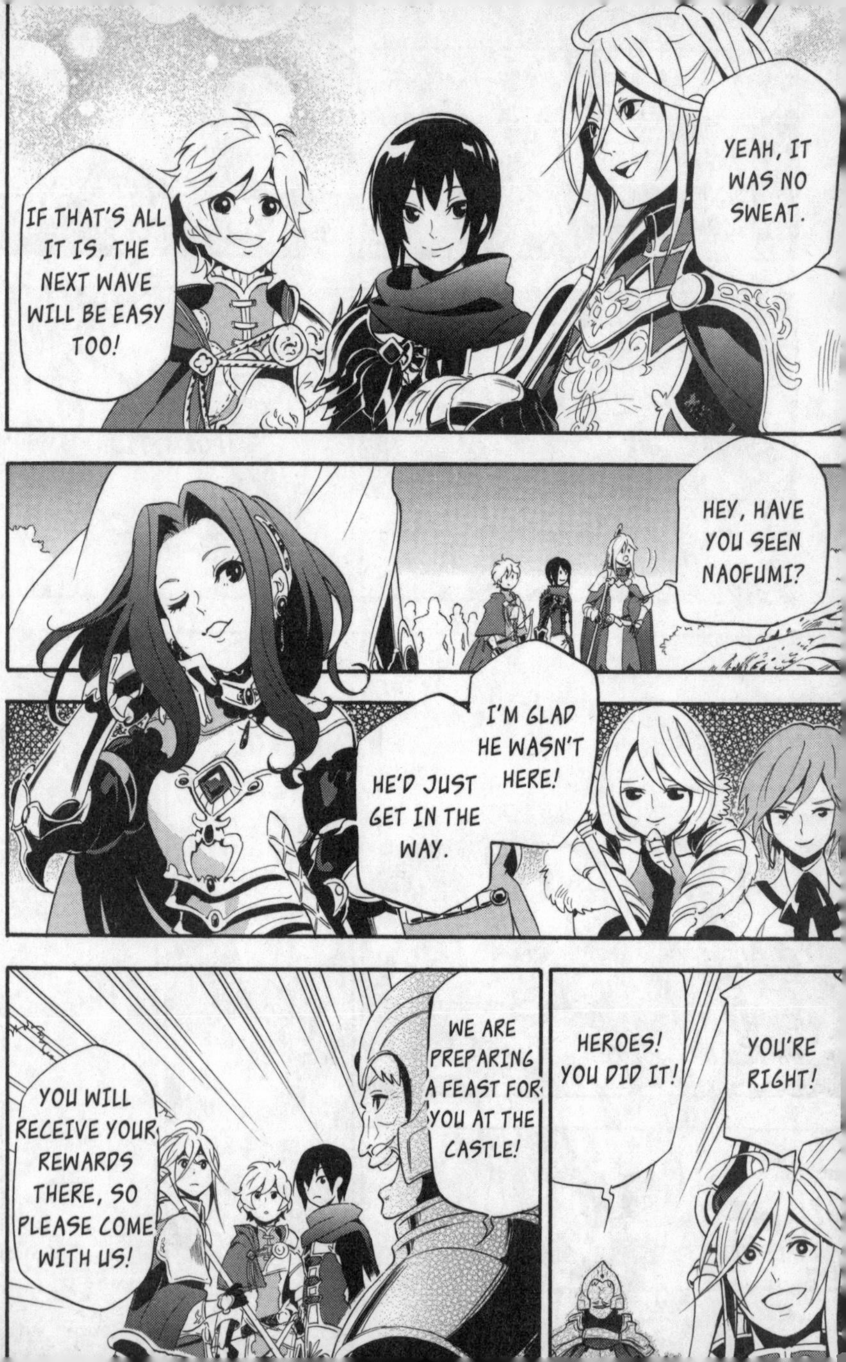
YEAH, IT WAS NO SWEAT.
IF THAT'S ALL IT IS, THE NEXT WAVE WILL BE EASY TOO!
HEY, HAVE YOU SEEN NAOFUMI?
I'M GLAD HE WASN'T HERE!
HE'D JUST GET IN THE WAY.
YOU'RE RIGHT!
HEROES! YOU DID IT!
WE ARE PREPARING A FEAST FOR YOU AT THE CASTLE!
YOU WILL RECEIVE YOUR REWARDS THERE, SO PLEASE COME WITH US!

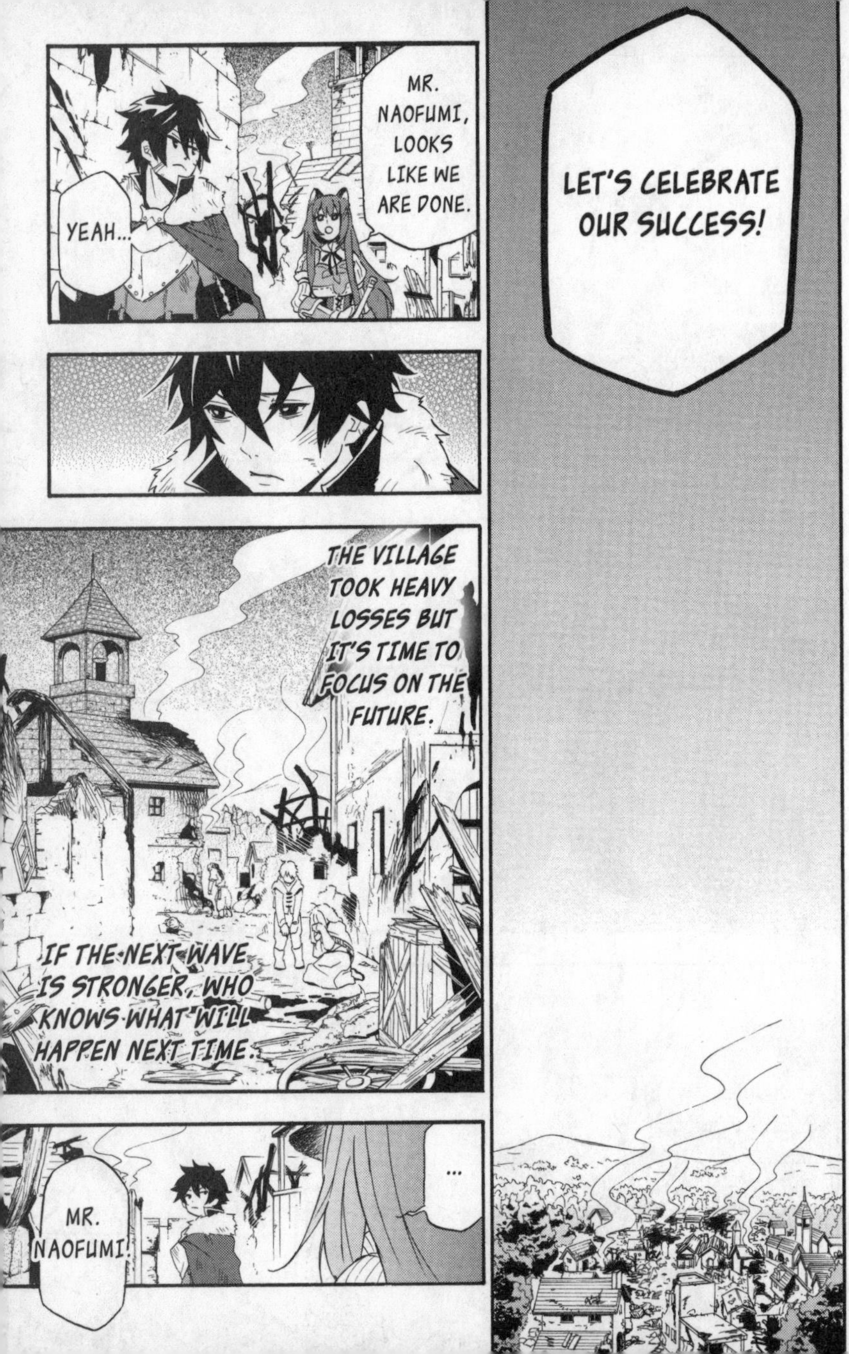
LET'S CELEBRATE OUR SUCCESS!
MR. NAOFUMI, LOOKS LIKE WE ARE DONE.
YEAH...
THE VILLAGE TOOK HEAVY LOSSES BUT IT'S TIME TO FOCUS ON THE FUTURE.
IF THE NEXT WAVE IS STRONGER, WHO KNOWS WHAT WILL HAPPEN NEXT TIME.
...
MR. NAOFUMI!

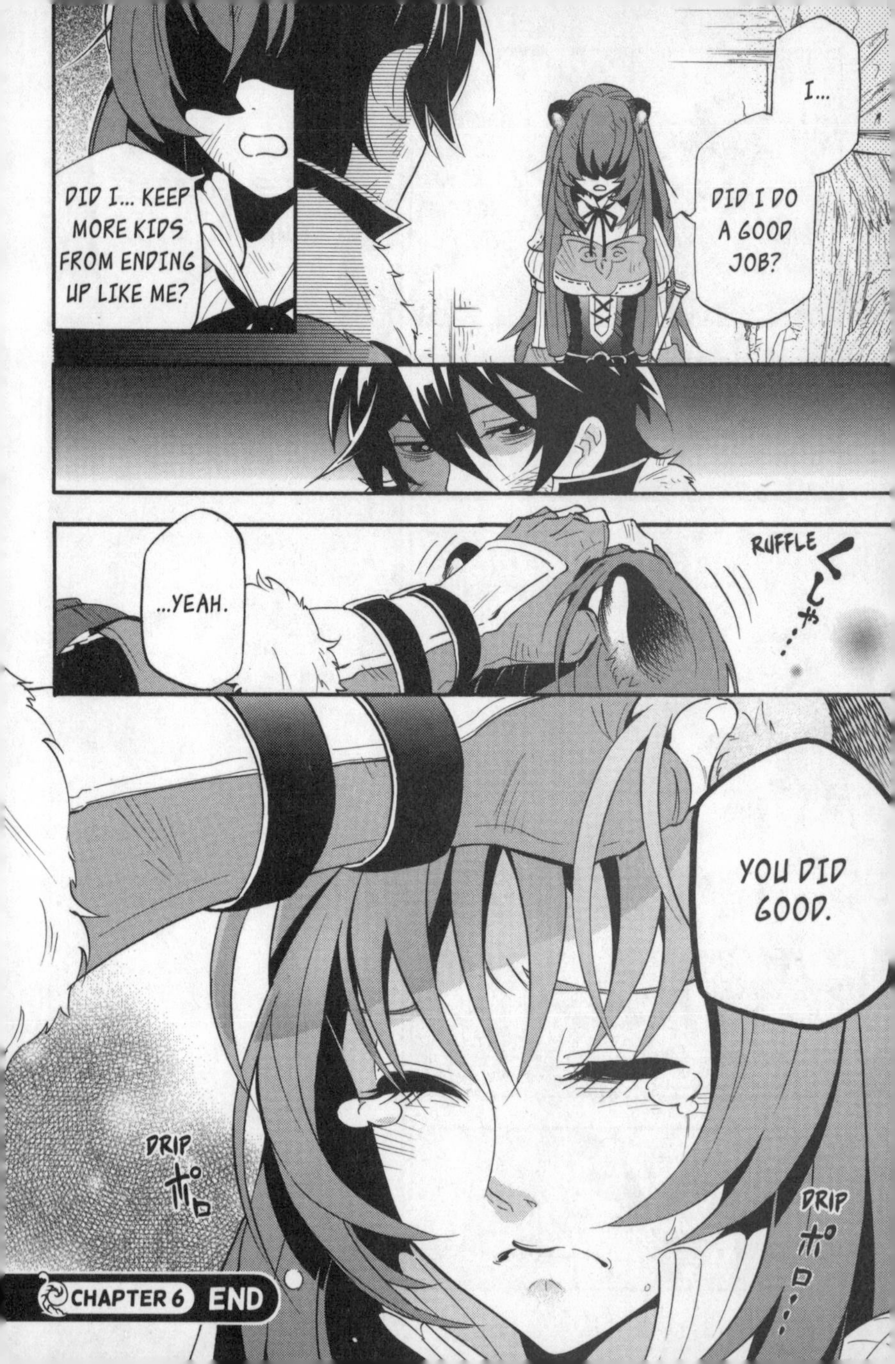
I...
DID I DO A GOOD JOB?
DID I... KEEP MORE KIDS FROM ENDING UP LIKE ME?
RUFFLE
...YEAH.
YOU DID GOOD.
DRIP
DRIP
CHAPTER 6 END

THE RISING OF 2 THE SHIELD HERO

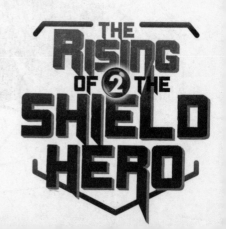

CHAPTER 7 THE DUEL

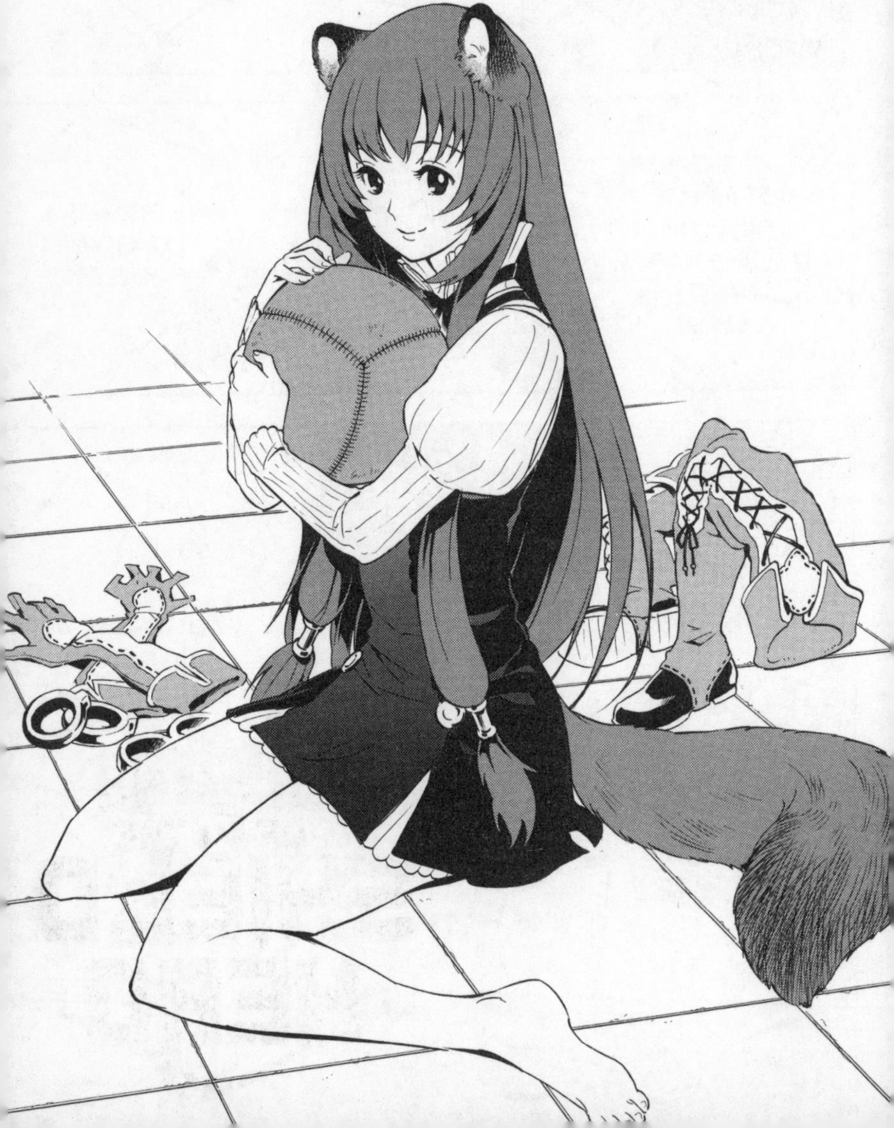

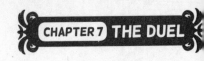

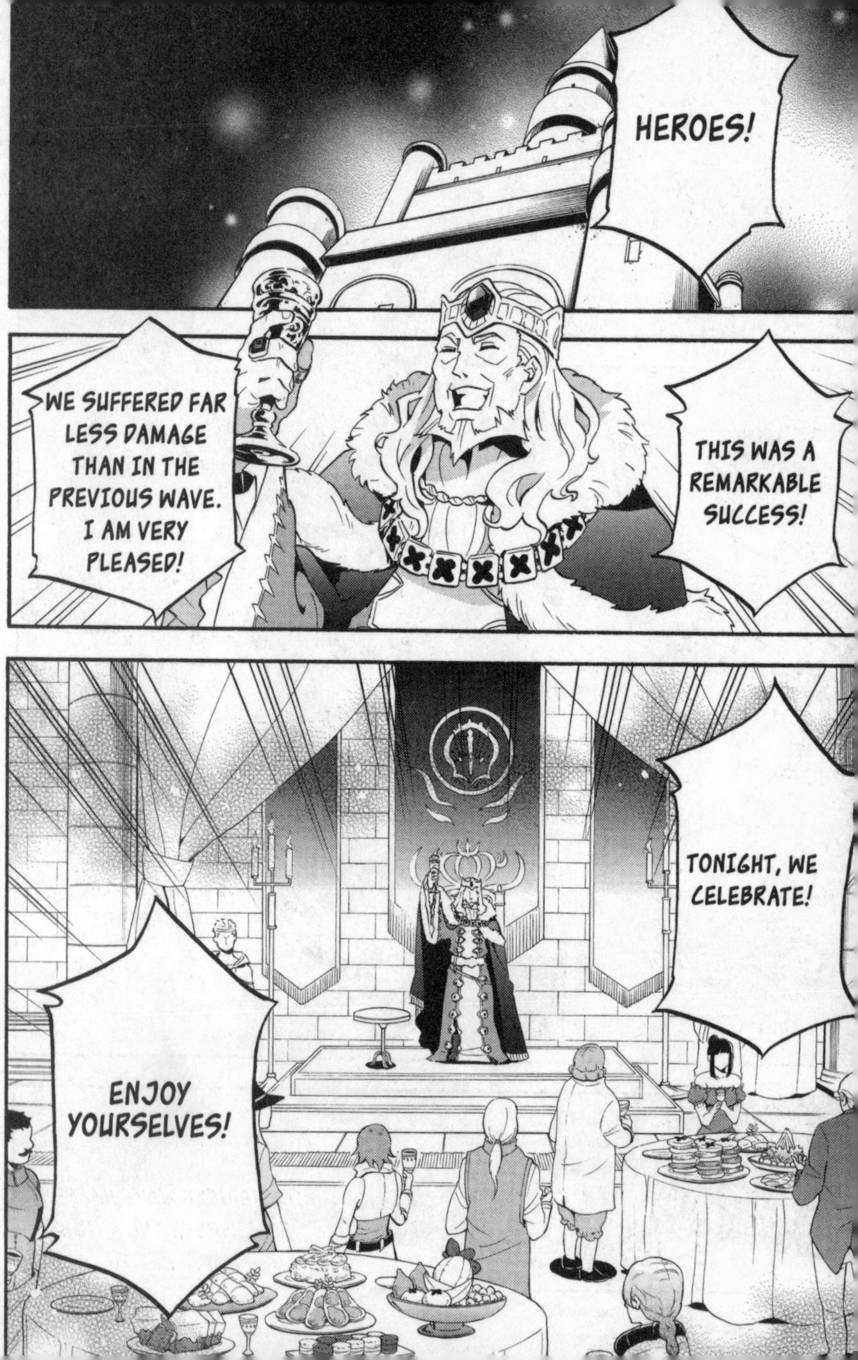
HEROES!
THIS WAS A REMARKABLE SUCCESS!
WE SUFFERED FAR LESS DAMAGE THAN IN THE PREVIOUS WAVE. I AM VERY PLEASED!
TONIGHT, WE CELEBRATE!
ENJOY YOURSELVES!

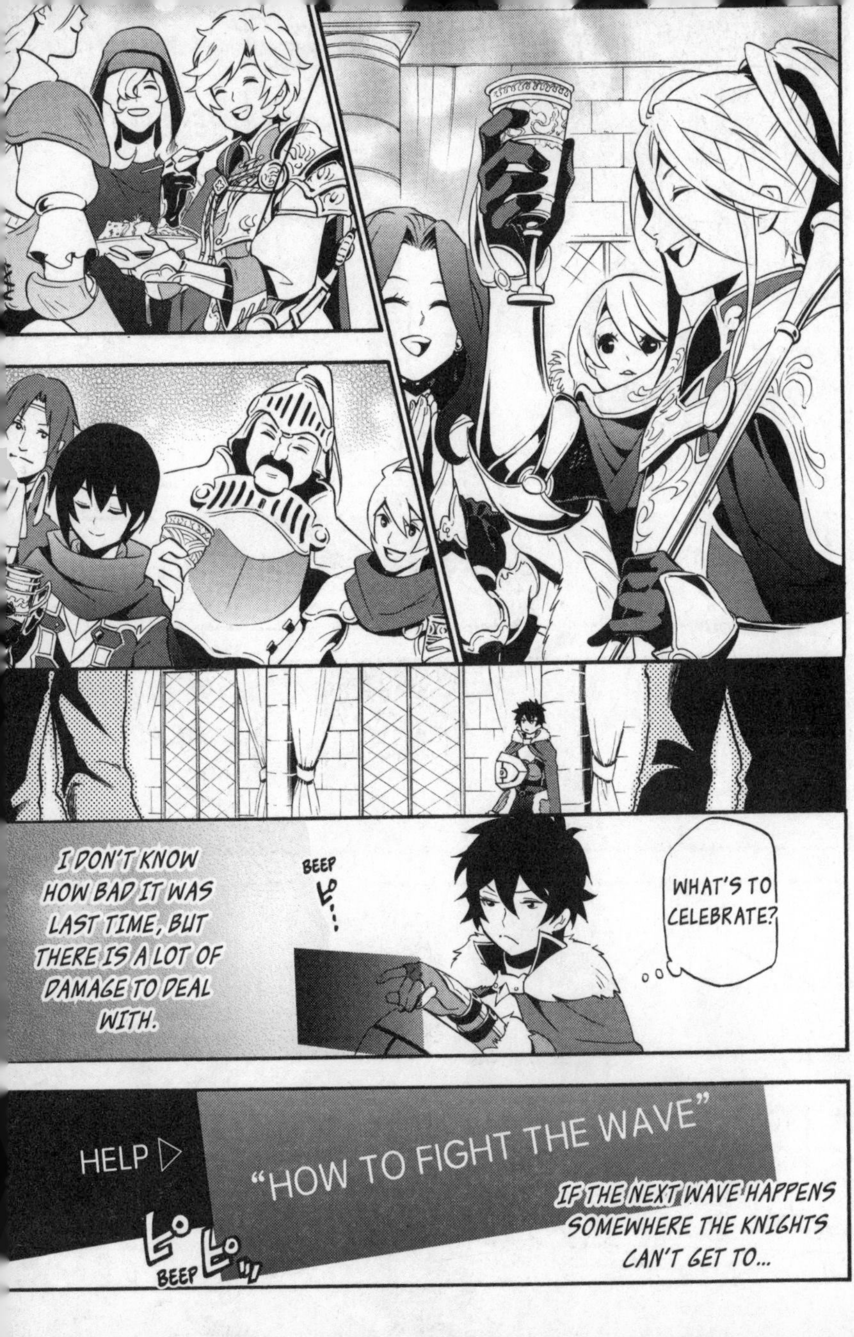

WHAT'S TO CELEBRATE?
BEEP
I DON'T KNOW HOW BAD IT WAS LAST TIME, BUT THERE IS A LOT OF DAMAGE TO DEAL WITH.
HELP ▷
"HOW TO FIGHT THE WAVE"
IF THE NEXT WAVE HAPPENS SOMEWHERE THE KNIGHTS CAN'T GET TO...
BEEP

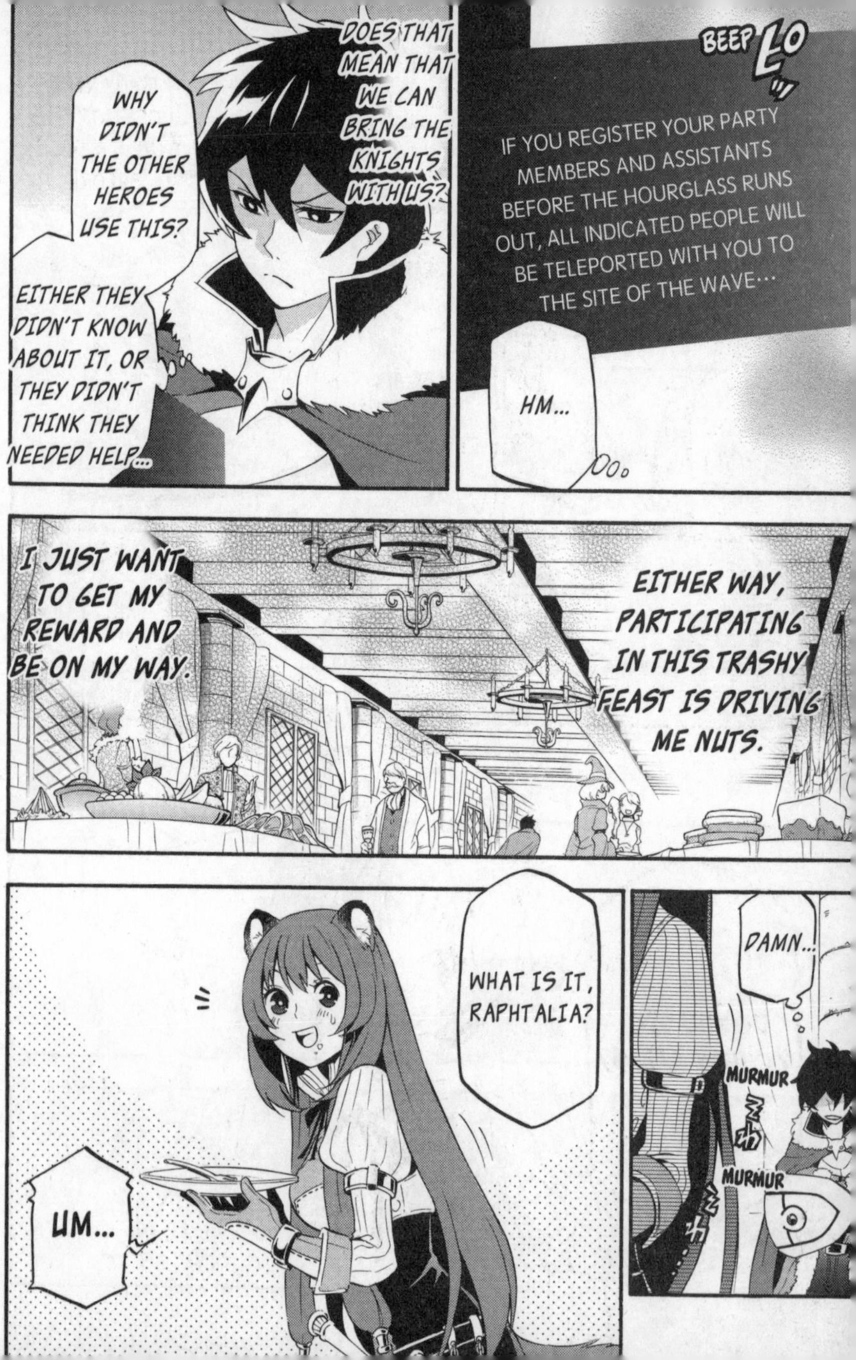
BEEP
IF YOU REGISTER YOUR PARTY MEMBERS AND ASSISTANTS BEFORE THE HOURGLASS RUNS OUT, ALL INDICATED PEOPLE WILL BE TELEPORTED WITH YOU TO THE SITE OF THE WAVE…
HM...
DOES THAT MEAN THAT WE CAN BRING THE KNIGHTS WITH US?
WHY DIDN'T THE OTHER HEROES USE THIS?
EITHER THEY DIDN'T KNOW ABOUT IT, OR THEY DIDN'T THINK THEY NEEDED HELP...
EITHER WAY, PARTICIPATING IN THIS TRASHY FEAST IS DRIVING ME NUTS.
I JUST WANT TO GET MY REWARD AND BE ON MY WAY.
DAMN...
MURMUR
MURMUR
WHAT IS IT, RAPHTALIA?
UM...

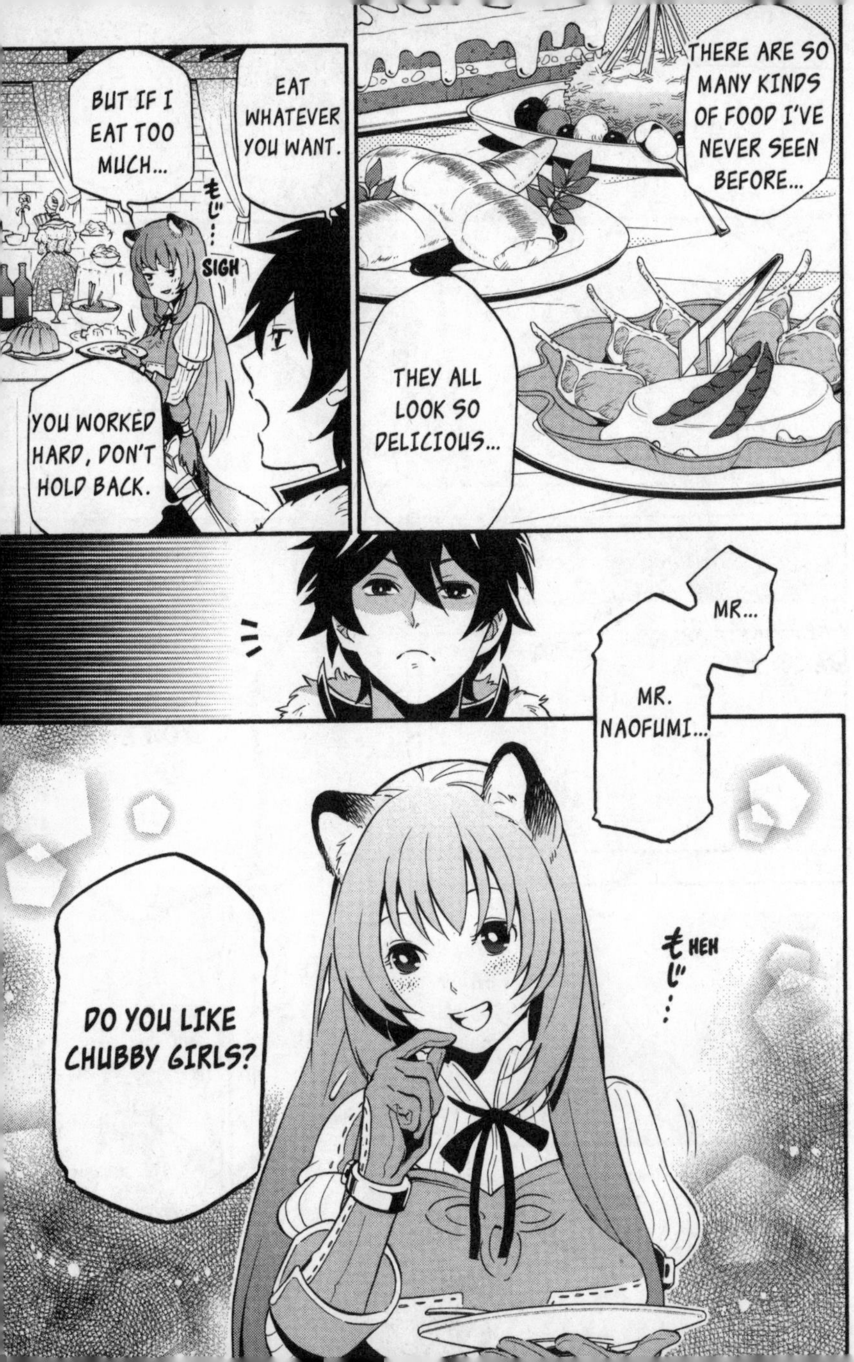
THERE ARE SO MANY KINDS OF FOOD I'VE NEVER SEEN BEFORE...
THEY ALL LOOK SO DELICIOUS...
EAT WHATEVER YOU WANT.
BUT IF I EAT TOO MUCH...
もじ…
SIGH
YOU WORKED HARD, DON'T HOLD BACK.
MR...
MR. NAOFUMI...
もじ…
HEH
DO YOU LIKE CHUBBY GIRLS?

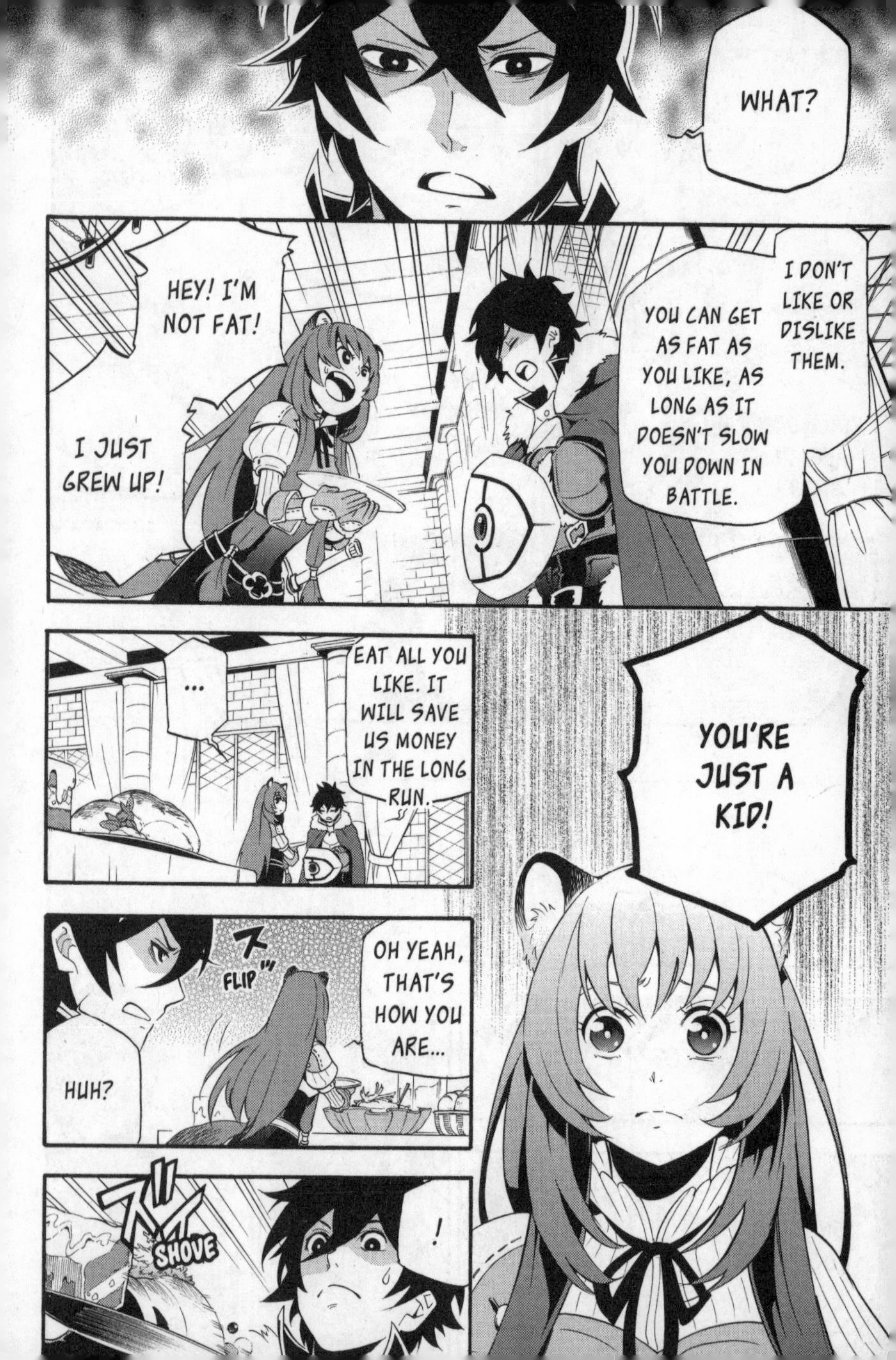
WHAT?
I DON'T LIKE OR DISLIKE THEM.
YOU CAN GET AS FAT AS YOU LIKE, AS LONG AS IT DOESN'T SLOW YOU DOWN IN BATTLE.
HEY! I'M NOT FAT!
I JUST GREW UP!
YOU'RE JUST A KID!
EAT ALL YOU LIKE. IT WILL SAVE US MONEY IN THE LONG RUN.
...
OH YEAH, THAT'S HOW YOU ARE...
FLIP
HUH?
!
SHOVE

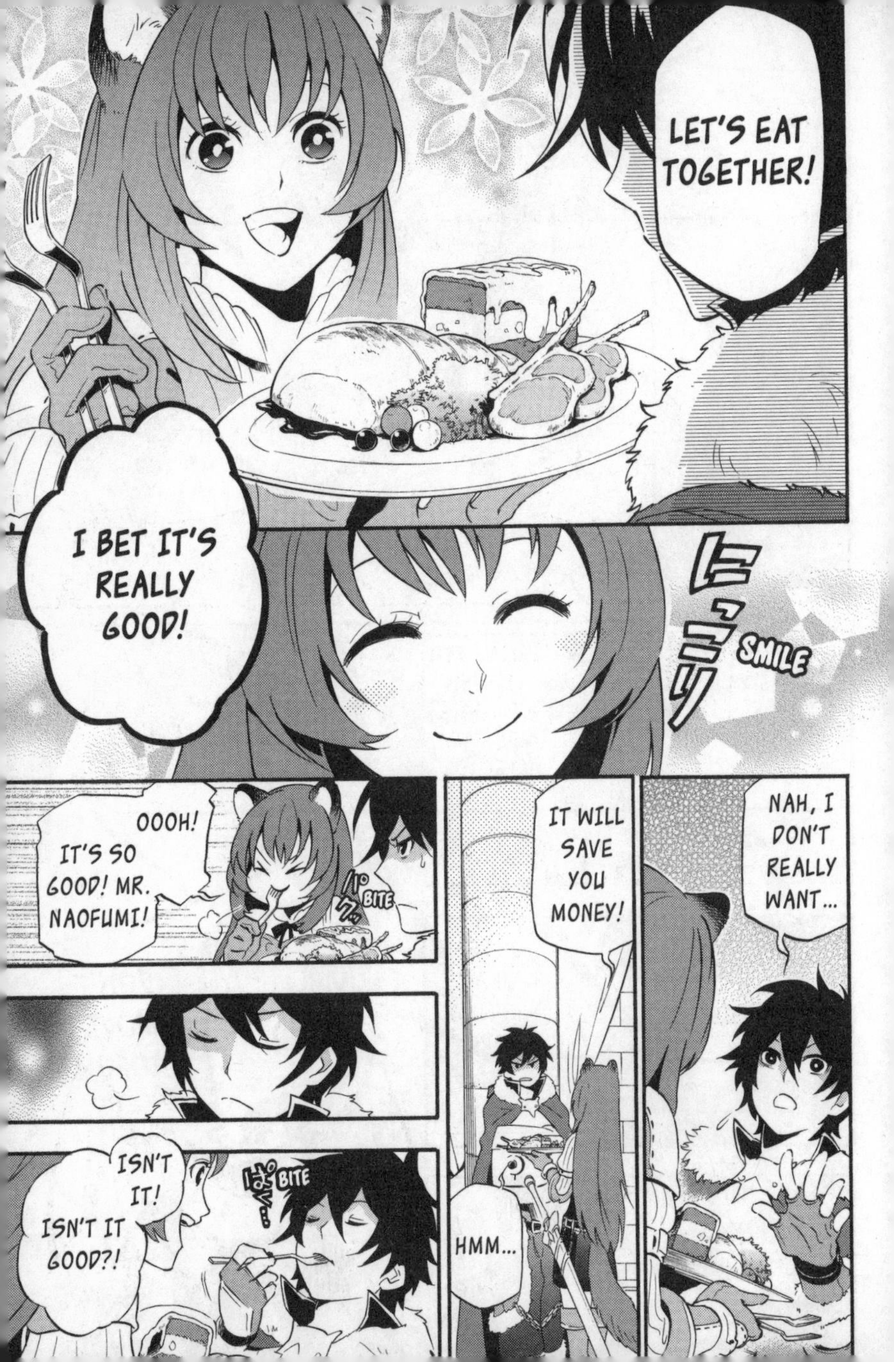
LET'S EAT TOGETHER!
I BET IT'S REALLY GOOD!
ニコッ
SMILE
NAH, I DON'T REALLY WANT...
IT WILL SAVE YOU MONEY!
HMM...
OOOH! IT'S SO GOOD! MR. NAOFUMI!
パク
BITE
ぱく…
BITE
ISN'T IT! ISN'T IT GOOD?!

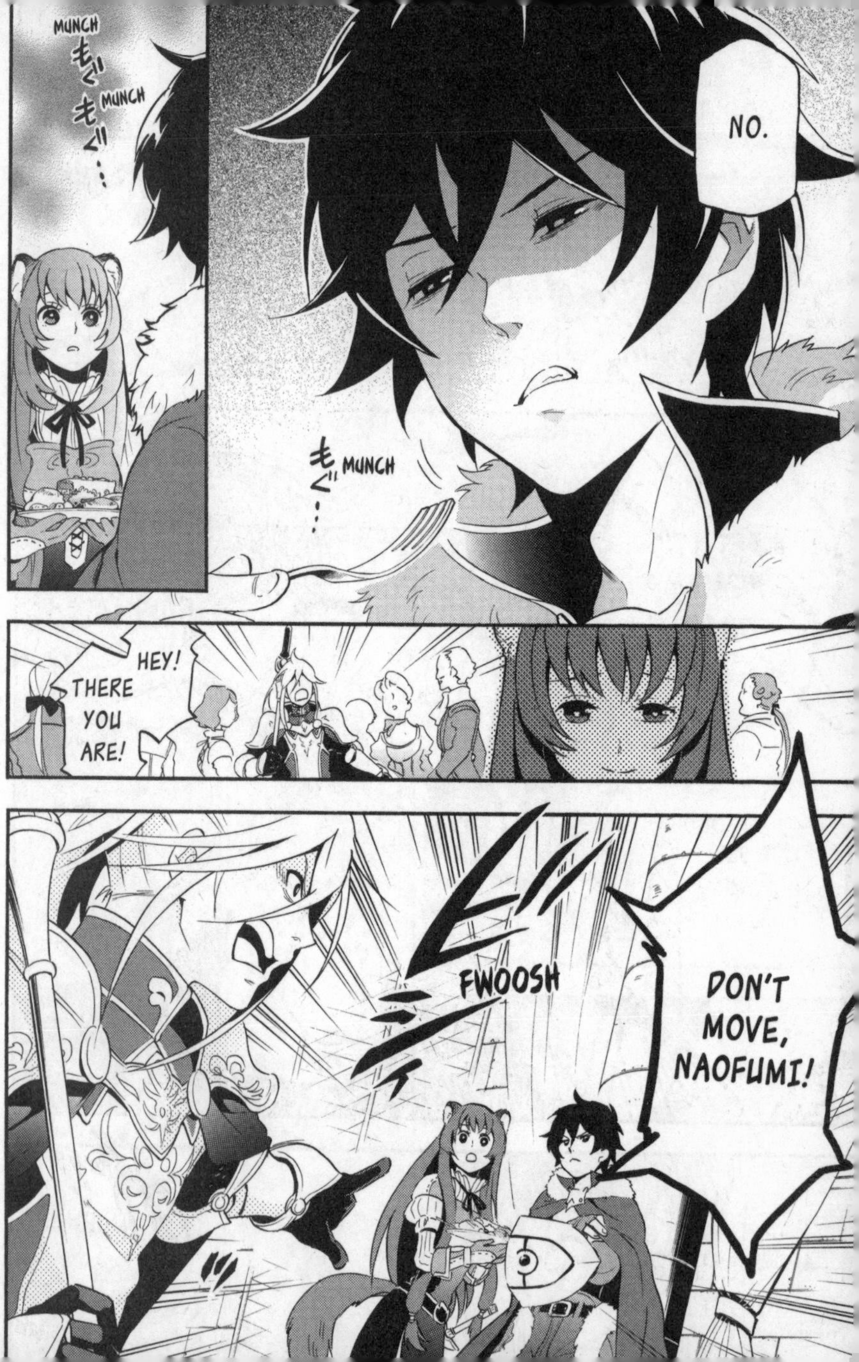
NO.
もぐ…
MUNCH
MUNCH
もぐ
MUNCH
もぐ…
HEY! THERE YOU ARE!
DON'T MOVE, NAOFUMI!
FWOOSH

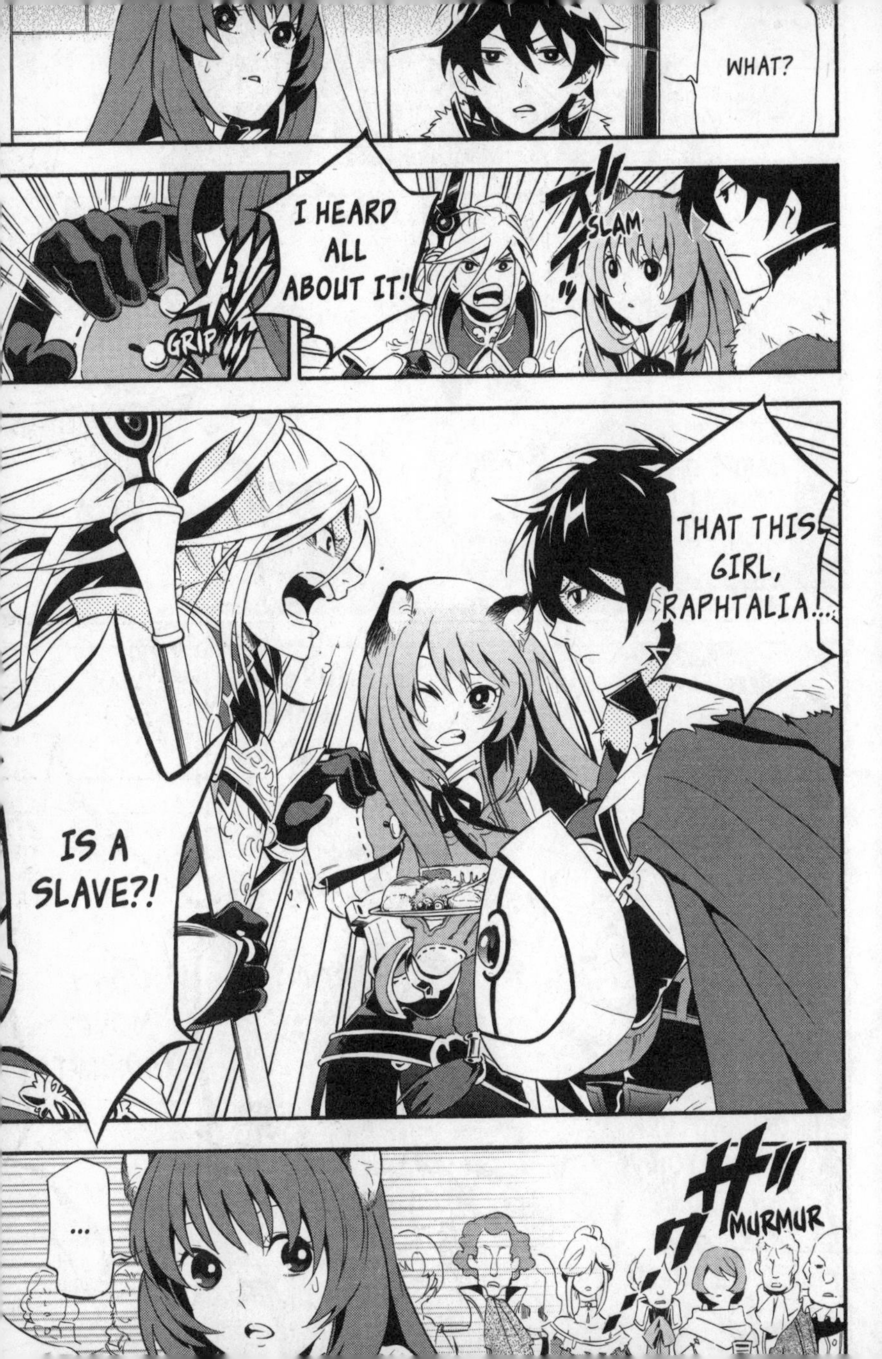

WHAT?
I HEARD ALL ABOUT IT!
SLAM
GRIP
THAT THIS GIRL, RAPHTALIA...
IS A SLAVE?!
MURMUR
...

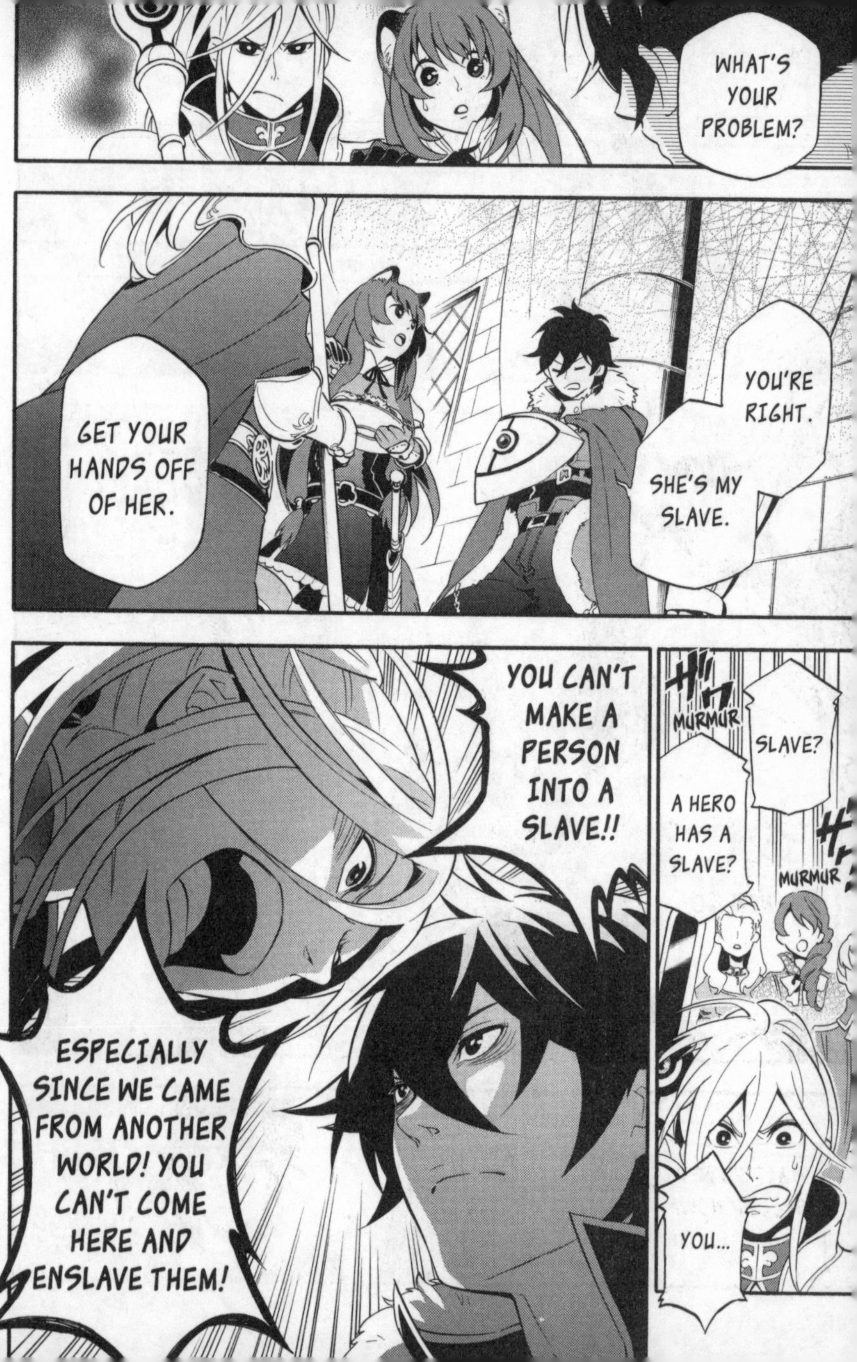
WHAT'S YOUR PROBLEM?
YOU'RE RIGHT.
SHE'S MY SLAVE.
GET YOUR HANDS OFF OF HER.
MURMUR
SLAVE?
A HERO HAS A SLAVE?
MURMUR
YOU...
YOU CAN'T MAKE A PERSON INTO A SLAVE!!
ESPECIALLY SINCE WE CAME FROM ANOTHER WORLD! YOU CAN'T COME HERE AND ENSLAVE THEM!

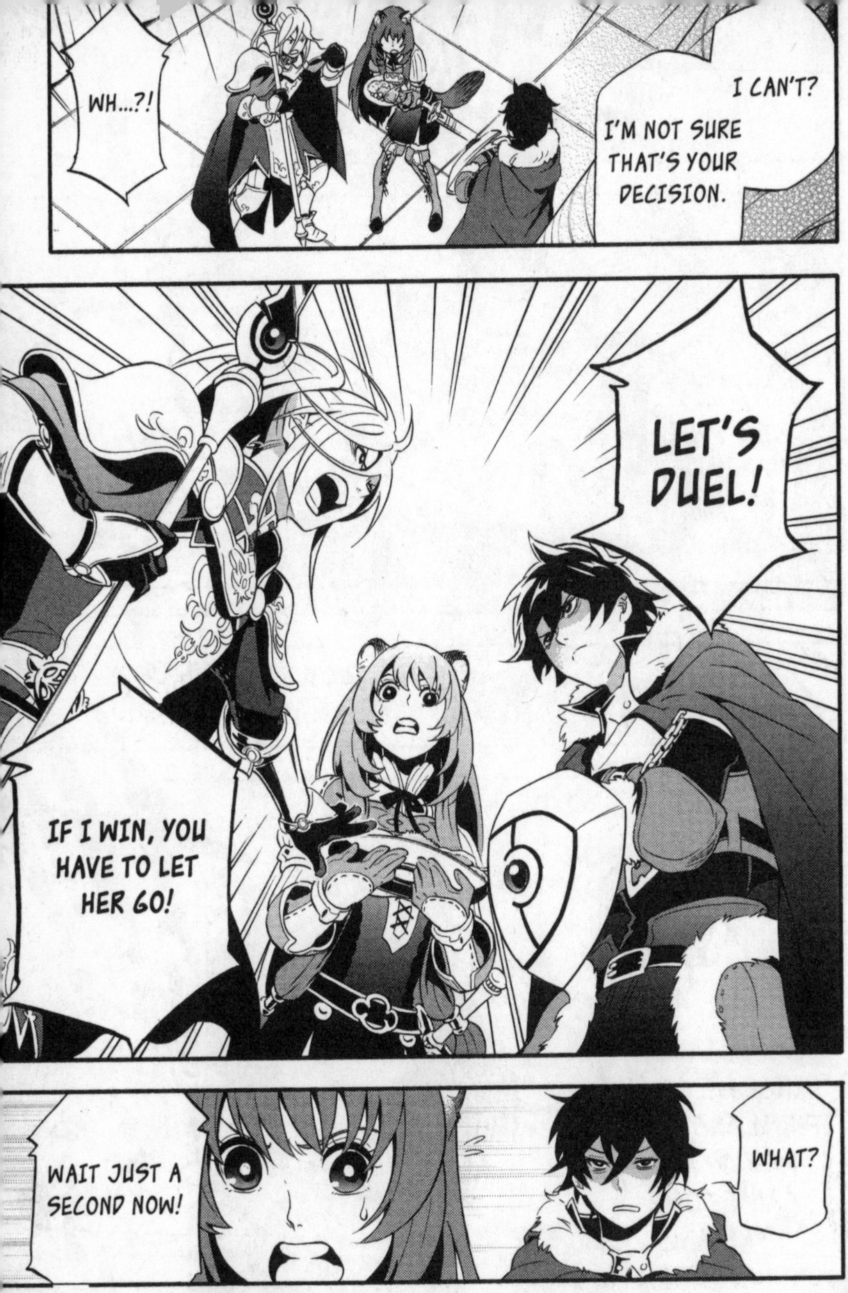
I CAN'T?
I'M NOT SURE THAT'S YOUR DECISION.
WH...?!
LET'S DUEL!
IF I WIN, YOU HAVE TO LET HER GO!
WHAT?
WAIT JUST A SECOND NOW!

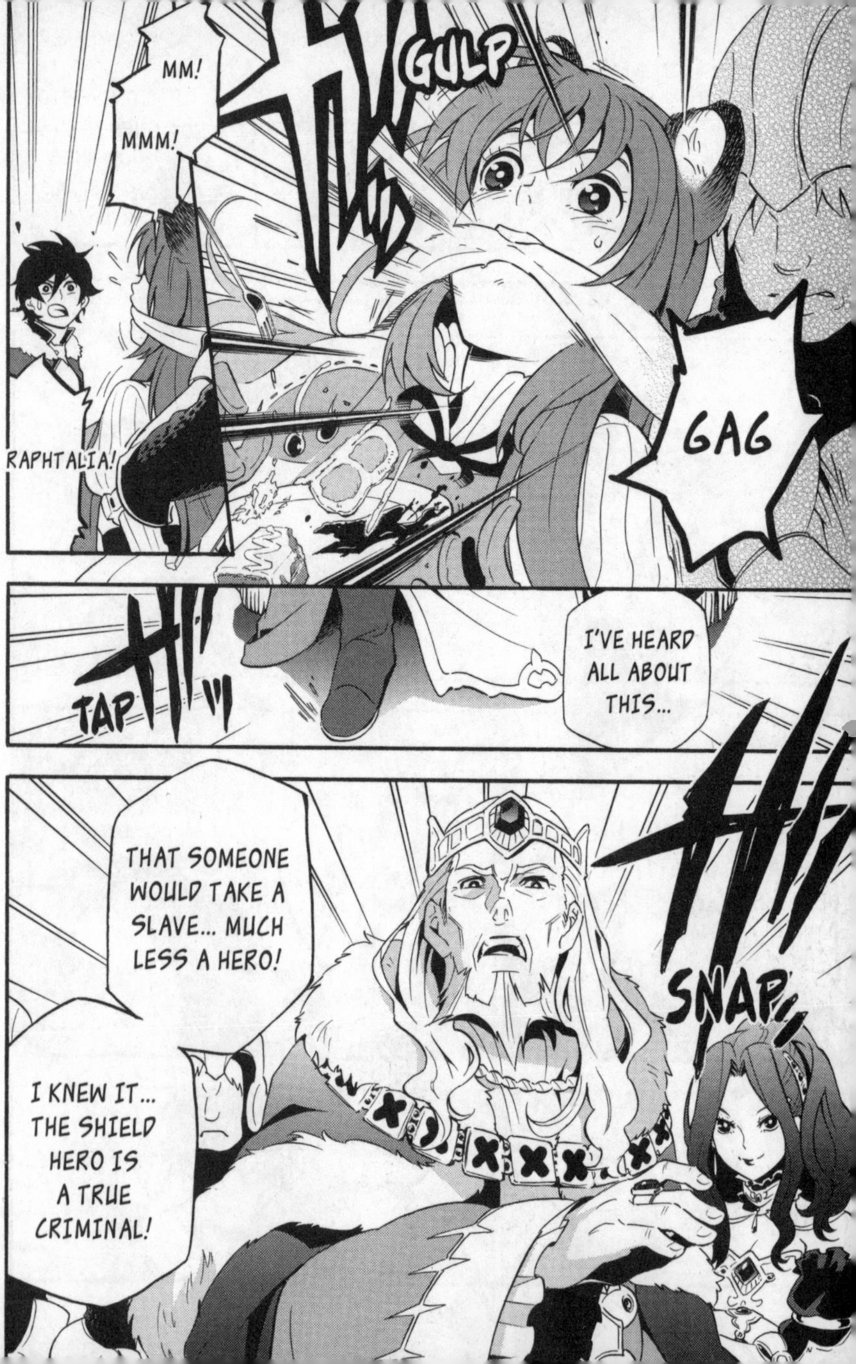
GULP
MM!
MMM!
GAG
RAPHTALIA!
TAP
I'VE HEARD ALL ABOUT THIS...
THAT SOMEONE WOULD TAKE A SLAVE... MUCH LESS A HERO!
SNAP
I KNEW IT... THE SHIELD HERO IS A TRUE CRIMINAL!

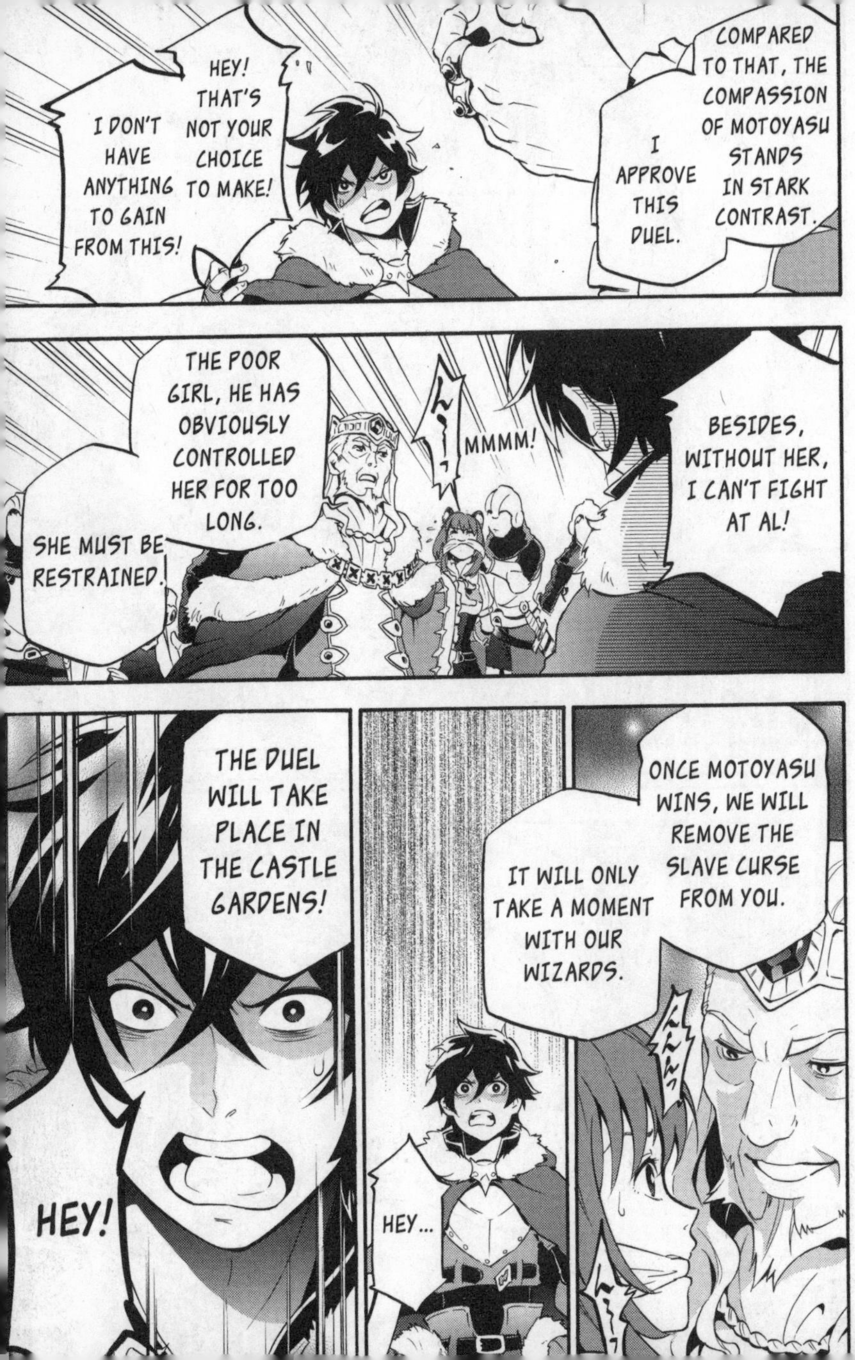
COMPARED TO THAT, THE COMPASSION OF MOTOYASU STANDS IN STARK CONTRAST.
I APPROVE THIS DUEL.
HEY! THAT'S NOT YOUR CHOICE TO MAKE!
I DON'T HAVE ANYTHING TO GAIN FROM THIS!
BESIDES, WITHOUT HER, I CAN'T FIGHT AT AL!
MMMM!
THE POOR GIRL, HE HAS OBVIOUSLY CONTROLLED HER FOR TOO LONG.
SHE MUST BE RESTRAINED!
ONCE MOTOYASU WINS, WE WILL REMOVE THE SLAVE CURSE FROM YOU.
IT WILL ONLY TAKE A MOMENT WITH OUR WIZARDS.
HEY...
THE DUEL WILL TAKE PLACE IN THE CASTLE GARDENS!
HEY!

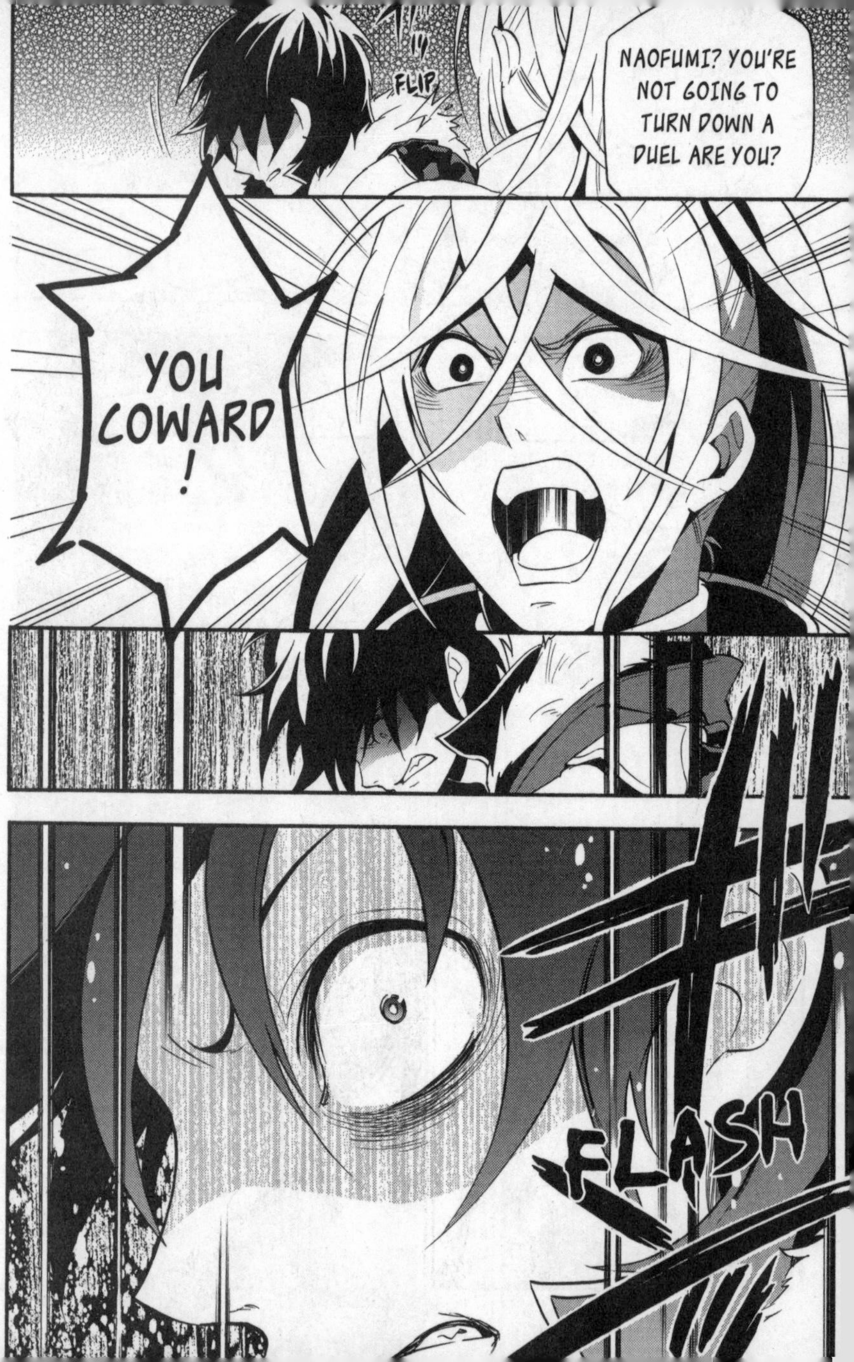
NAOFUMI? YOU'RE NOT GOING TO TURN DOWN A DUEL ARE YOU?
FLIP
YOU COWARD!
FLASH

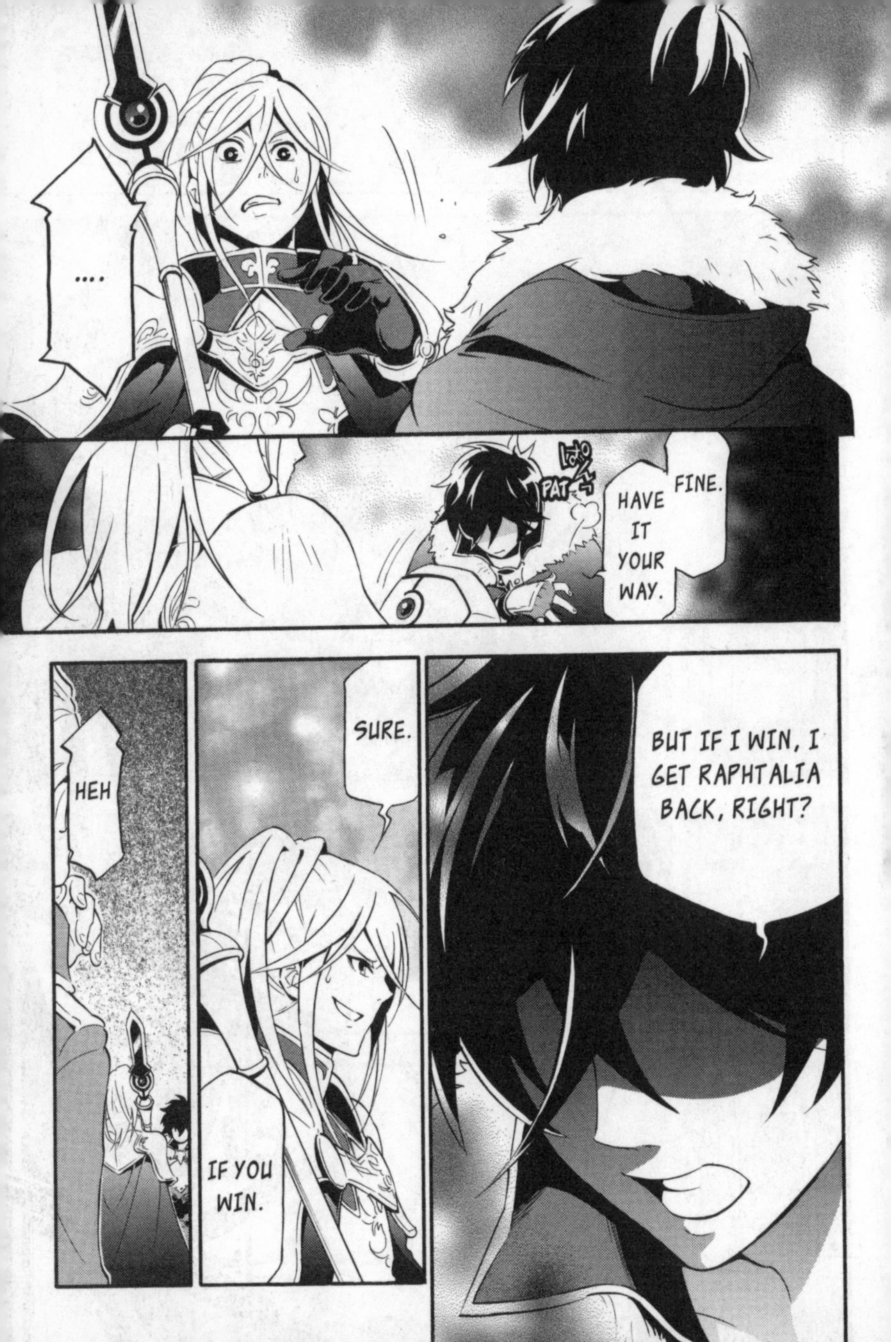
....
FINE.
HAVE IT YOUR WAY.
PAT
BUT IF I WIN, I GET RAPHTALIA BACK, RIGHT?
SURE.
IF YOU WIN.
HEH

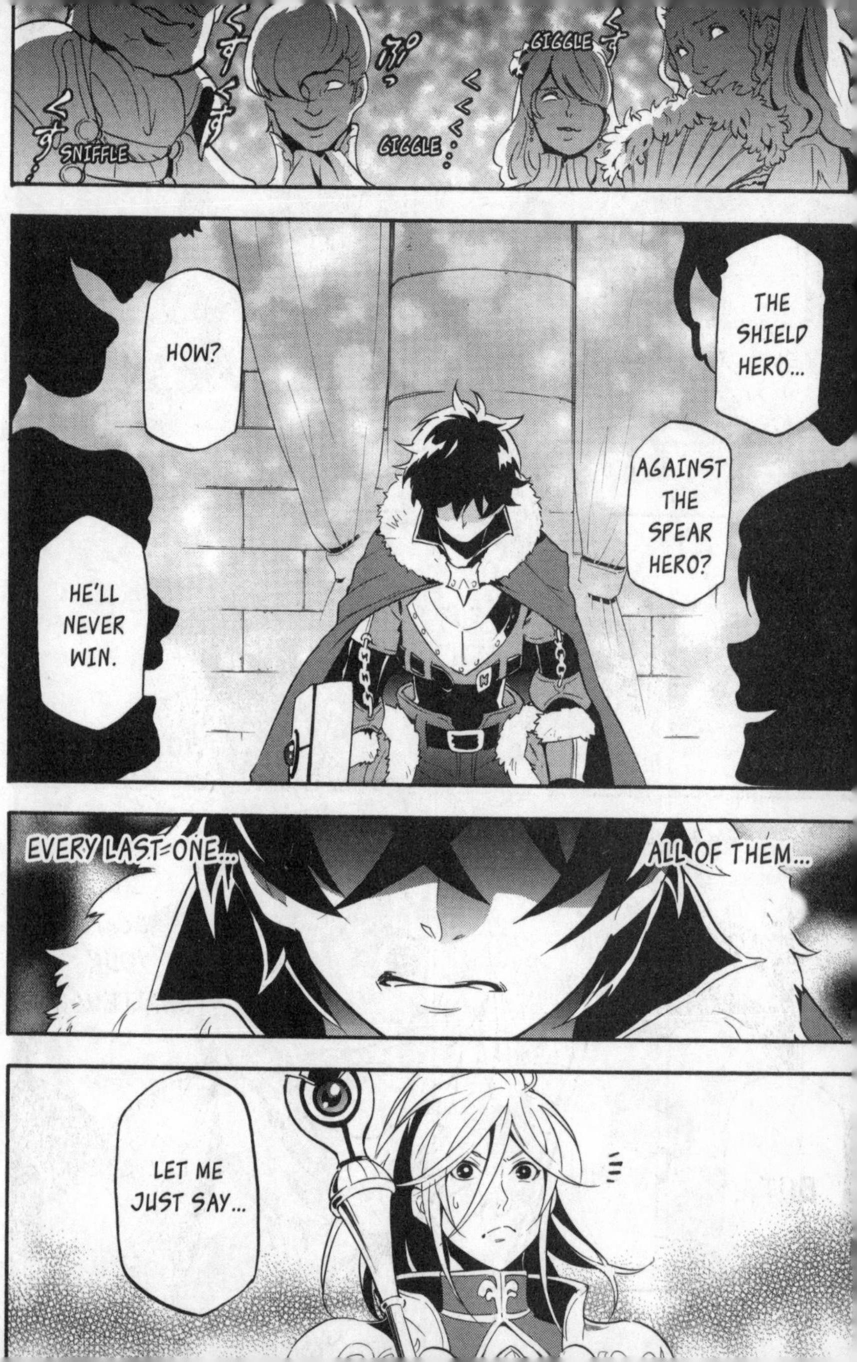

くす
GIGGLE
くくく…
GIGGLE
ぷっ
くすくす
くす
SNIFFLE
THE SHIELD HERO...
AGAINST THE SPEAR HERO?
HOW?
HE'LL NEVER WIN.
ALL OF THEM...
EVERY LAST ONE...
LET ME JUST SAY...

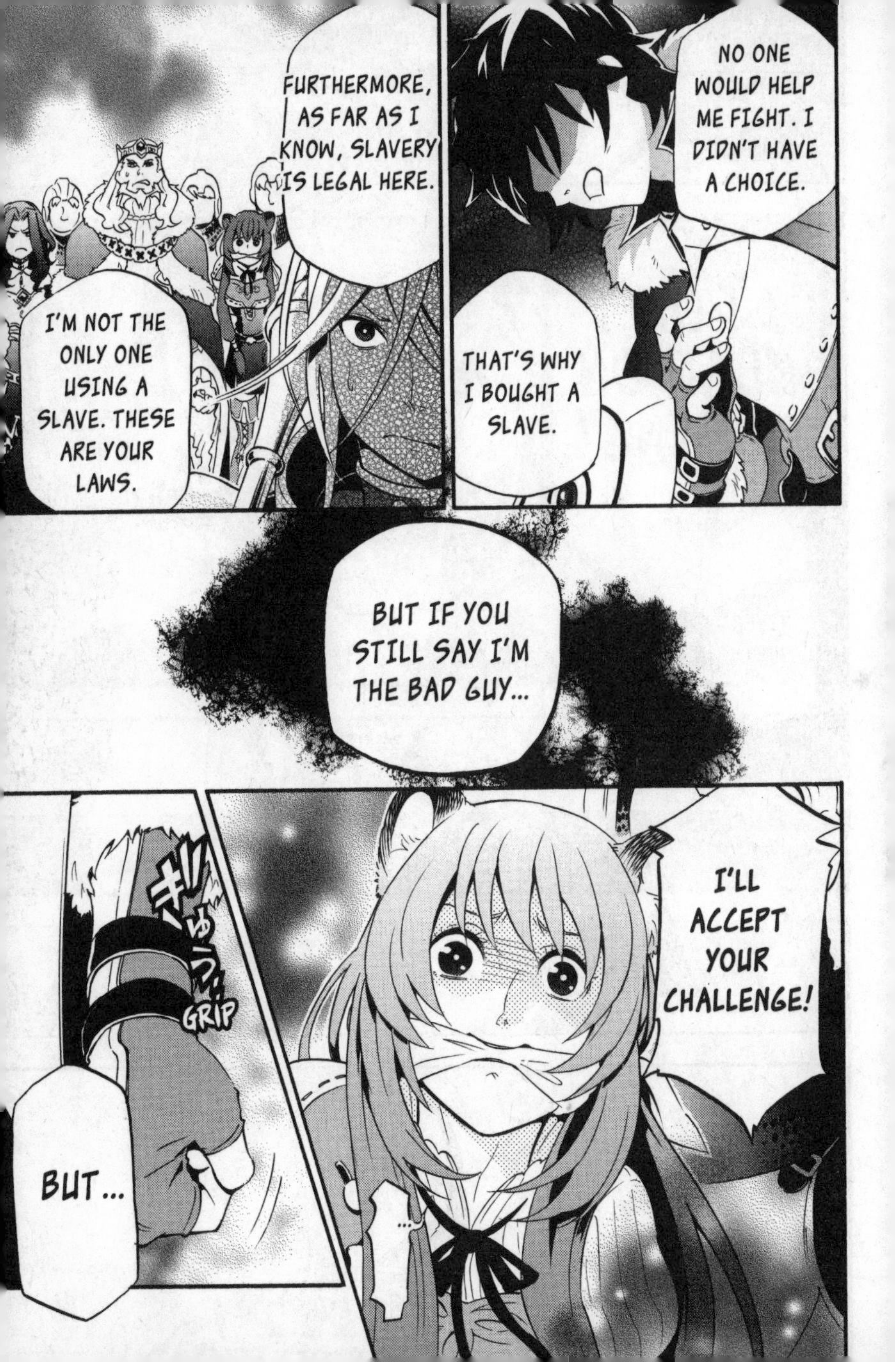
NO ONE WOULD HELP ME FIGHT. I DIDN'T HAVE A CHOICE.
THAT'S WHY I BOUGHT A SLAVE.
FURTHERMORE, AS FAR AS I KNOW, SLAVERY IS LEGAL HERE.
I'M NOT THE ONLY ONE USING A SLAVE. THESE ARE YOUR LAWS.
BUT IF YOU STILL SAY I'M THE BAD GUY...
I'LL ACCEPT YOUR CHALLENGE!
...
GRIP
BUT...

I DON'T PLAN ON LOSING!

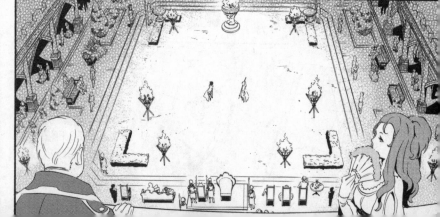

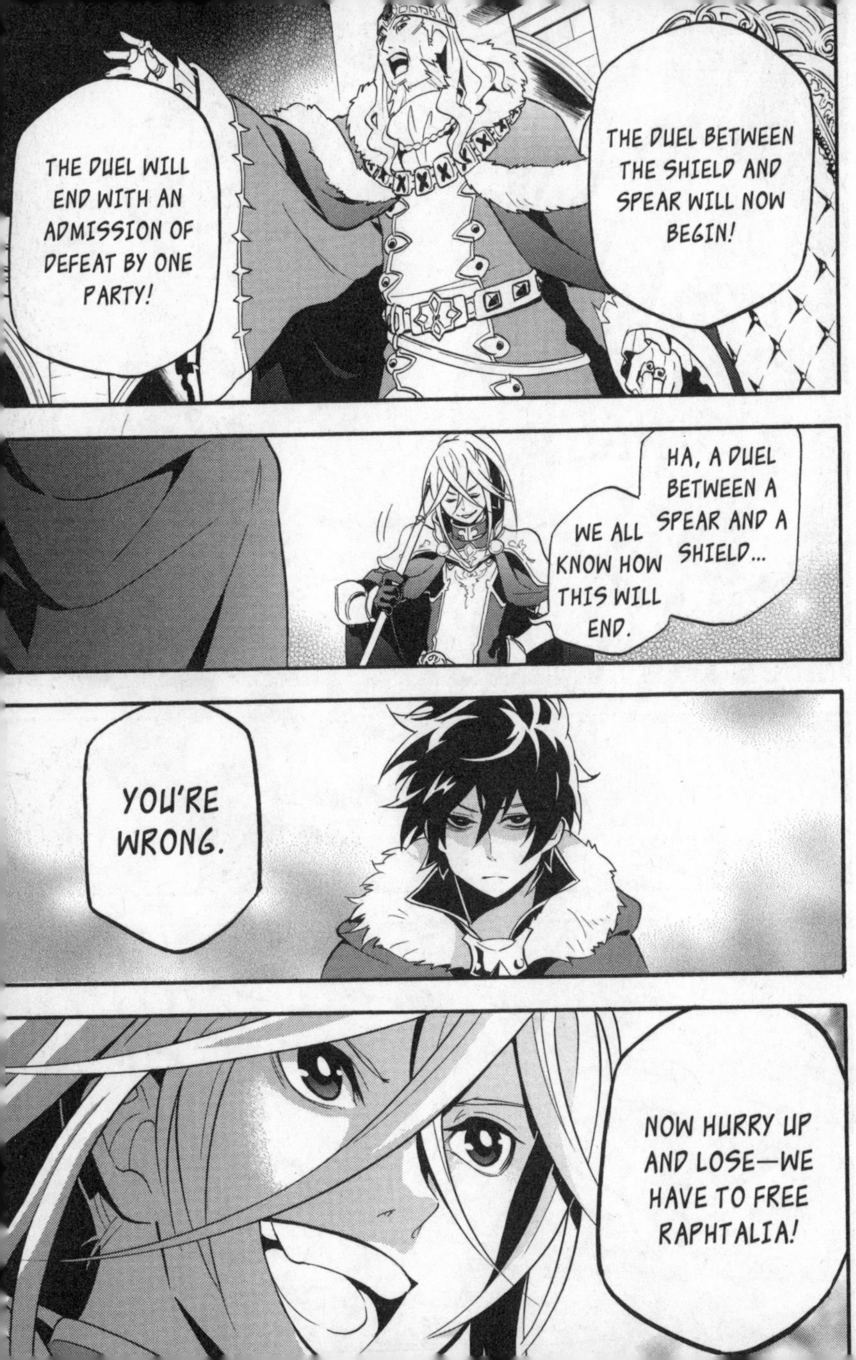
THE DUEL BETWEEN THE SHIELD AND SPEAR WILL NOW BEGIN!
THE DUEL WILL END WITH AN ADMISSION OF DEFEAT BY ONE PARTY!
HA, A DUEL BETWEEN A SPEAR AND A SHIELD...
WE ALL KNOW HOW THIS WILL END.
YOU'RE WRONG.
NOW HURRY UP AND LOSE—WE HAVE TO FREE RAPHTALIA!

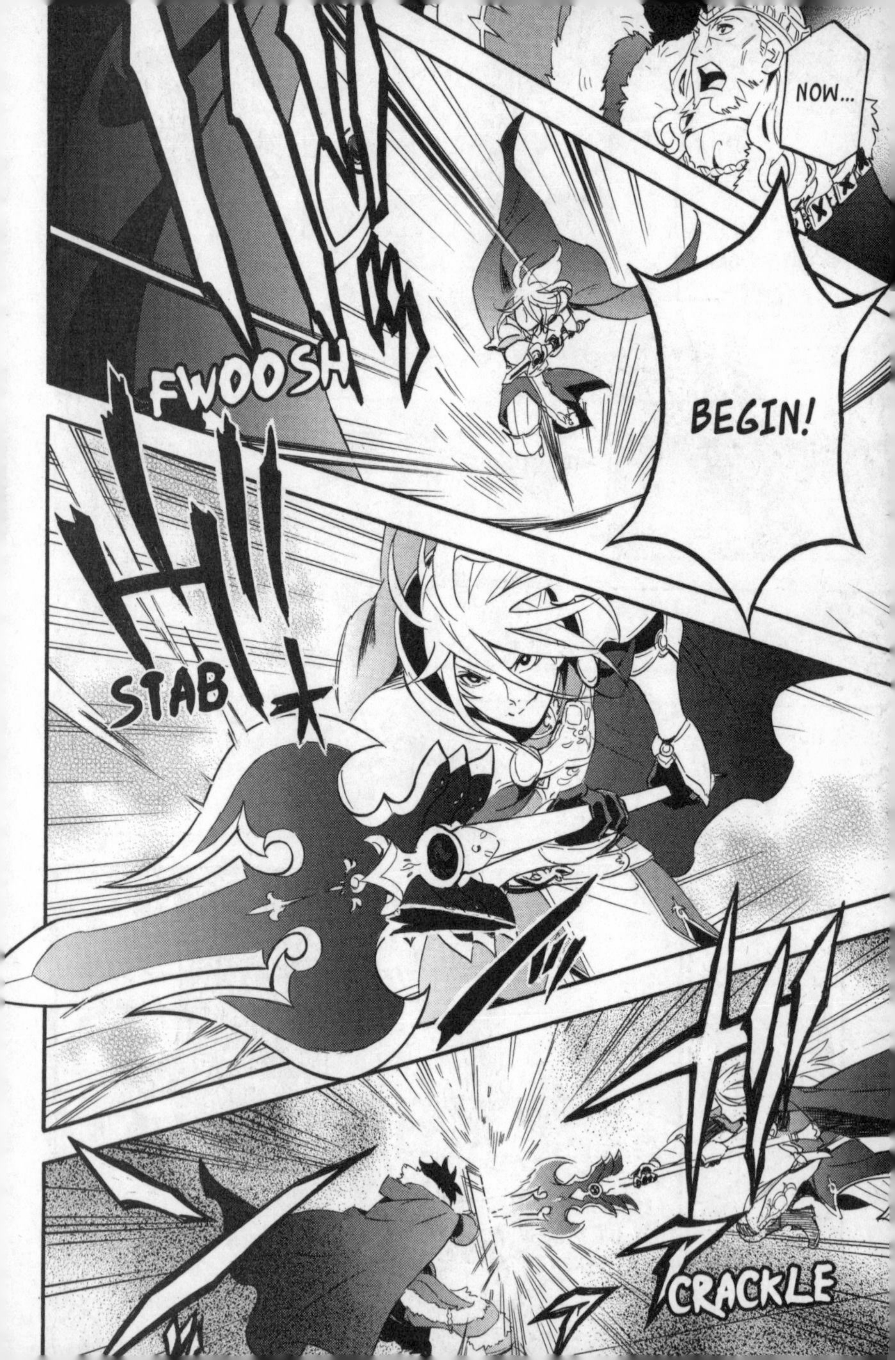
NOW...
BEGIN!
FWOOSH
STAB
CRACKLE

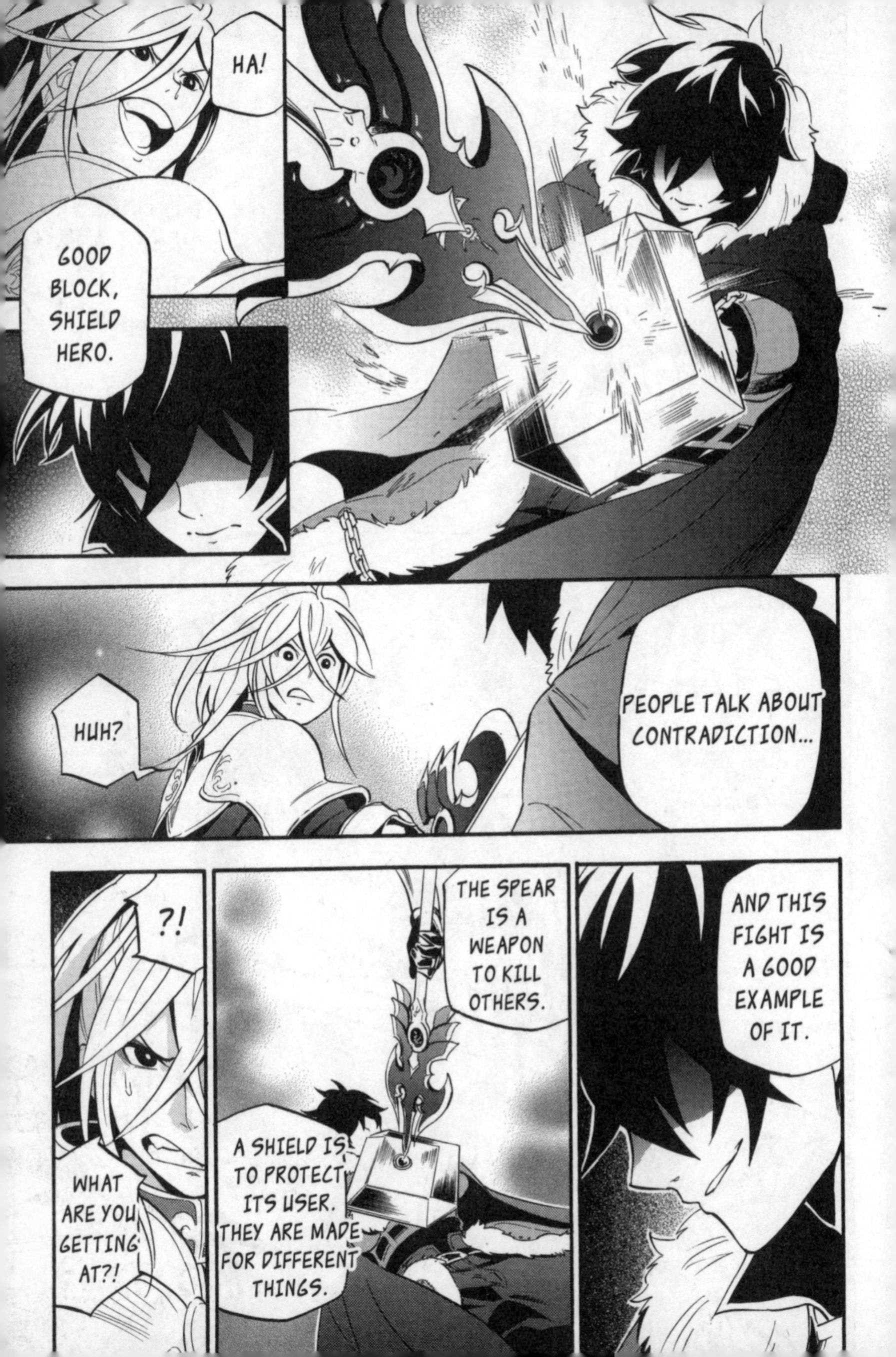
HA!
GOOD BLOCK, SHIELD HERO.
PEOPLE TALK ABOUT CONTRADICTION...
HUH?
AND THIS FIGHT IS A GOOD EXAMPLE OF IT.
THE SPEAR IS A WEAPON TO KILL OTHERS.
A SHIELD IS TO PROTECT ITS USER. THEY ARE MADE FOR DIFFERENT THINGS.
?!
WHAT ARE YOU GETTING AT?!

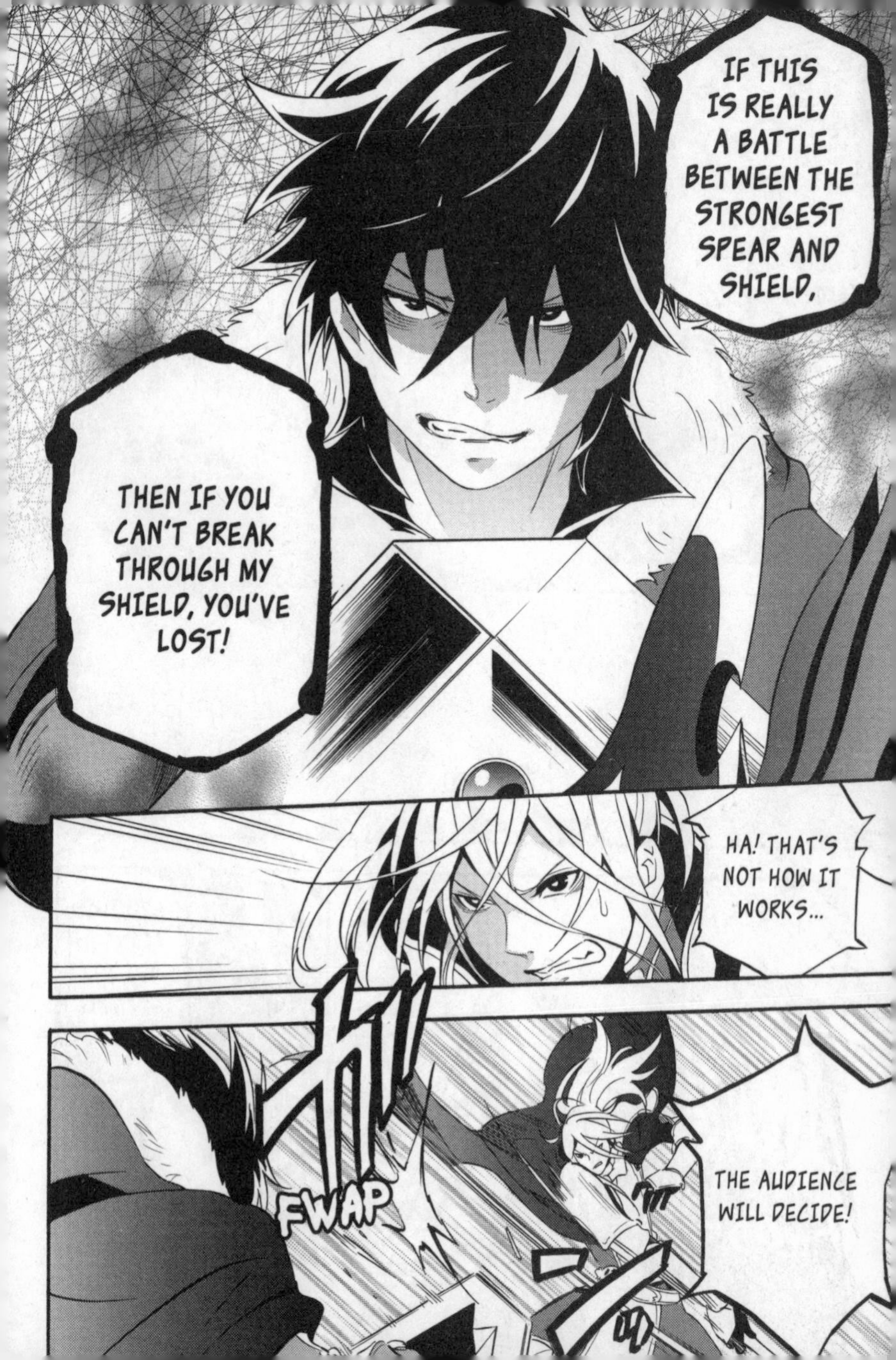
IF THIS IS REALLY A BATTLE BETWEEN THE STRONGEST SPEAR AND SHIELD,
THEN IF YOU CAN'T BREAK THROUGH MY SHIELD, YOU'VE LOST!
HA! THAT'S NOT HOW IT WORKS...
THE AUDIENCE WILL DECIDE!
FWAP

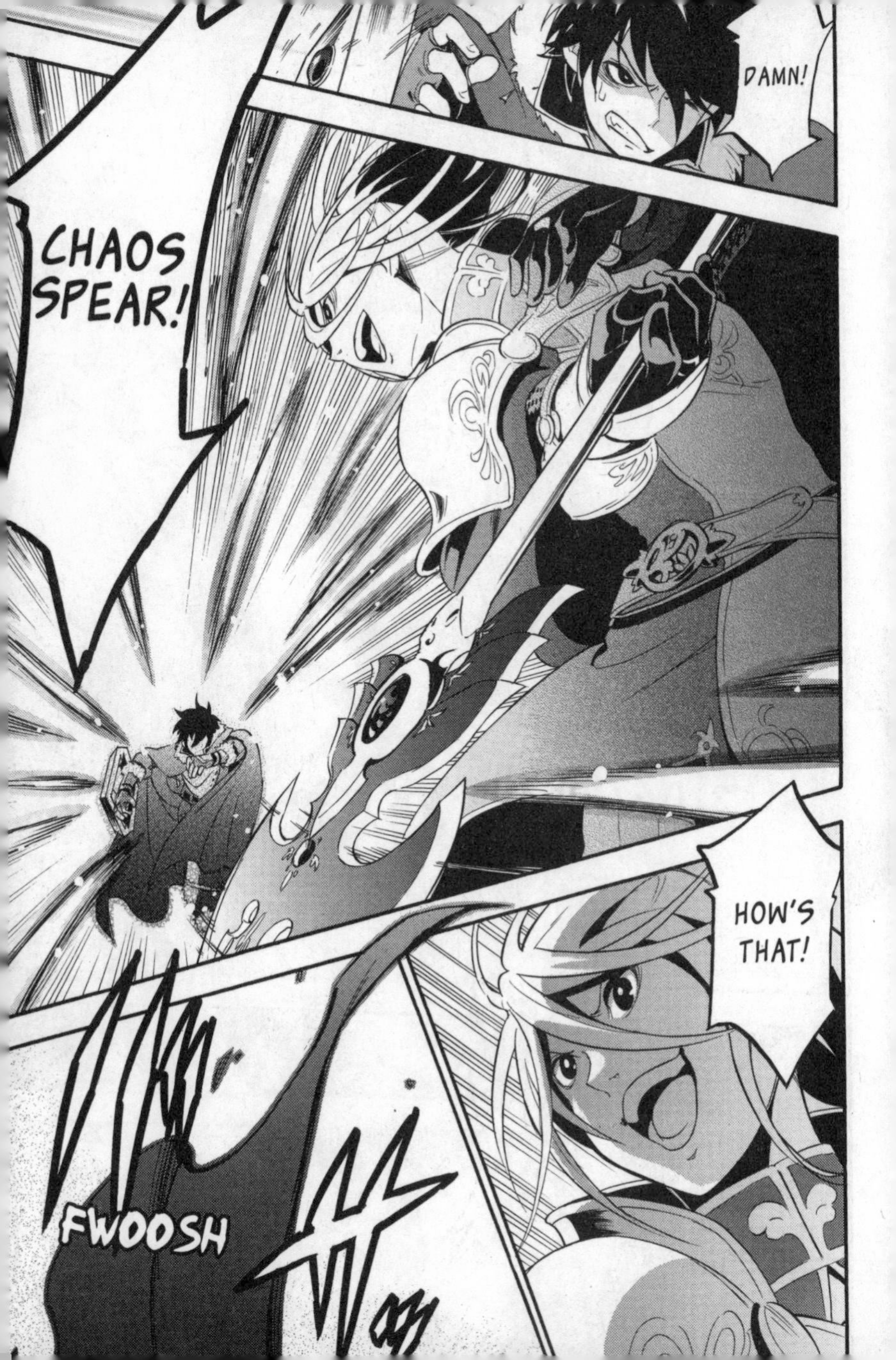

DAMN!
CHAOS SPEAR!
HOW'S THAT!
FWOOSH

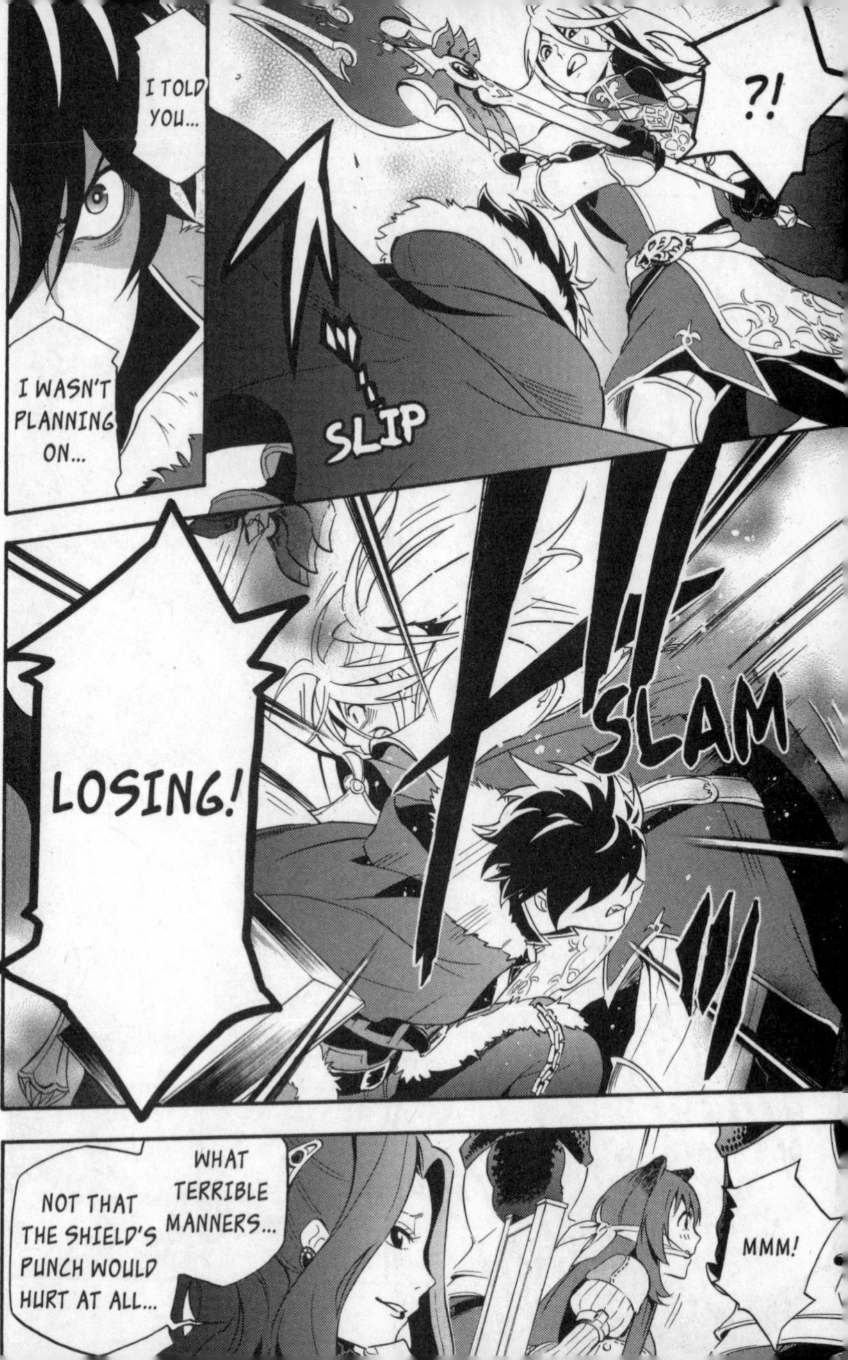
?!
SLIP
I TOLD YOU...
I WASN'T PLANNING ON...
SLAM
LOSING!
MMM!
WHAT TERRIBLE MANNERS...
NOT THAT THE SHIELD'S PUNCH WOULD HURT AT ALL...

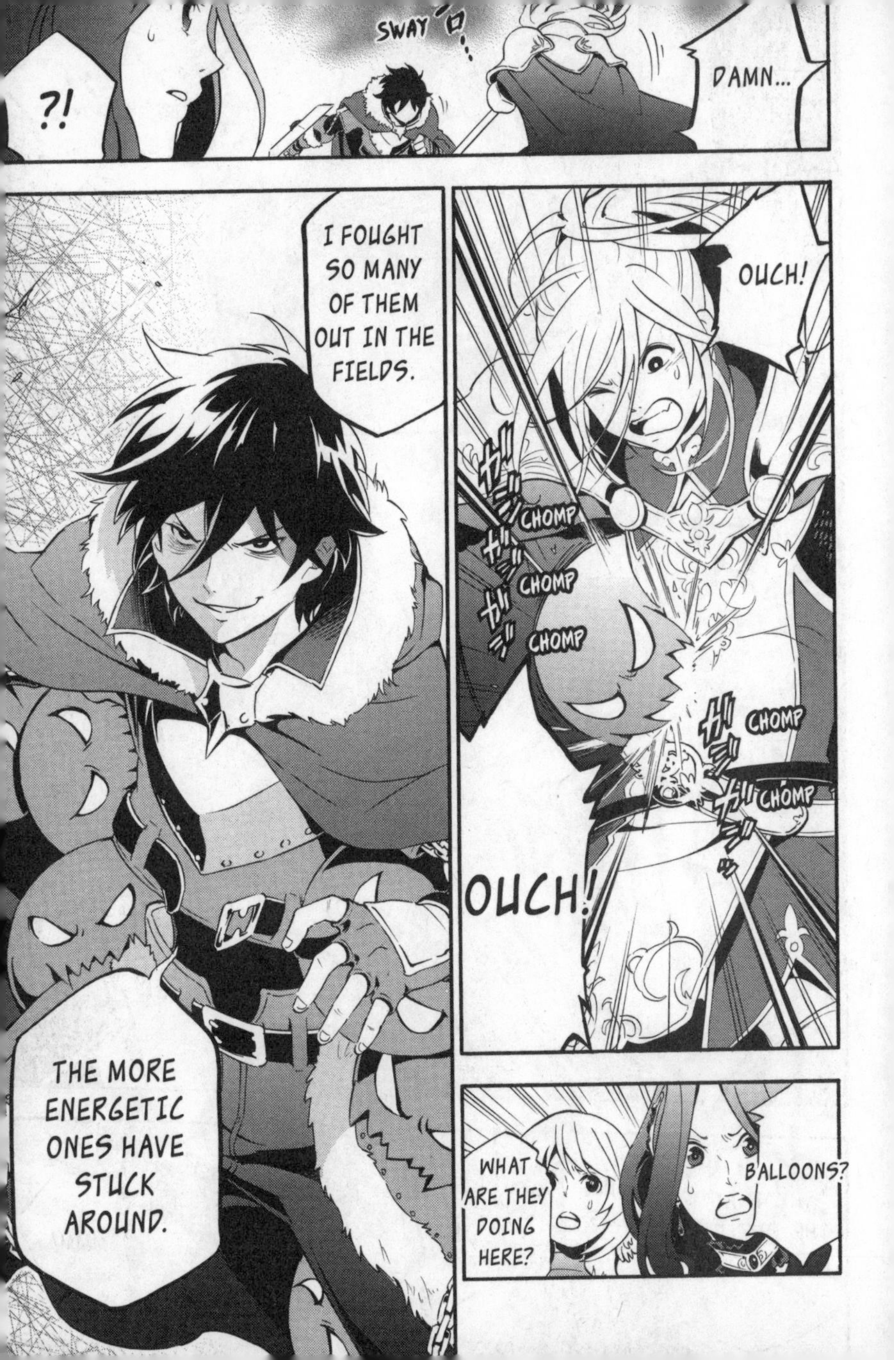
DAMN...
SWAY
?!
OUCH!
CHOMP
CHOMP
CHOMP
CHOMP
CHOMP
OUCH!
BALLOONS?
WHAT ARE THEY DOING HERE?
I FOUGHT SO MANY OF THEM OUT IN THE FIELDS.
THE MORE ENERGETIC ONES HAVE STUCK AROUND.

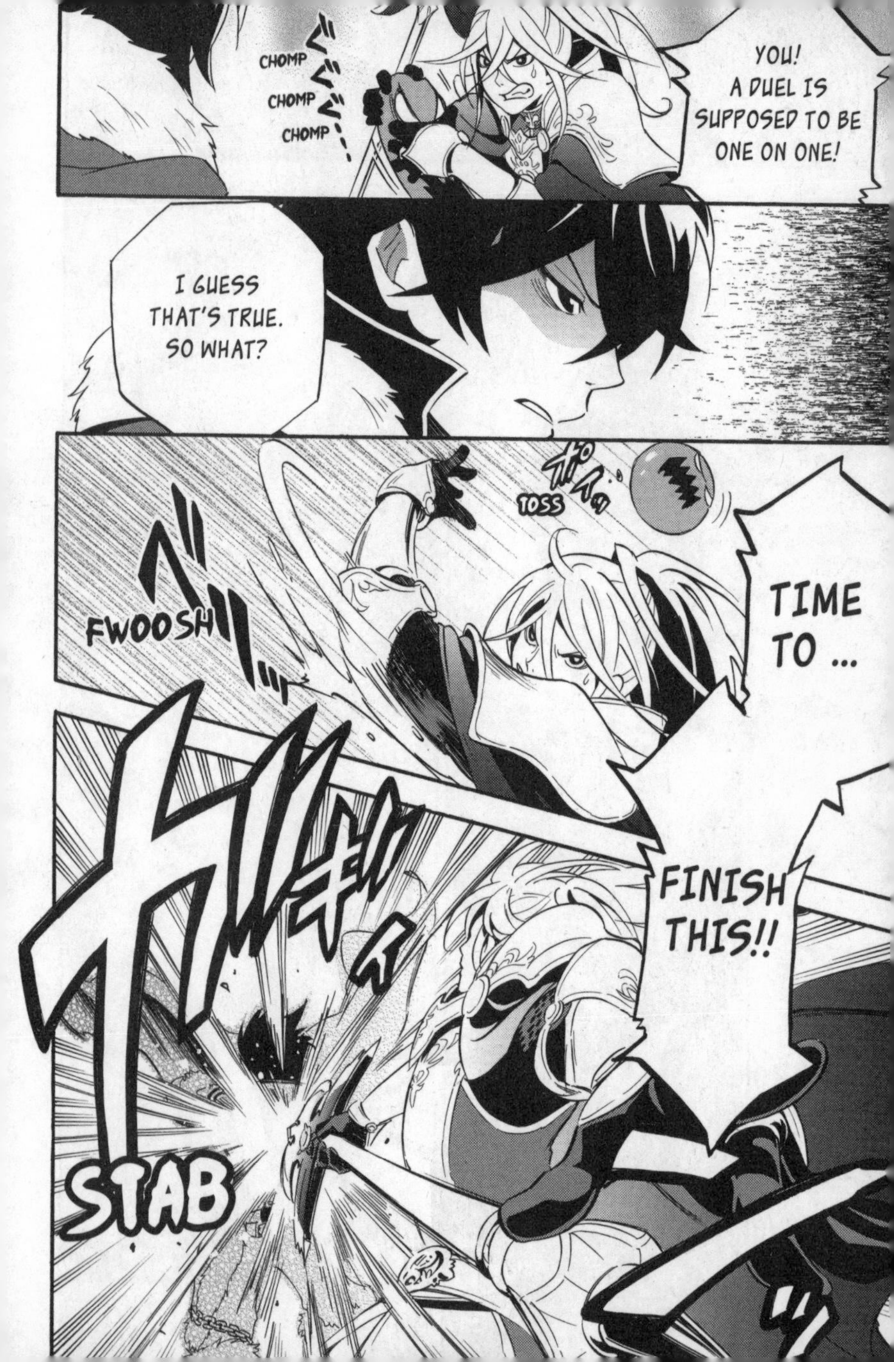
YOU!
A DUEL IS SUPPOSED TO BE ONE ON ONE!
CHOMP
CHOMP
CHOMP
I GUESS THAT'S TRUE. SO WHAT?
TIME TO ...
TOSS
FWOOSH
FINISH THIS!!
STAB

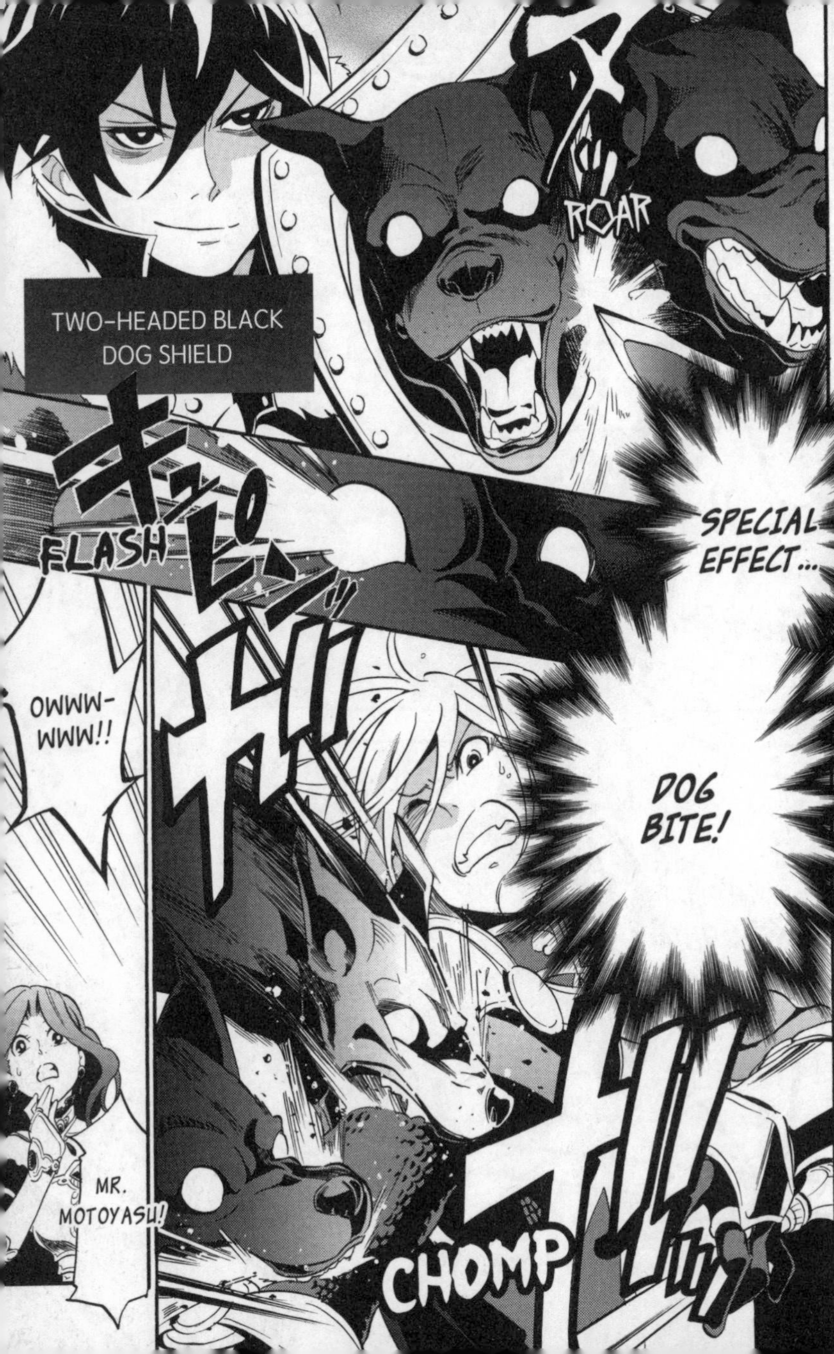
ROAR
TWO-HEADED BLACK DOG SHIELD
FLASH
SPECIAL EFFECT...
DOG BITE!
CHOMP
OWWW-WWW!!
MR. MOTOYASU!

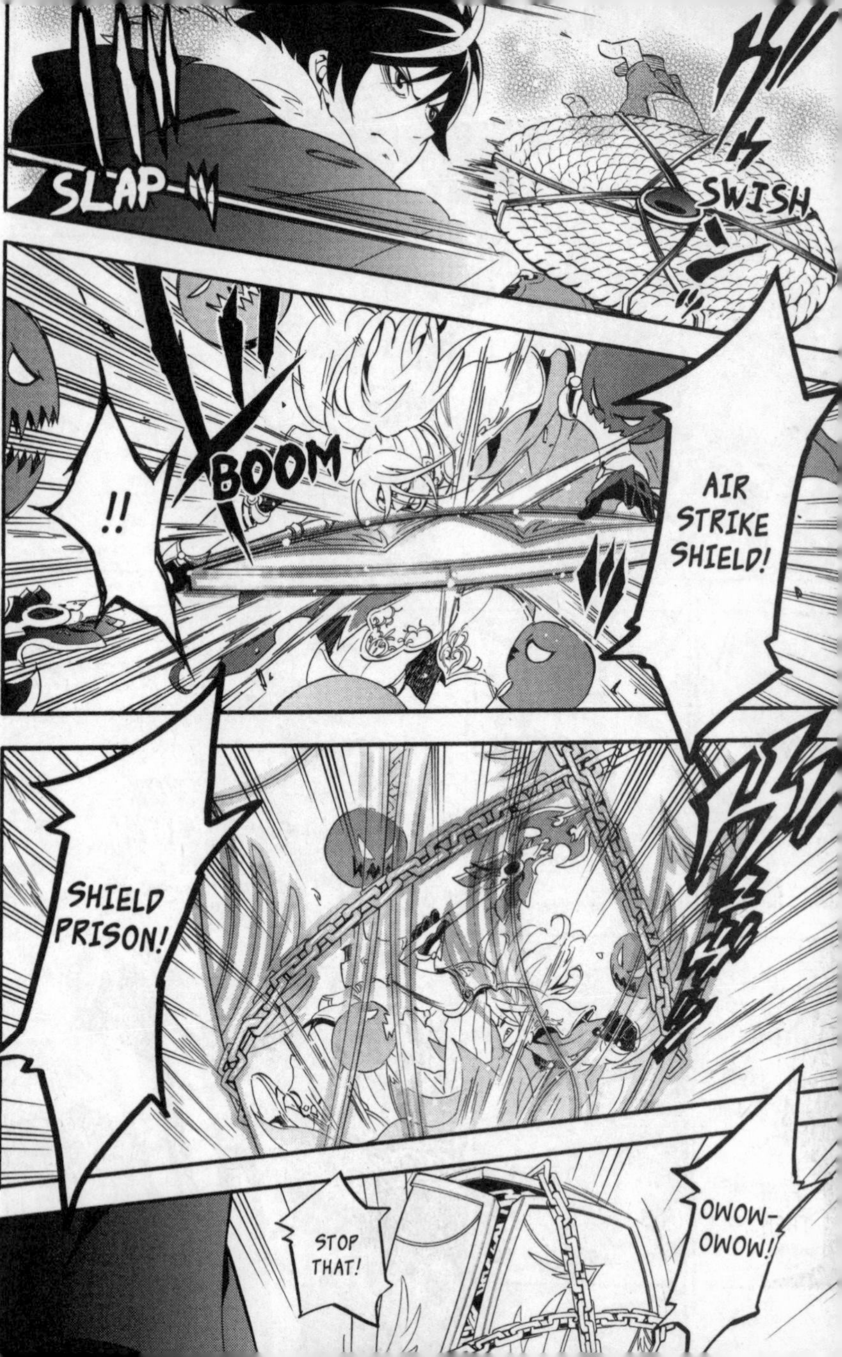
SWISH
SLAP
AIR STRIKE SHIELD!
BOOM
!!
SHIELD PRISON!
OWOW-OWOW!
STOP THAT!

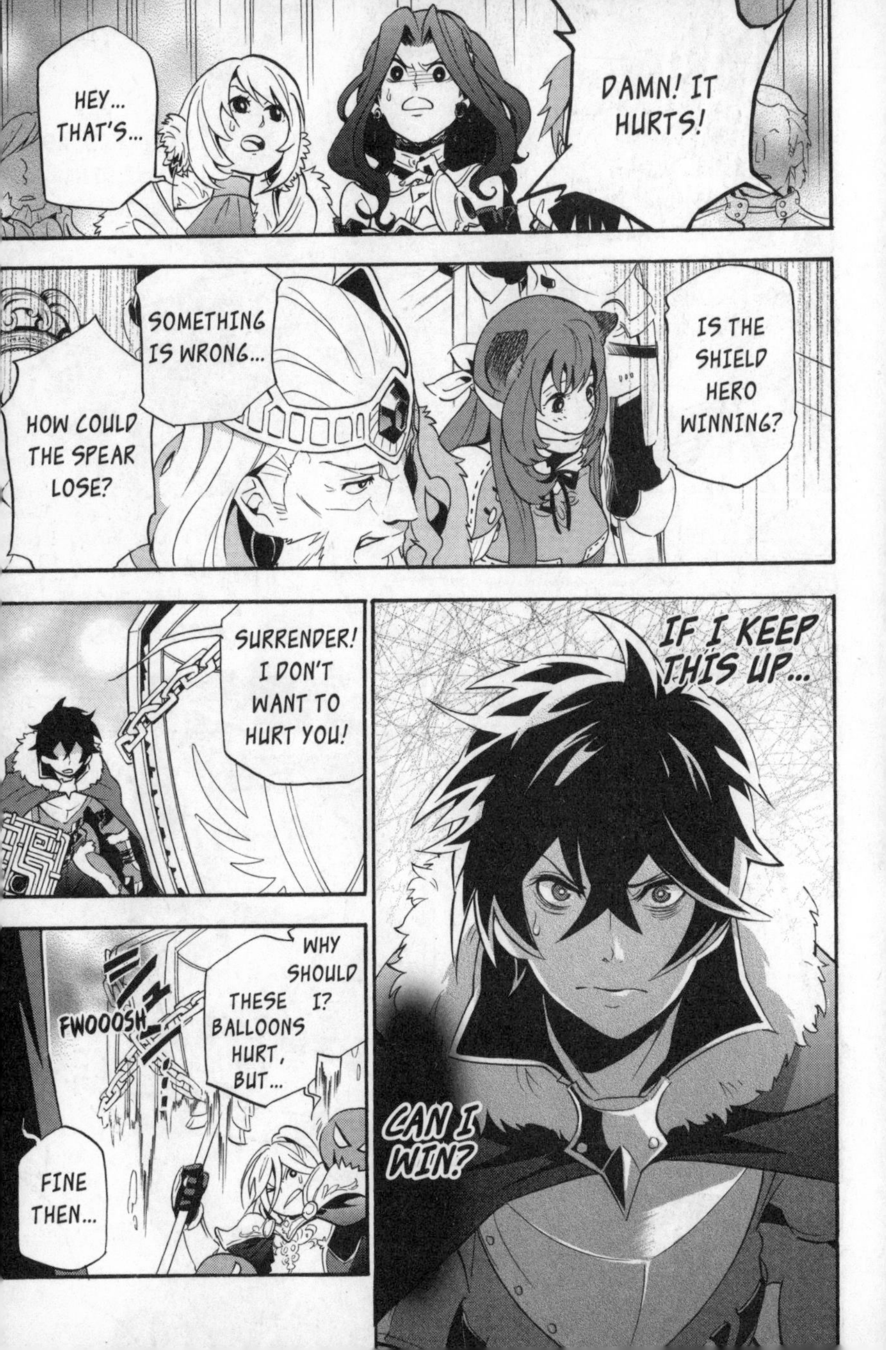
DAMN! IT HURTS!
HEY... THAT'S...
IS THE SHIELD HERO WINNING?
SOMETHING IS WRONG...
HOW COULD THE SPEAR LOSE?
IF I KEEP THIS UP...
CAN I WIN?
SURRENDER! I DON'T WANT TO HURT YOU!
WHY SHOULD I?
THESE BALLOONS HURT, BUT...
FWOOOSH
FINE THEN...

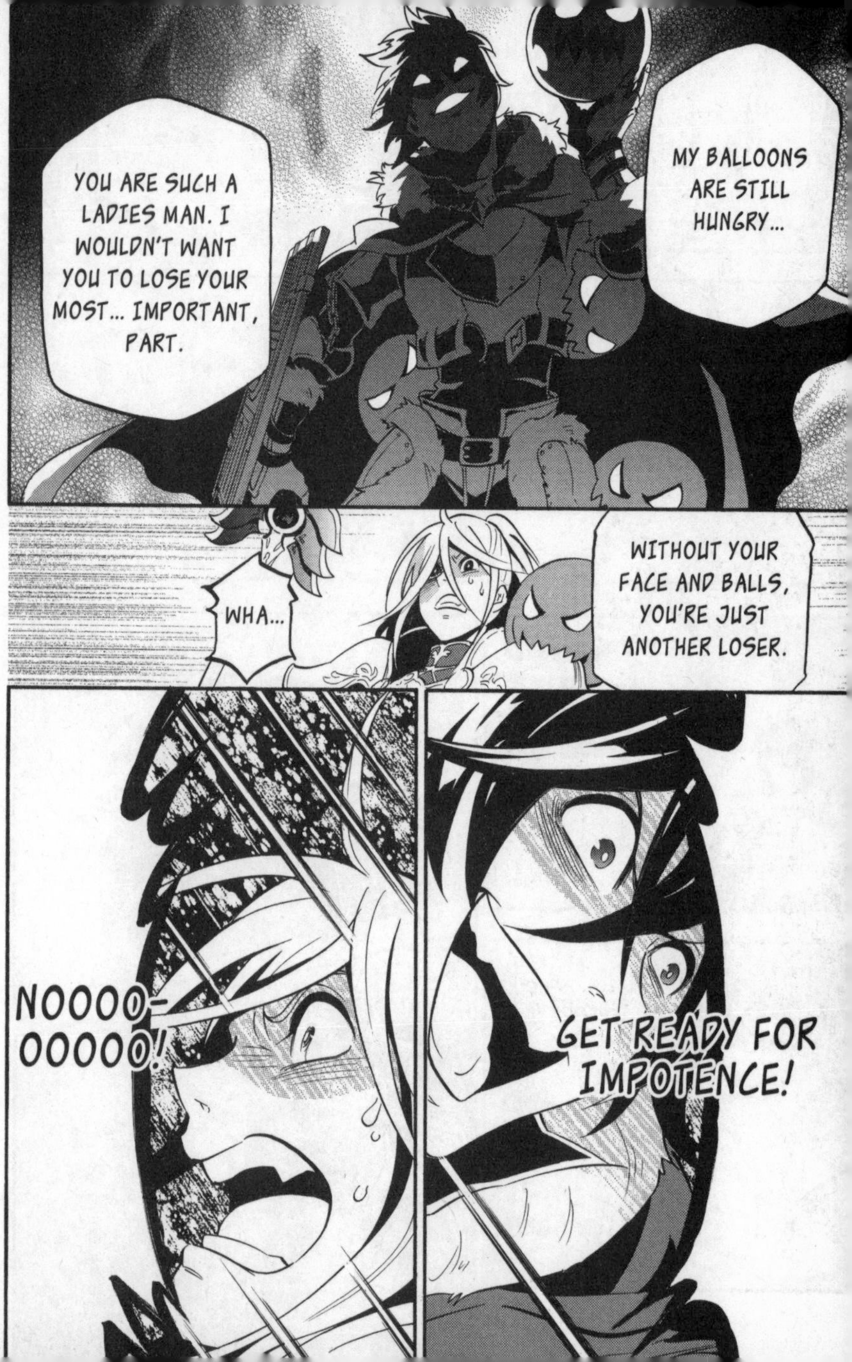
MY BALLOONS ARE STILL HUNGRY...
YOU ARE SUCH A LADIES MAN. I WOULDN'T WANT YOU TO LOSE YOUR MOST... IMPORTANT, PART.
WITHOUT YOUR FACE AND BALLS, YOU'RE JUST ANOTHER LOSER.
WHA...
GET READY FOR IMPOTENCE!
NOOOO-OOOOO!

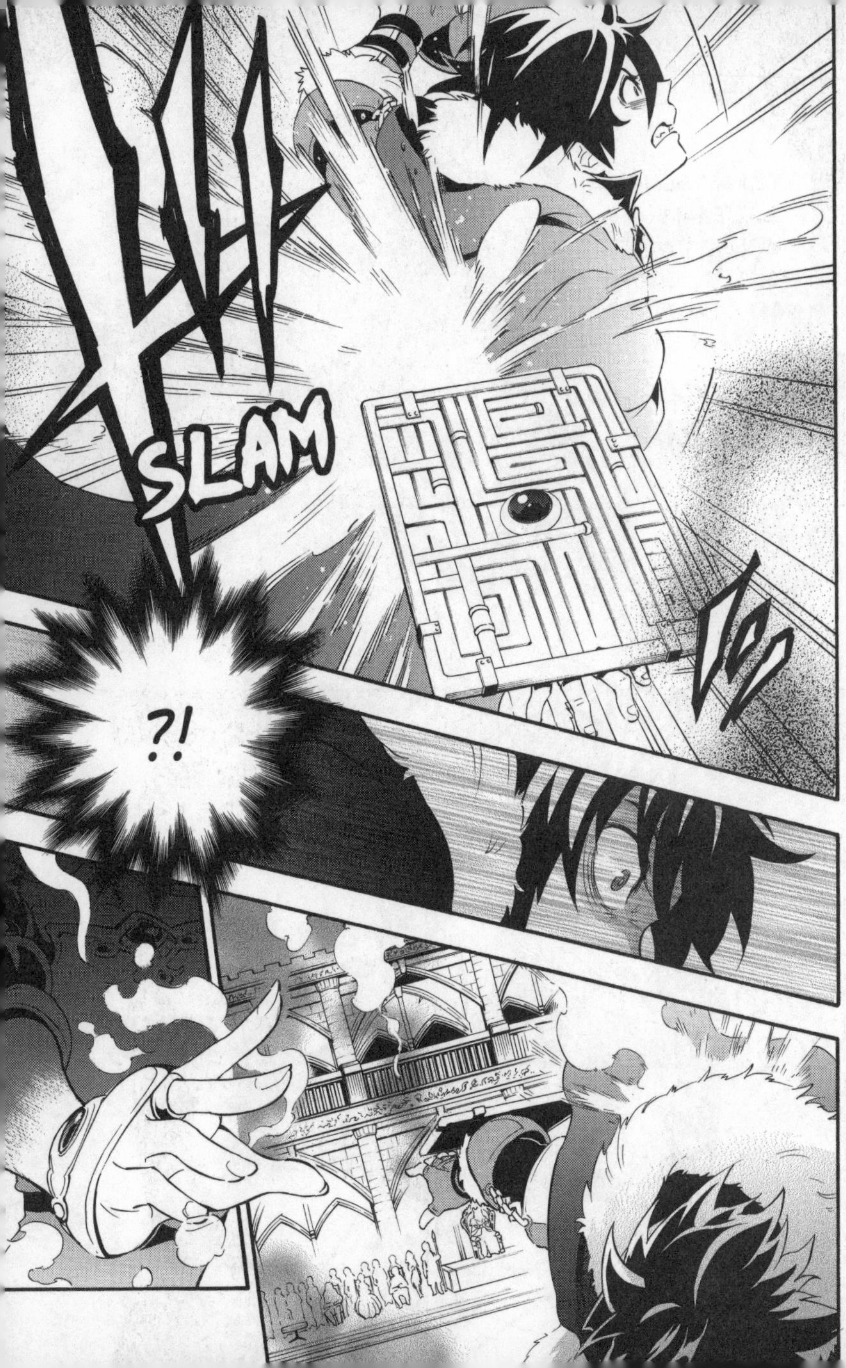
SLAM
?!

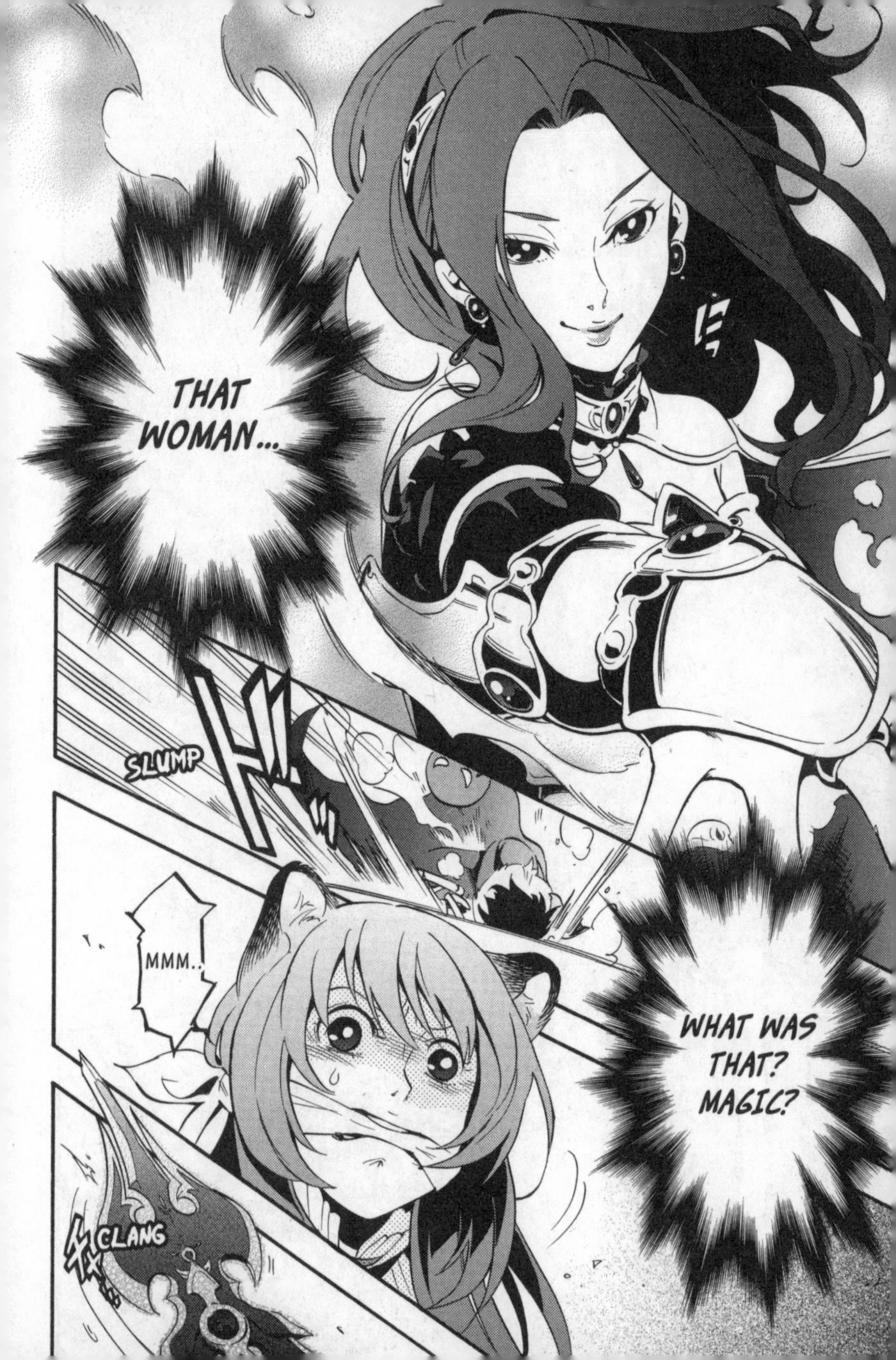
THAT WOMAN...
SLUMP
WHAT WAS THAT? MAGIC?
MMM..
CLANG

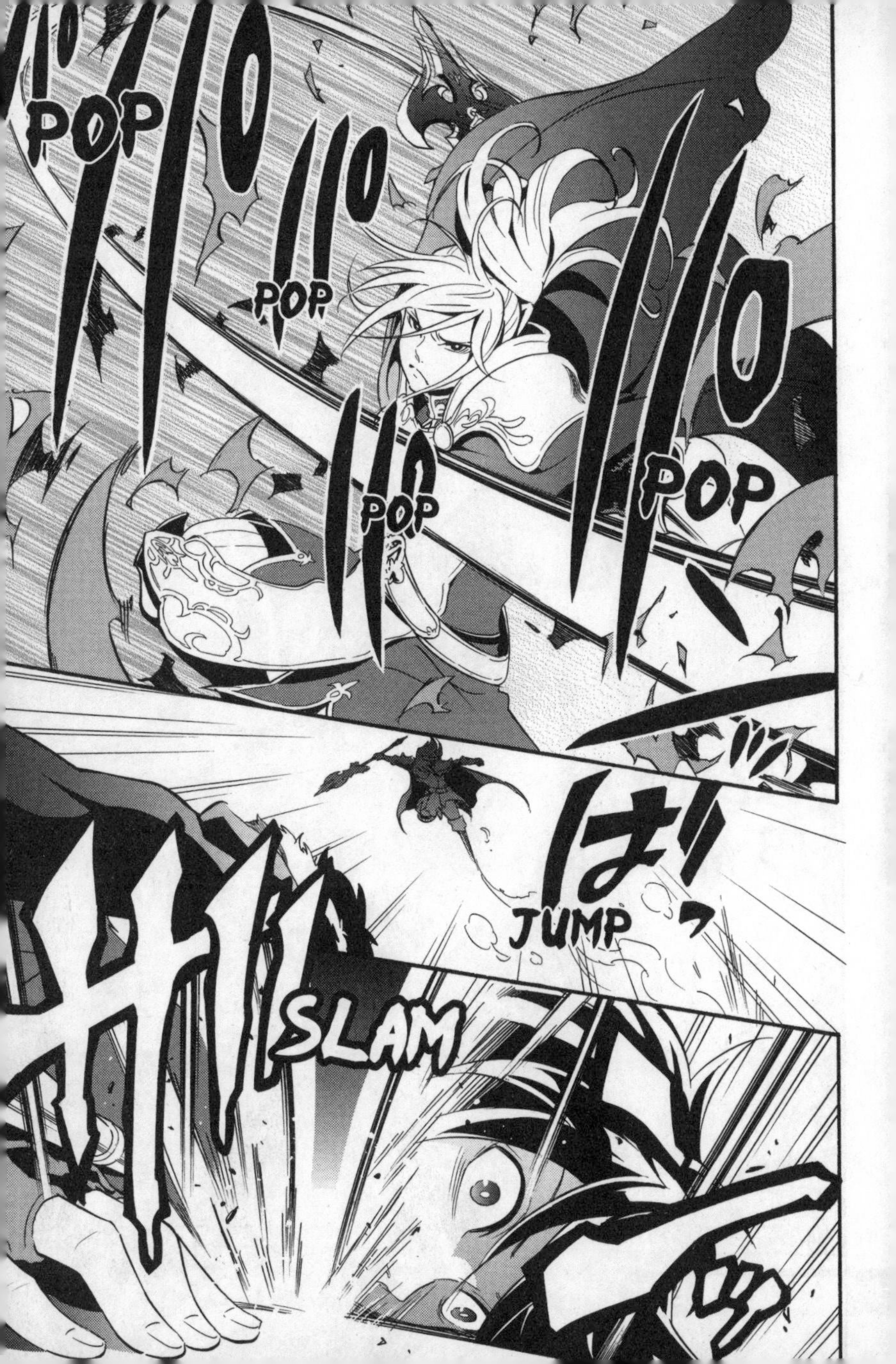
POP
POP
POP
POP
JUMP
SLAM

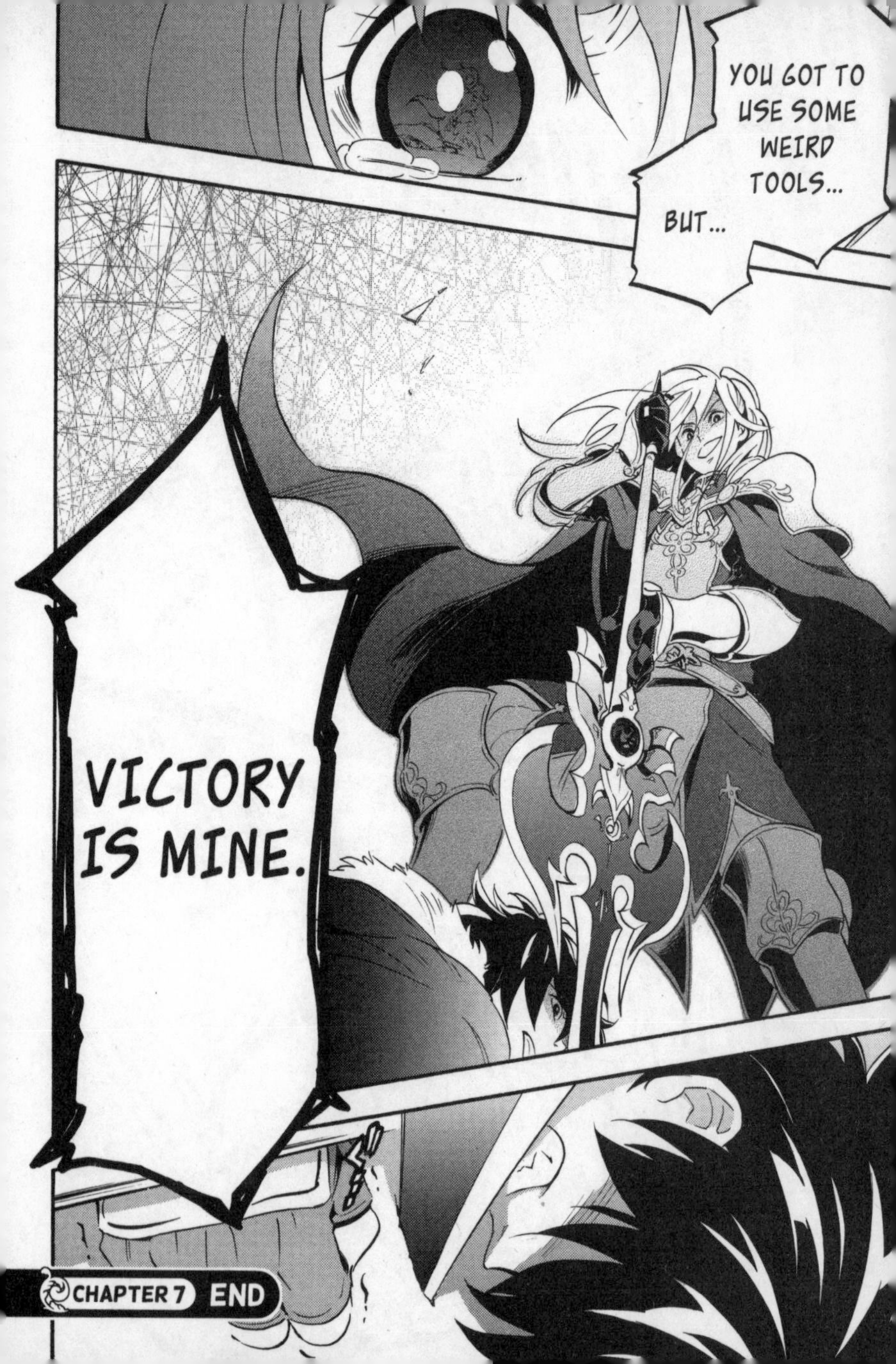
YOU GOT TO USE SOME WEIRD TOOLS...
BUT...
VICTORY IS MINE.
CHAPTER 7 END

THE RISING OF THE SHIELD HERO 2

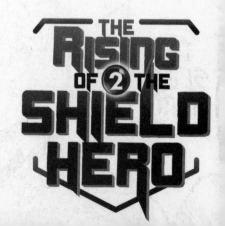

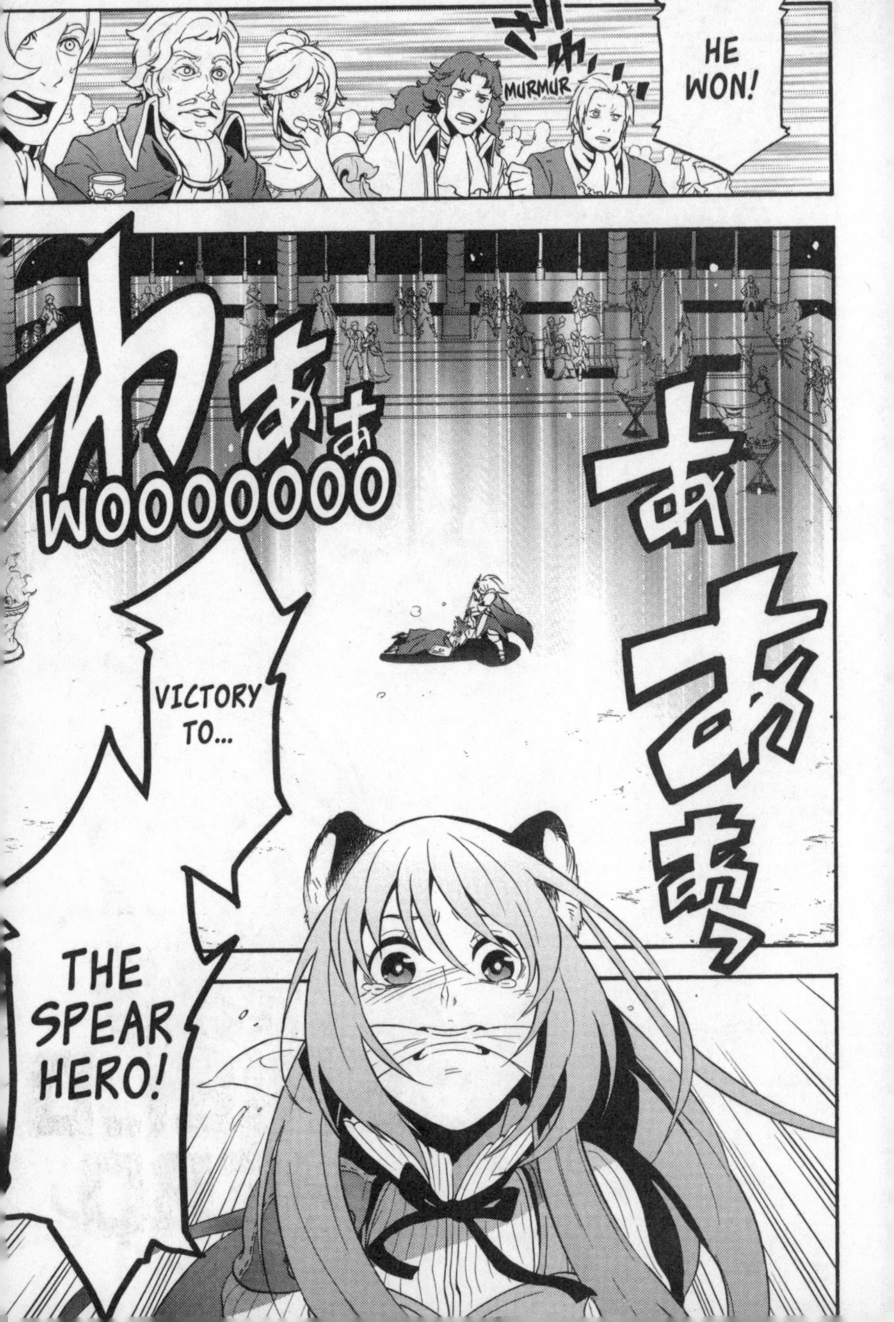
HE WON!
MURMUR
WOOOOOOO
VICTORY TO...
THE SPEAR HERO!

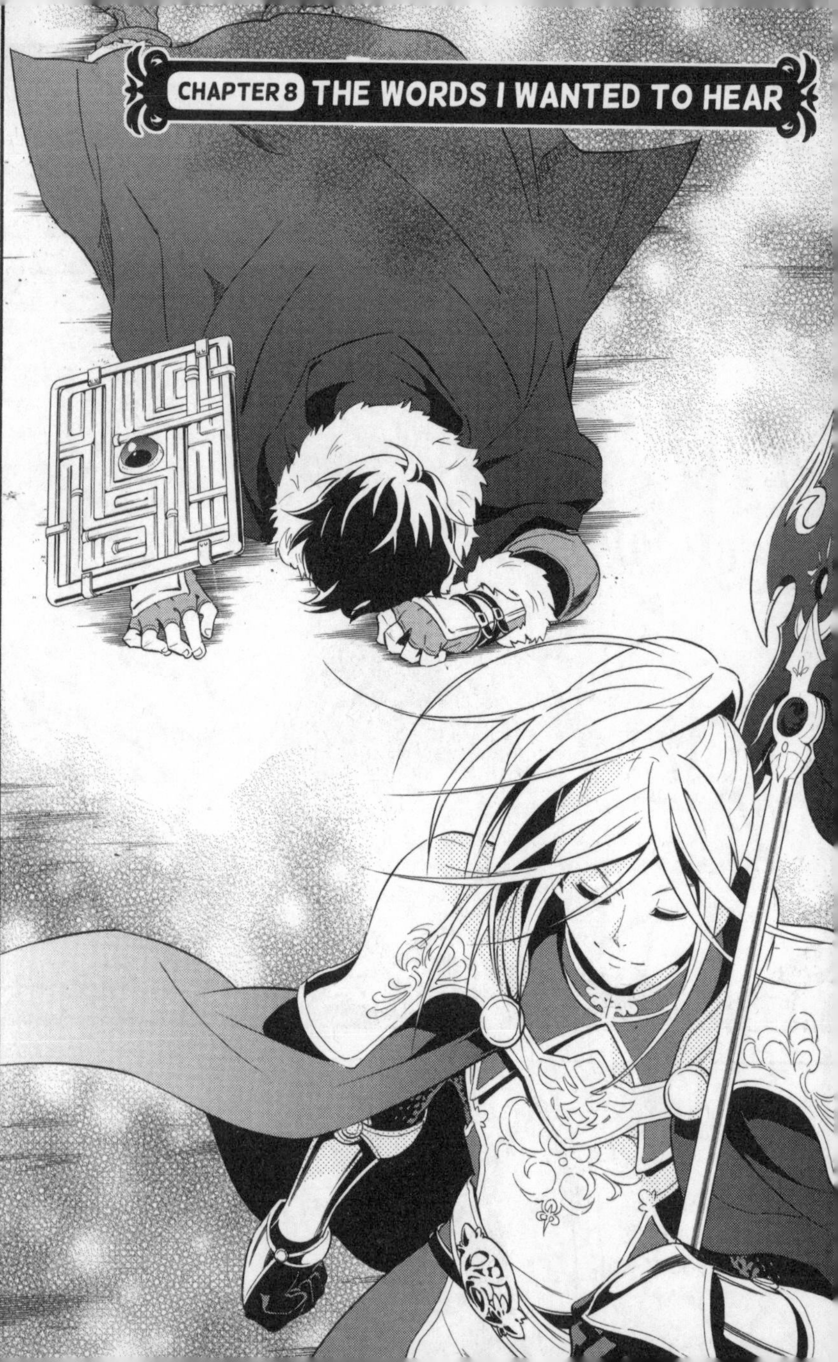
CHAPTER 8 THE WORDS I WANTED TO HEAR

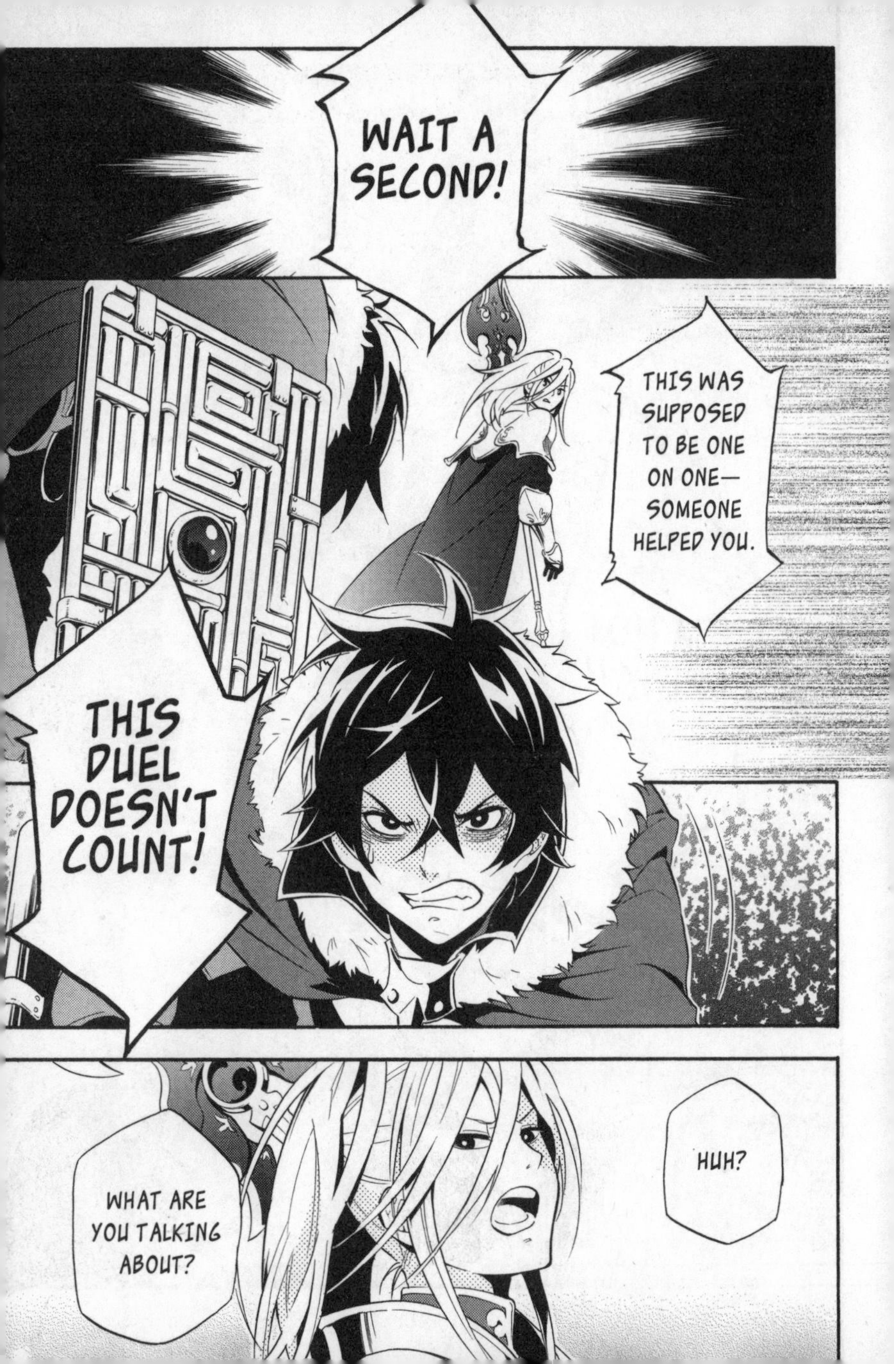
WAIT A SECOND!
THIS WAS SUPPOSED TO BE ONE ON ONE— SOMEONE HELPED YOU.
THIS DUEL DOESN'T COUNT!
HUH?
WHAT ARE YOU TALKING ABOUT?

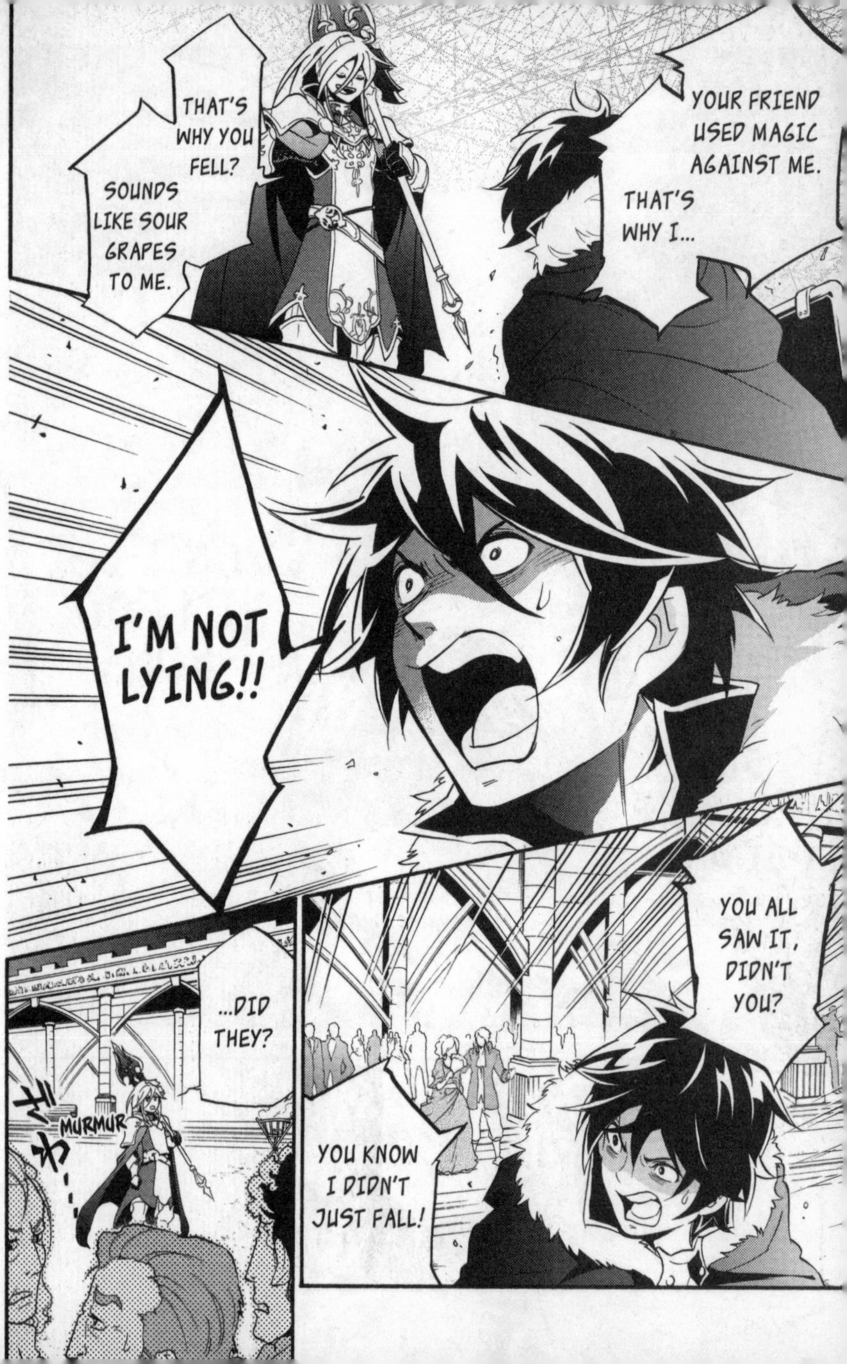
YOUR FRIEND USED MAGIC AGAINST ME.
THAT'S WHY I...
THAT'S WHY YOU FELL?
SOUNDS LIKE SOUR GRAPES TO ME.
I'M NOT LYING!!
YOU ALL SAW IT, DIDN'T YOU?
YOU KNOW I DIDN'T JUST FALL!
...DID THEY?
MURMUR

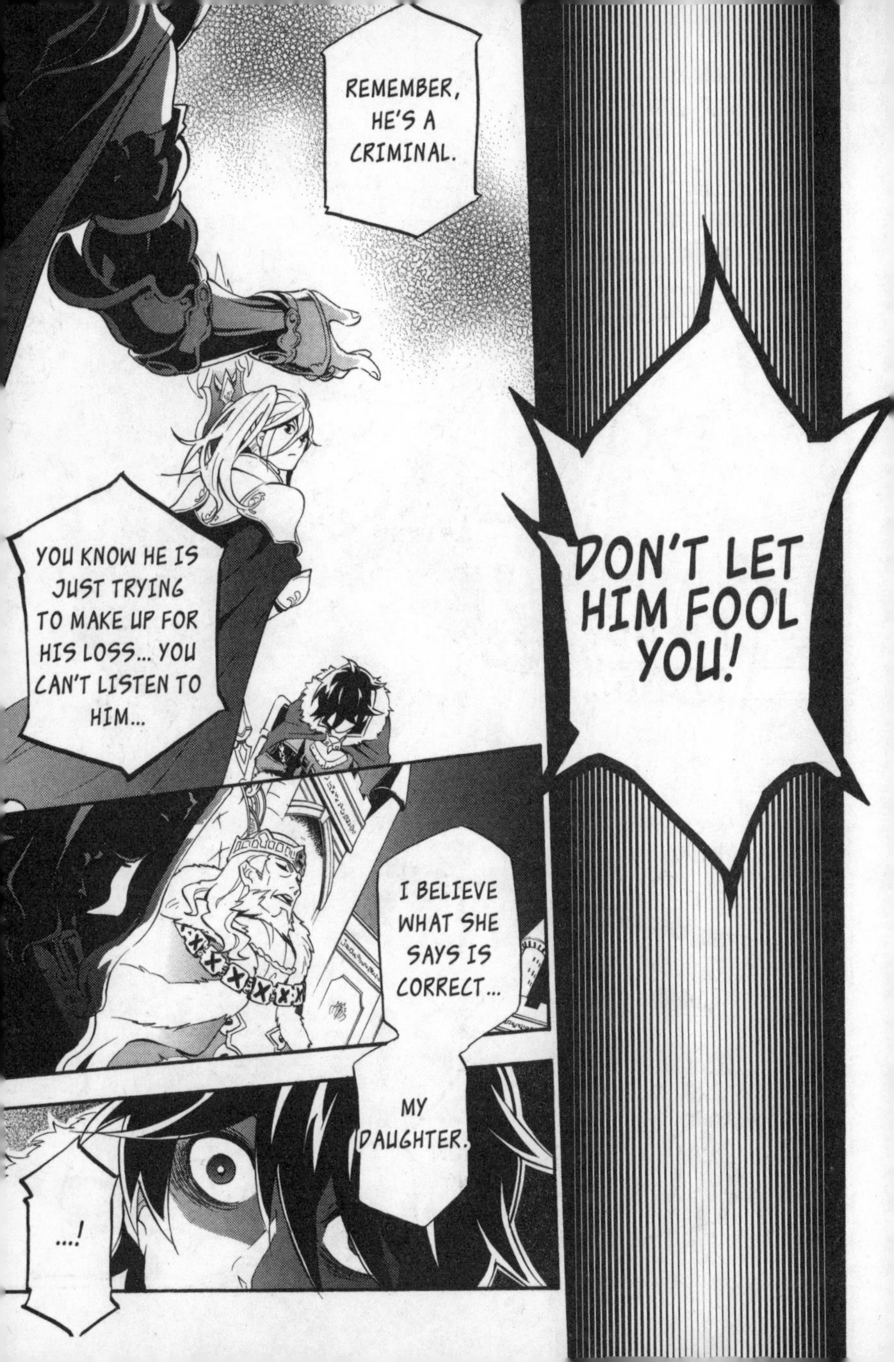
DON'T LET HIM FOOL YOU!
REMEMBER, HE'S A CRIMINAL.
YOU KNOW HE IS JUST TRYING TO MAKE UP FOR HIS LOSS... YOU CAN'T LISTEN TO HIM...
I BELIEVE WHAT SHE SAYS IS CORRECT...
MY DAUGHTER.
...!

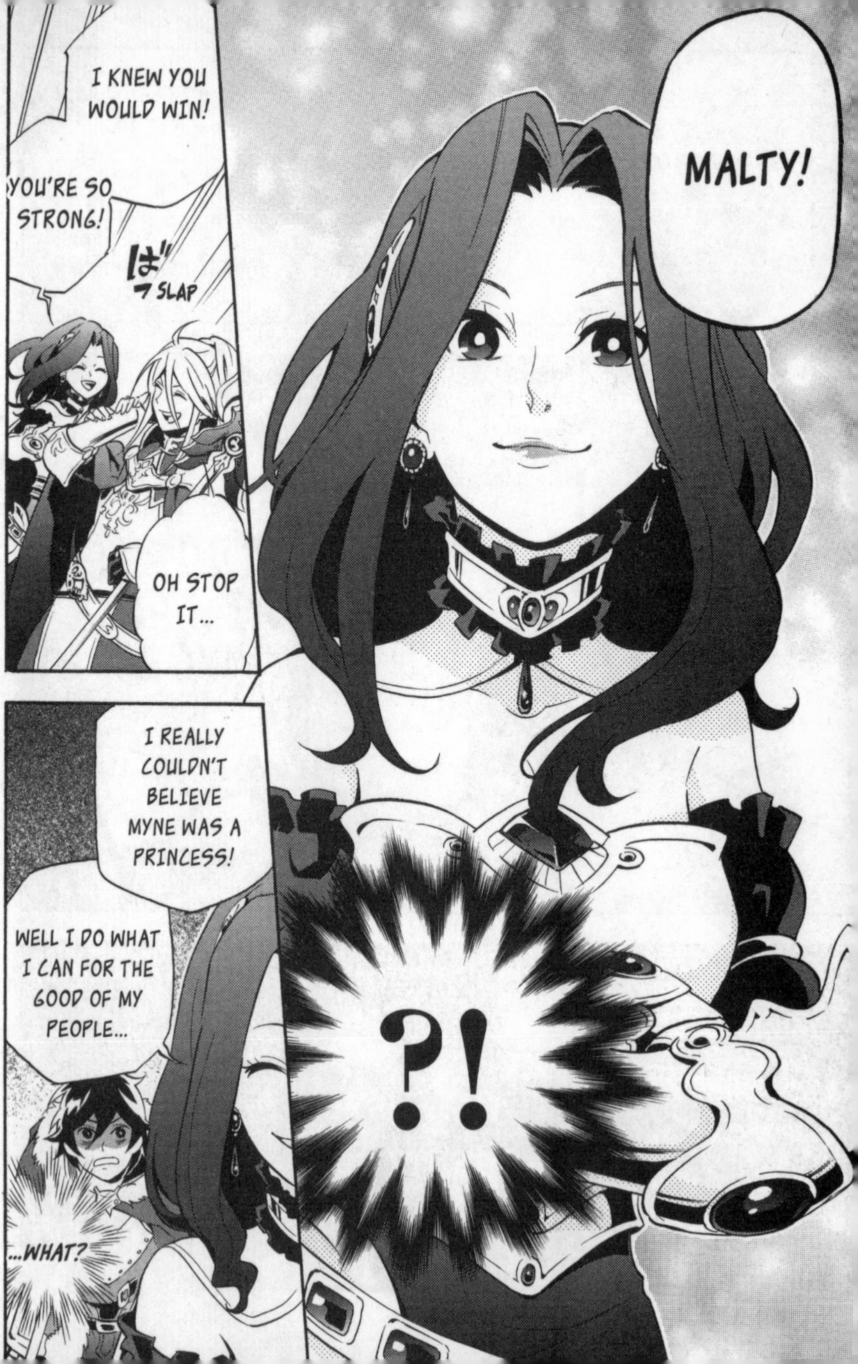
MALTY!
?!
I KNEW YOU WOULD WIN!
YOU'RE SO STRONG!
ばっ
SLAP
OH STOP IT...
I REALLY COULDN'T BELIEVE MYNE WAS A PRINCESS!
WELL I DO WHAT I CAN FOR THE GOOD OF MY PEOPLE...
...WHAT?

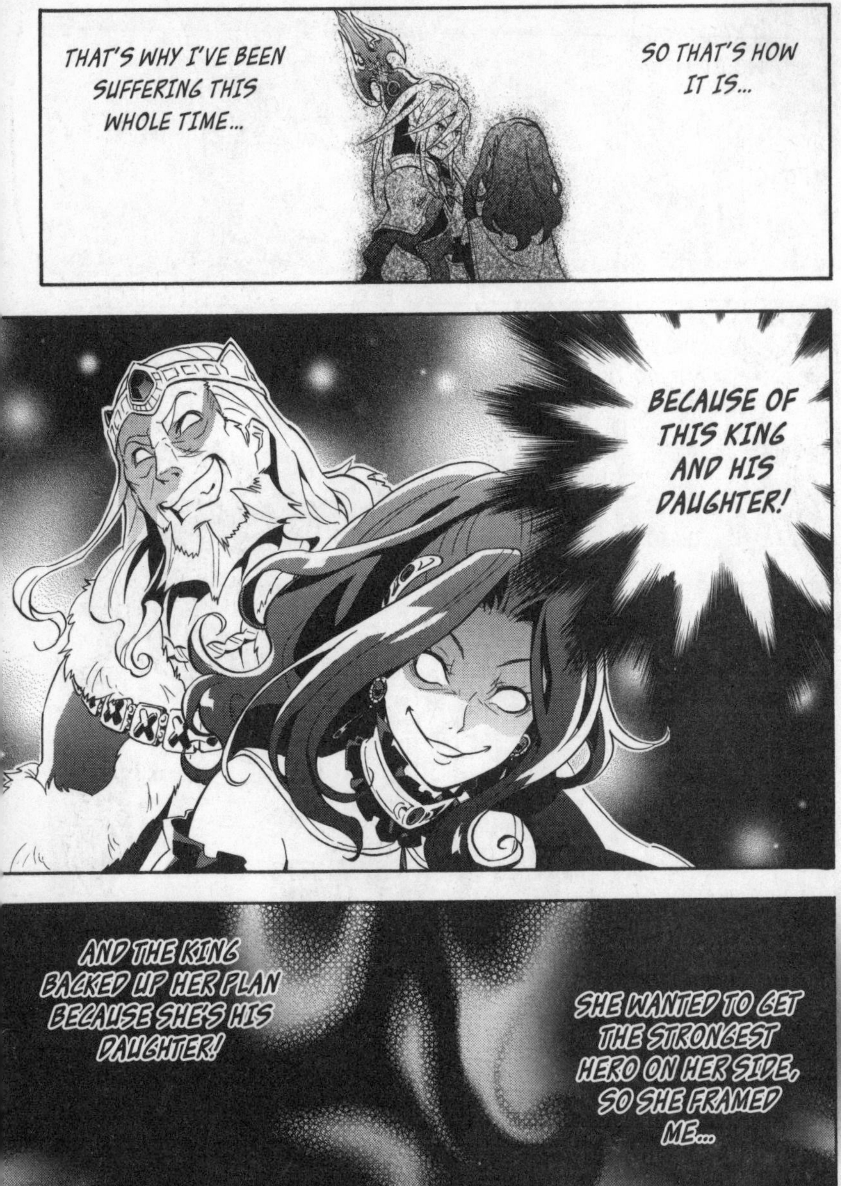
SO THAT'S HOW IT IS...
THAT'S WHY I'VE BEEN SUFFERING THIS WHOLE TIME...
BECAUSE OF THIS KING AND HIS DAUGHTER!
SHE WANTED TO GET THE STRONGEST HERO ON HER SIDE, SO SHE FRAMED ME...
AND THE KING BACKED UP HER PLAN BECAUSE SHE'S HIS DAUGHTER!

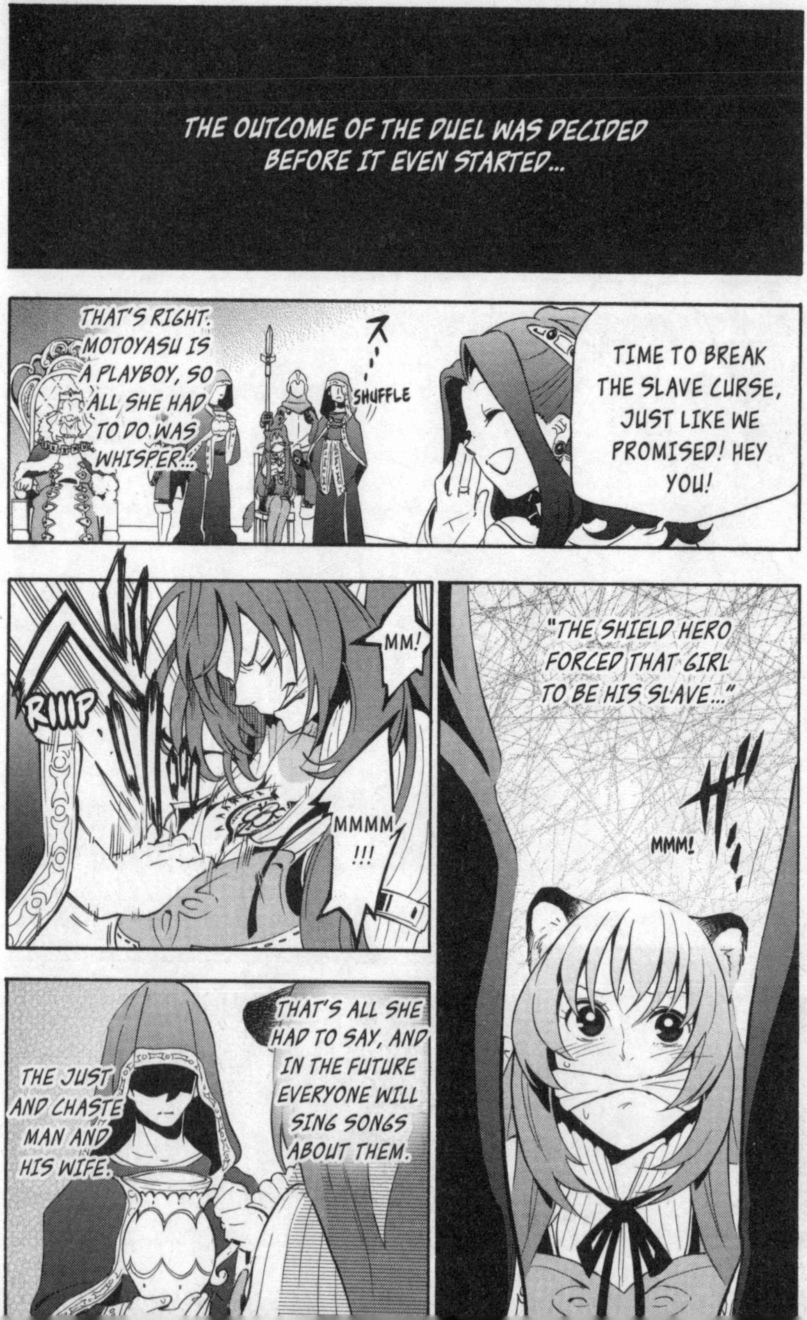
THE OUTCOME OF THE DUEL WAS DECIDED BEFORE IT EVEN STARTED...
TIME TO BREAK THE SLAVE CURSE, JUST LIKE WE PROMISED! HEY YOU!
SHUFFLE
THAT'S RIGHT. MOTOYASU IS A PLAYBOY, SO ALL SHE HAD TO DO WAS WHISPER...
"THE SHIELD HERO FORCED THAT GIRL TO BE HIS SLAVE..."
MMM!
MM!
RIIIP
MMMM !!!
THAT'S ALL SHE HAD TO SAY, AND IN THE FUTURE EVERYONE WILL SING SONGS ABOUT THEM.
THE JUST AND CHASTE MAN AND HIS WIFE.

DRIP

THEY'LL SAY
THEY SAVED A
GIRL FROM THE
EVIL HERO

SIZZLE

SIZZLE

THE SPEAR
HERO WILL
GO-DOWN-IN
HISTORY...

SMILE

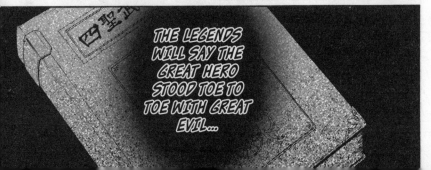

THE LEGENDS
WILL SAY THE
GREAT HERO
STOOD TOE TO
TOE WITH GREAT
EVIL...

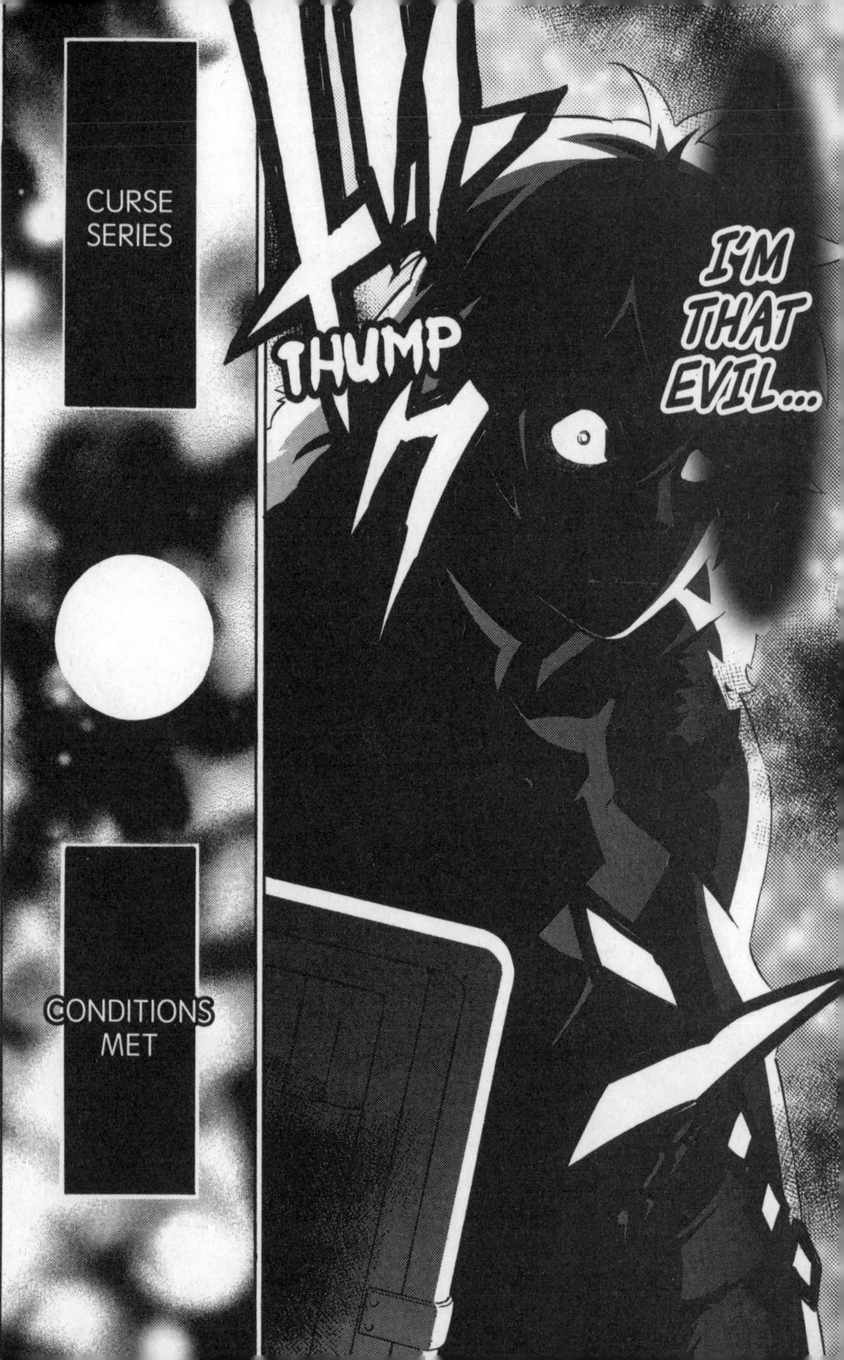
I'M THAT EVIL...
THUMP
CURSE SERIES
CONDITIONS MET

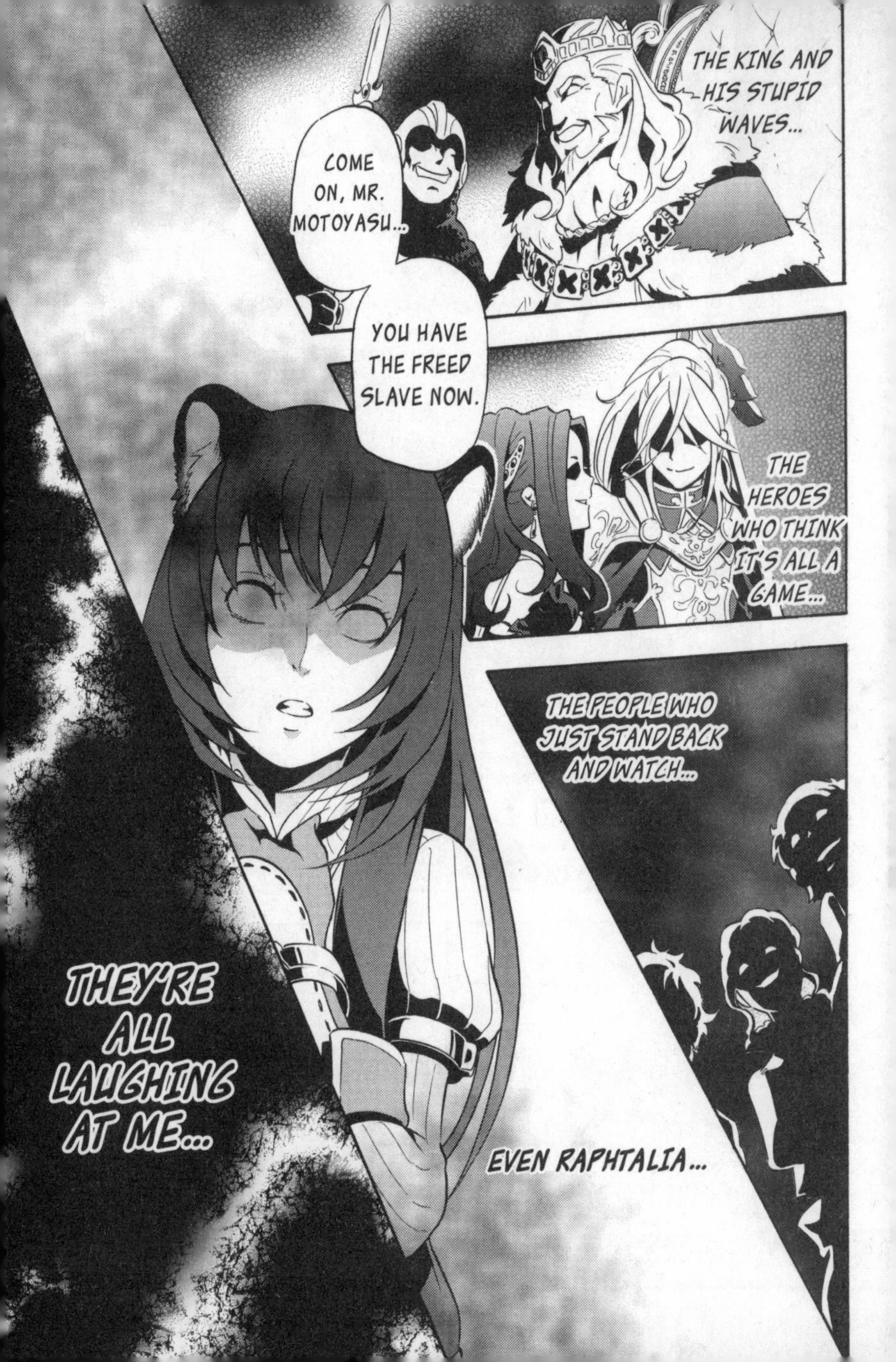
THE KING AND HIS STUPID WAVES...
COME ON, MR. MOTOYASU...
YOU HAVE THE FREED SLAVE NOW.
THE HEROES WHO THINK IT'S ALL A GAME...
THE PEOPLE WHO JUST STAND BACK AND WATCH...
EVEN RAPHTALIA...
THEY'RE ALL LAUGHING AT ME...

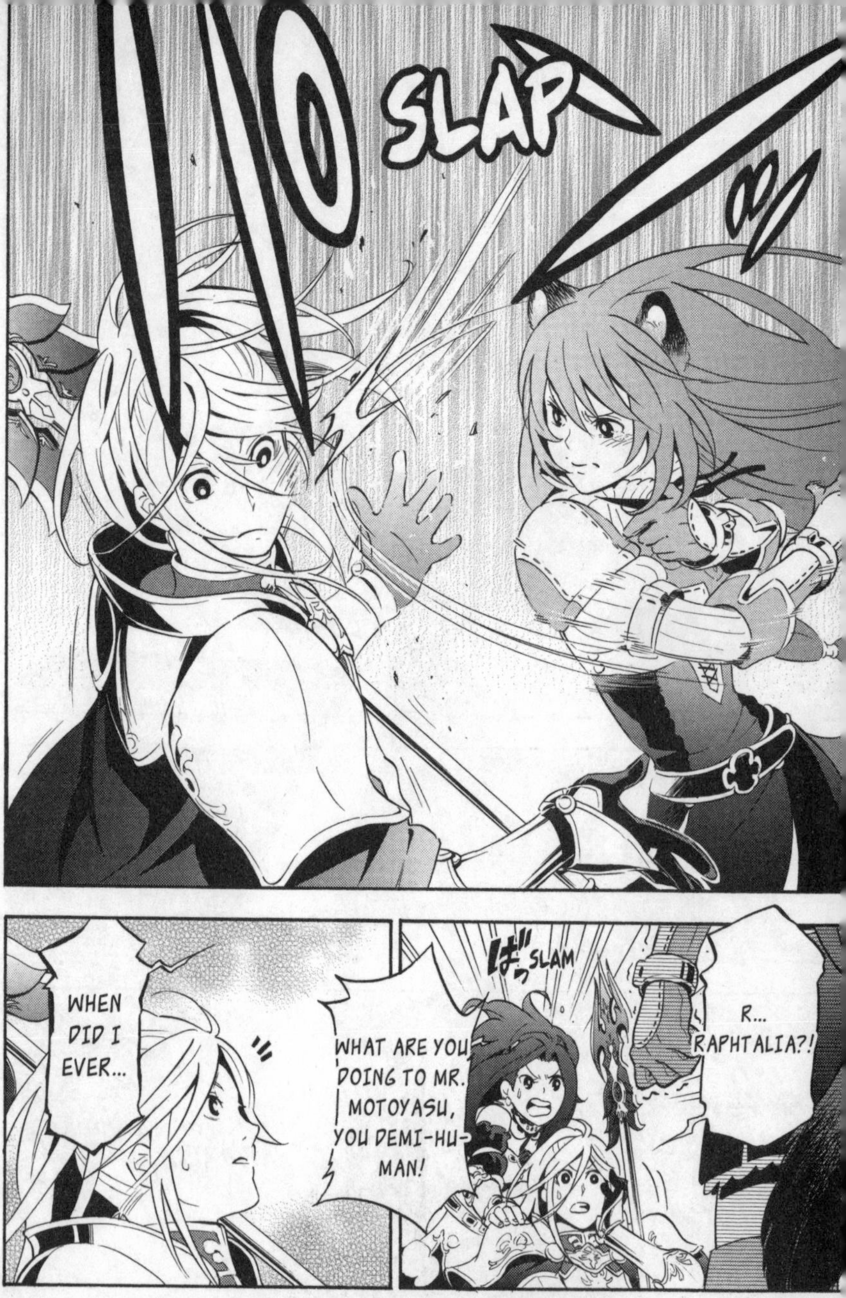
SLAP
R... RAPHTALIA?!
ばっ SLAM
WHAT ARE YOU DOING TO MR. MOTOYASU, YOU DEMI-HU-MAN!
WHEN DID I EVER...

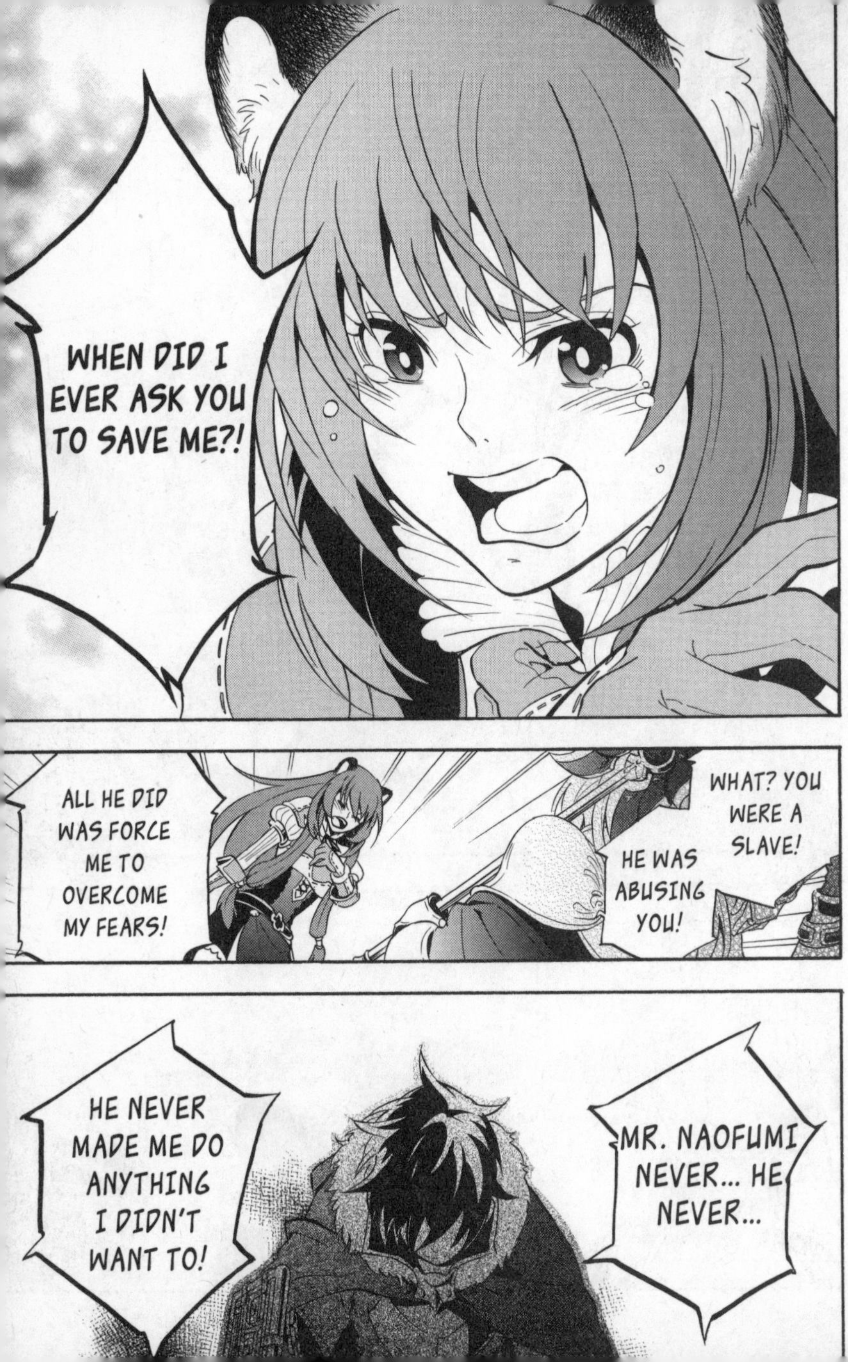
WHEN DID I EVER ASK YOU TO SAVE ME?!
WHAT? YOU WERE A SLAVE!
HE WAS ABUSING YOU!
ALL HE DID WAS FORCE ME TO OVERCOME MY FEARS!
MR. NAOFUMI NEVER... HE NEVER...
HE NEVER MADE ME DO ANYTHING I DIDN'T WANT TO!

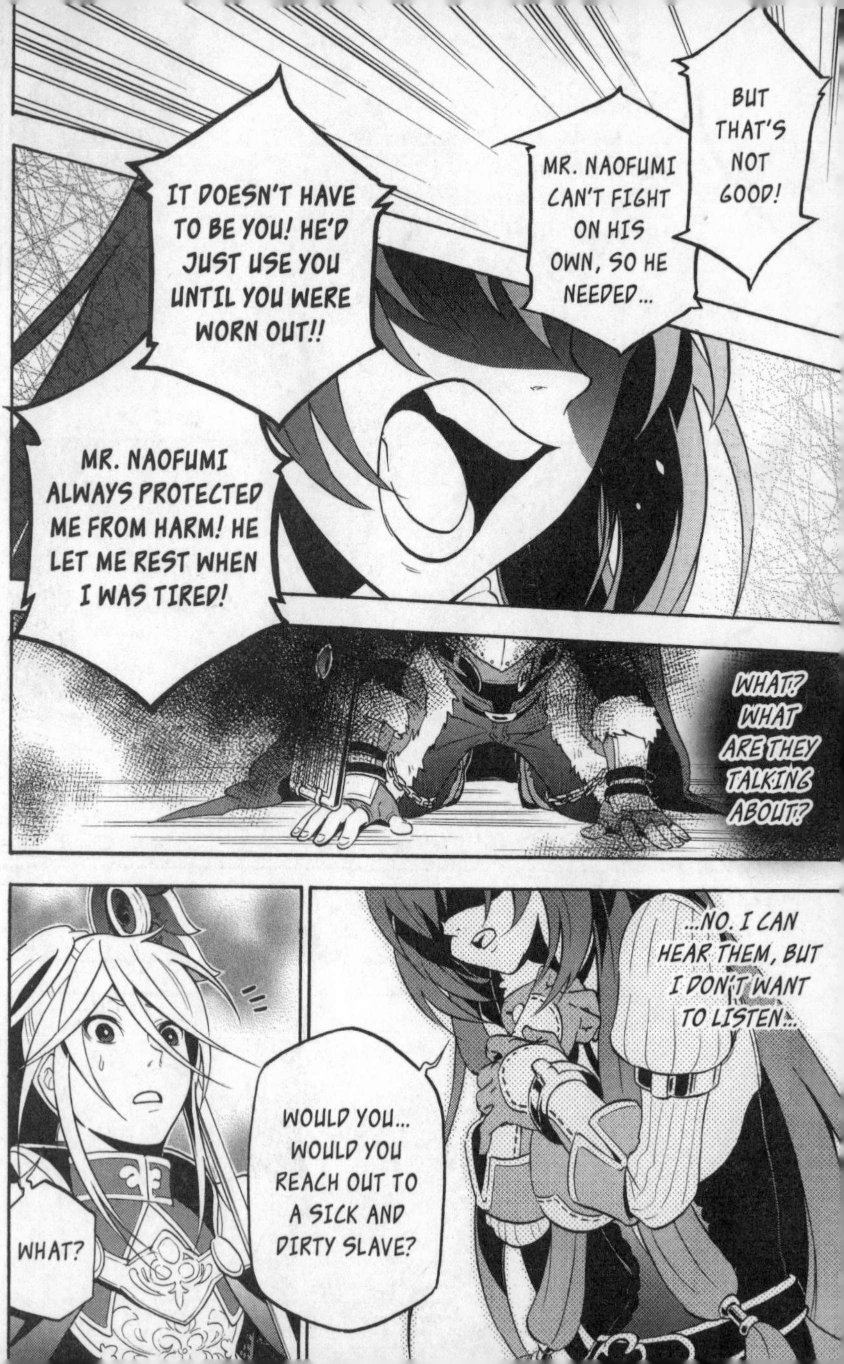
BUT THAT'S NOT GOOD!
MR. NAOFUMI CAN'T FIGHT ON HIS OWN, SO HE NEEDED...
IT DOESN'T HAVE TO BE YOU! HE'D JUST USE YOU UNTIL YOU WERE WORN OUT!!
MR. NAOFUMI ALWAYS PROTECTED ME FROM HARM! HE LET ME REST WHEN I WAS TIRED!
WHAT? WHAT ARE THEY TALKING ABOUT?
...NO. I CAN HEAR THEM, BUT I DON'T WANT TO LISTEN...
WOULD YOU... WOULD YOU REACH OUT TO A SICK AND DIRTY SLAVE?
WHAT?

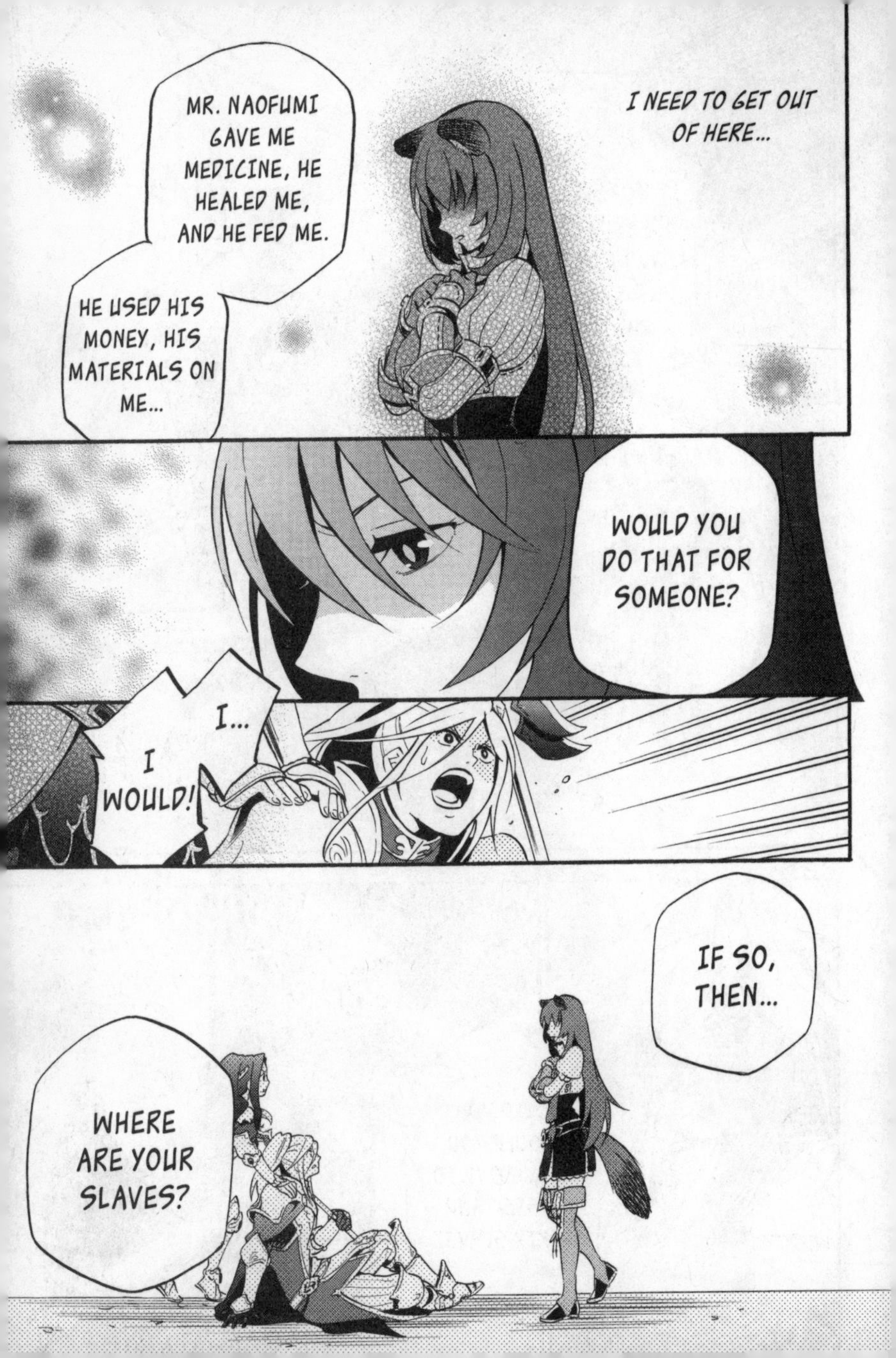
I NEED TO GET OUT OF HERE...
MR. NAOFUMI GAVE ME MEDICINE, HE HEALED ME, AND HE FED ME.
HE USED HIS MONEY, HIS MATERIALS ON ME...
WOULD YOU DO THAT FOR SOMEONE?
I...
I WOULD!
IF SO, THEN...
WHERE ARE YOUR SLAVES?

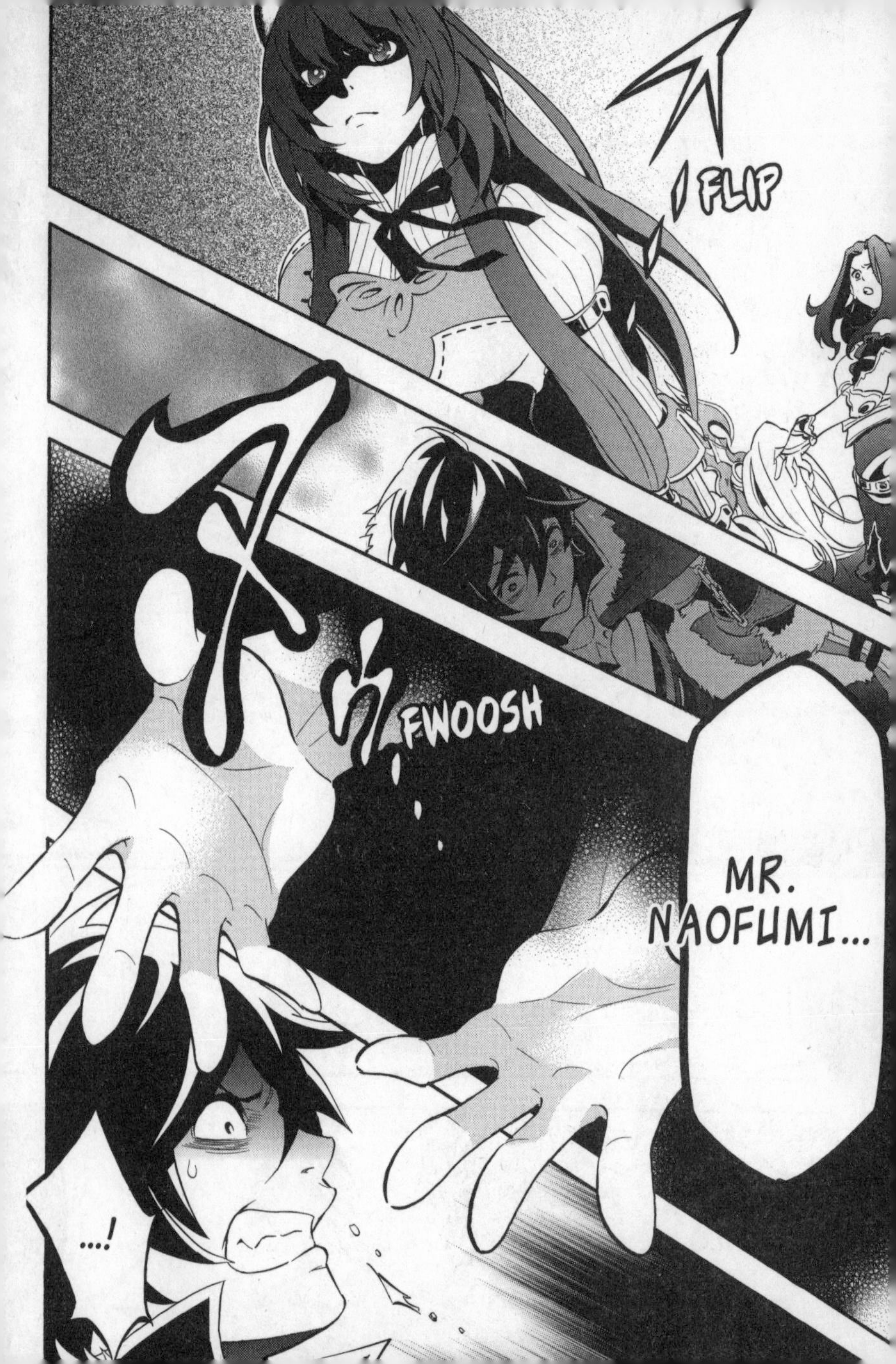
FLIP
FWOOSH
MR. NAOFUMI...
...!

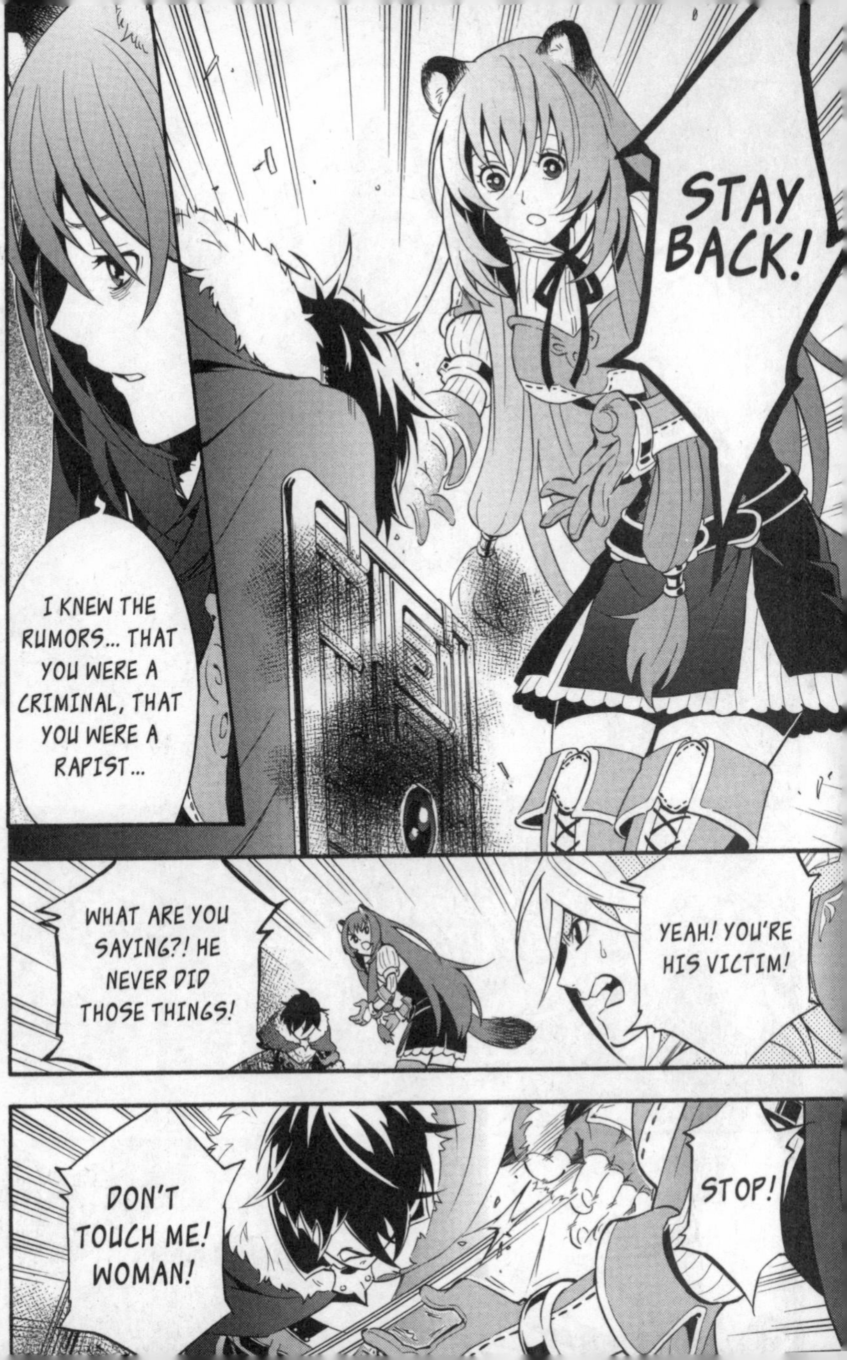
STAY BACK!
I KNEW THE RUMORS... THAT YOU WERE A CRIMINAL, THAT YOU WERE A RAPIST...
YEAH! YOU'RE HIS VICTIM!
WHAT ARE YOU SAYING?! HE NEVER DID THOSE THINGS!
STOP!
DON'T TOUCH ME! WOMAN!

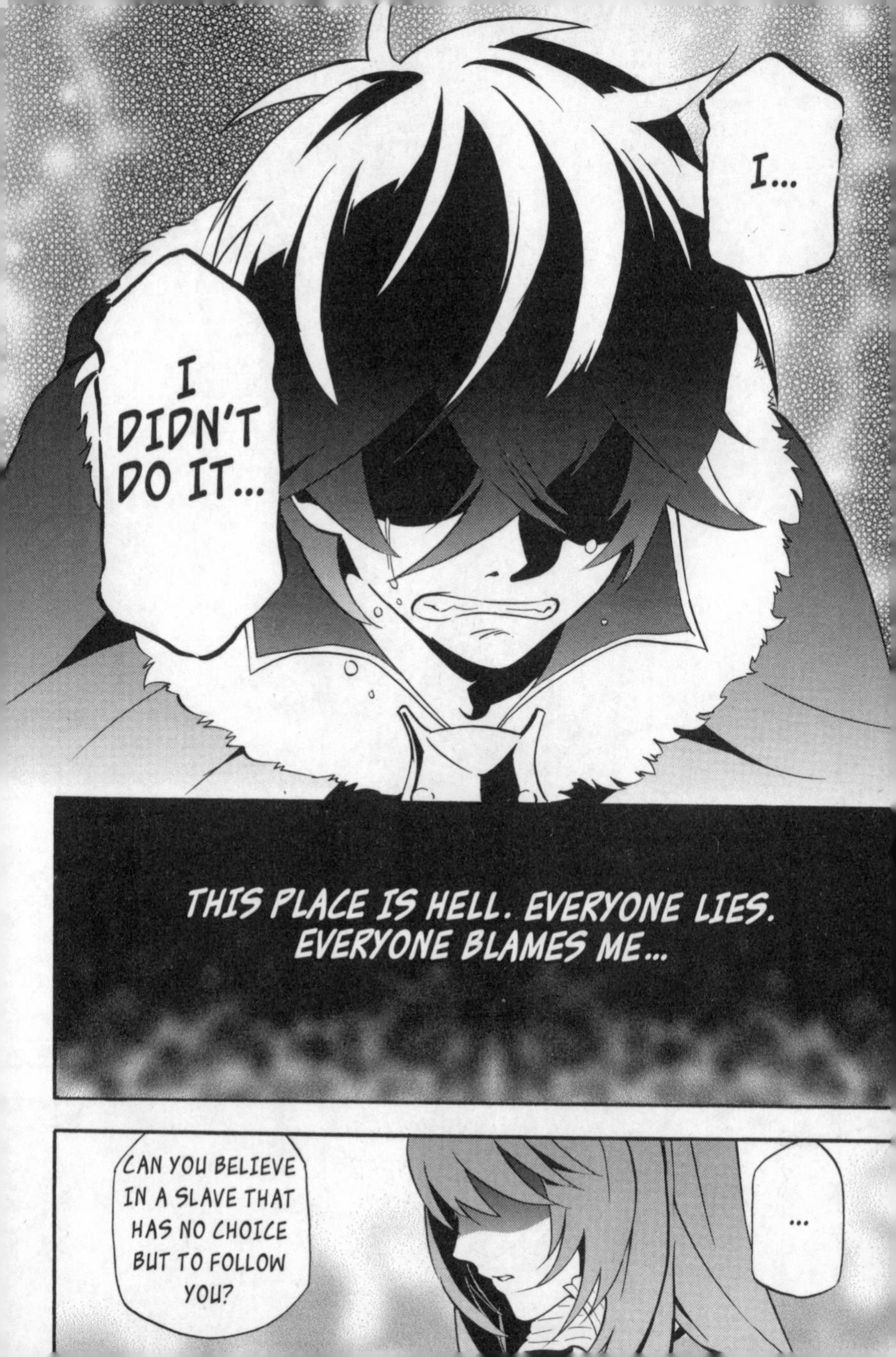
I...
I DIDN'T DO IT...
THIS PLACE IS HELL. EVERYONE LIES. EVERYONE BLAMES ME...
...
CAN YOU BELIEVE IN A SLAVE THAT HAS NO CHOICE BUT TO FOLLOW YOU?

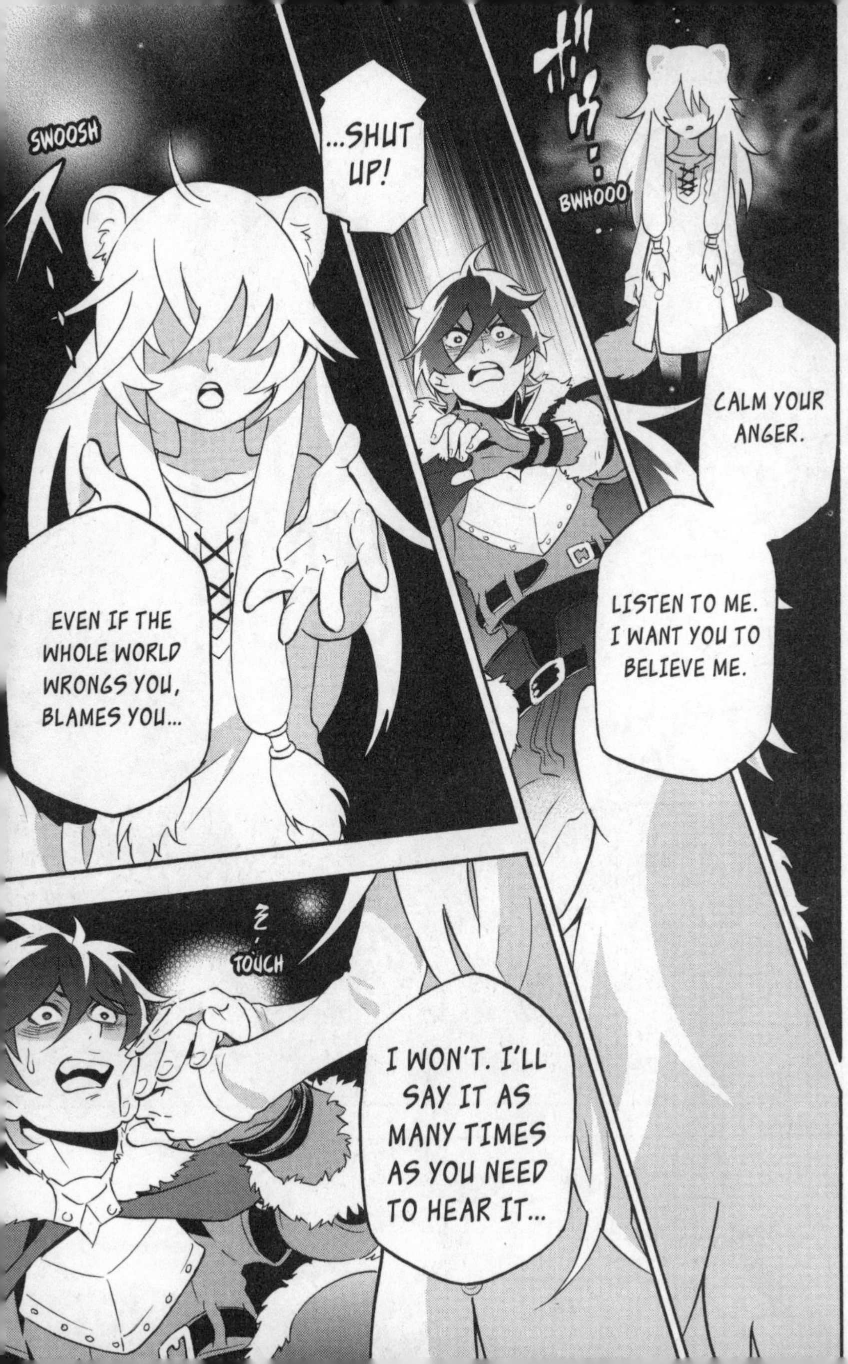
BWHOOO
CALM YOUR ANGER.
LISTEN TO ME. I WANT YOU TO BELIEVE ME.
...SHUT UP!
SWOOSH
EVEN IF THE WHOLE WORLD WRONGS YOU, BLAMES YOU...
TOUCH
I WON'T. I'LL SAY IT AS MANY TIMES AS YOU NEED TO HEAR IT...

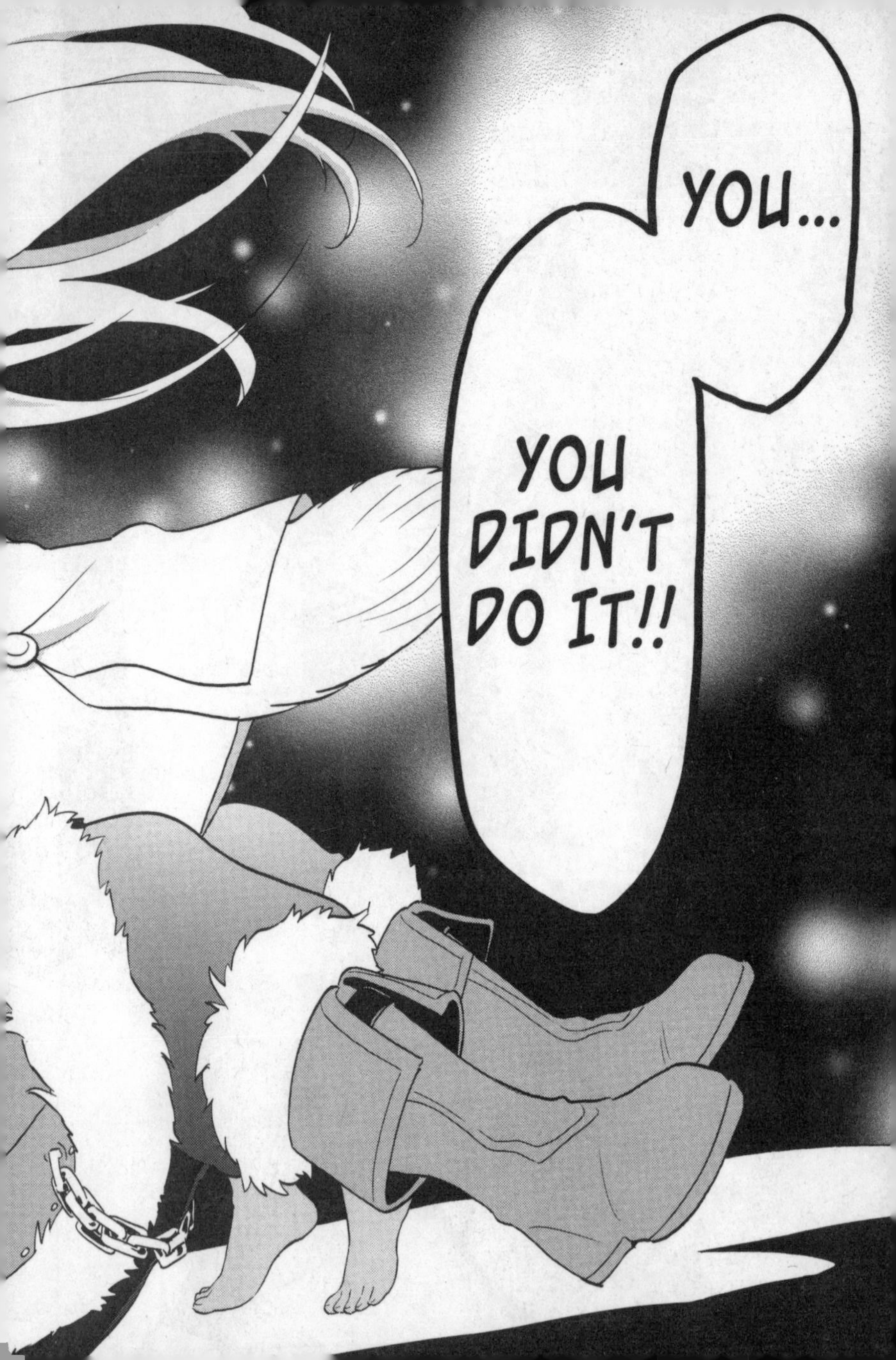
YOU...
YOU DIDN'T DO IT!!

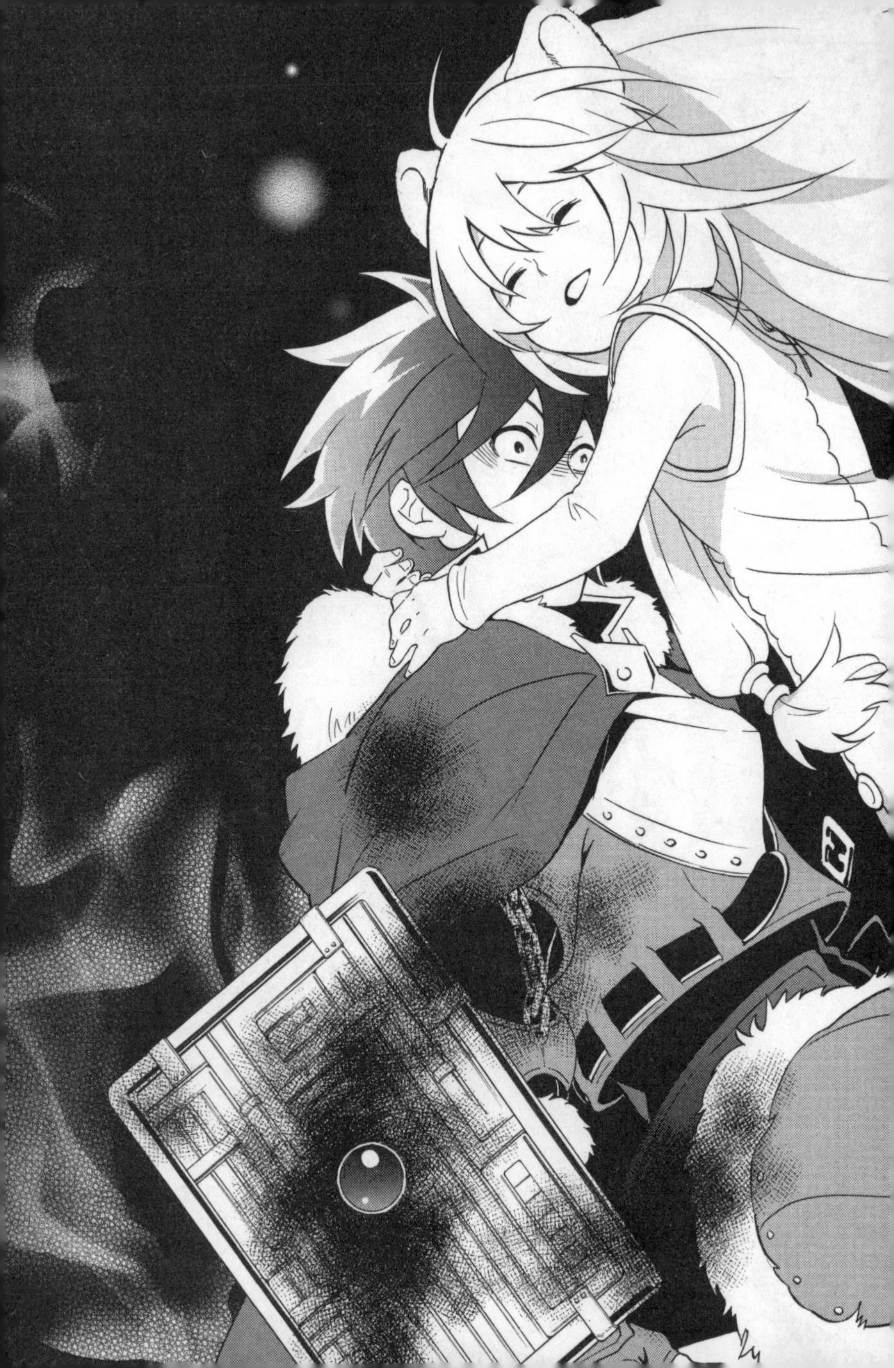

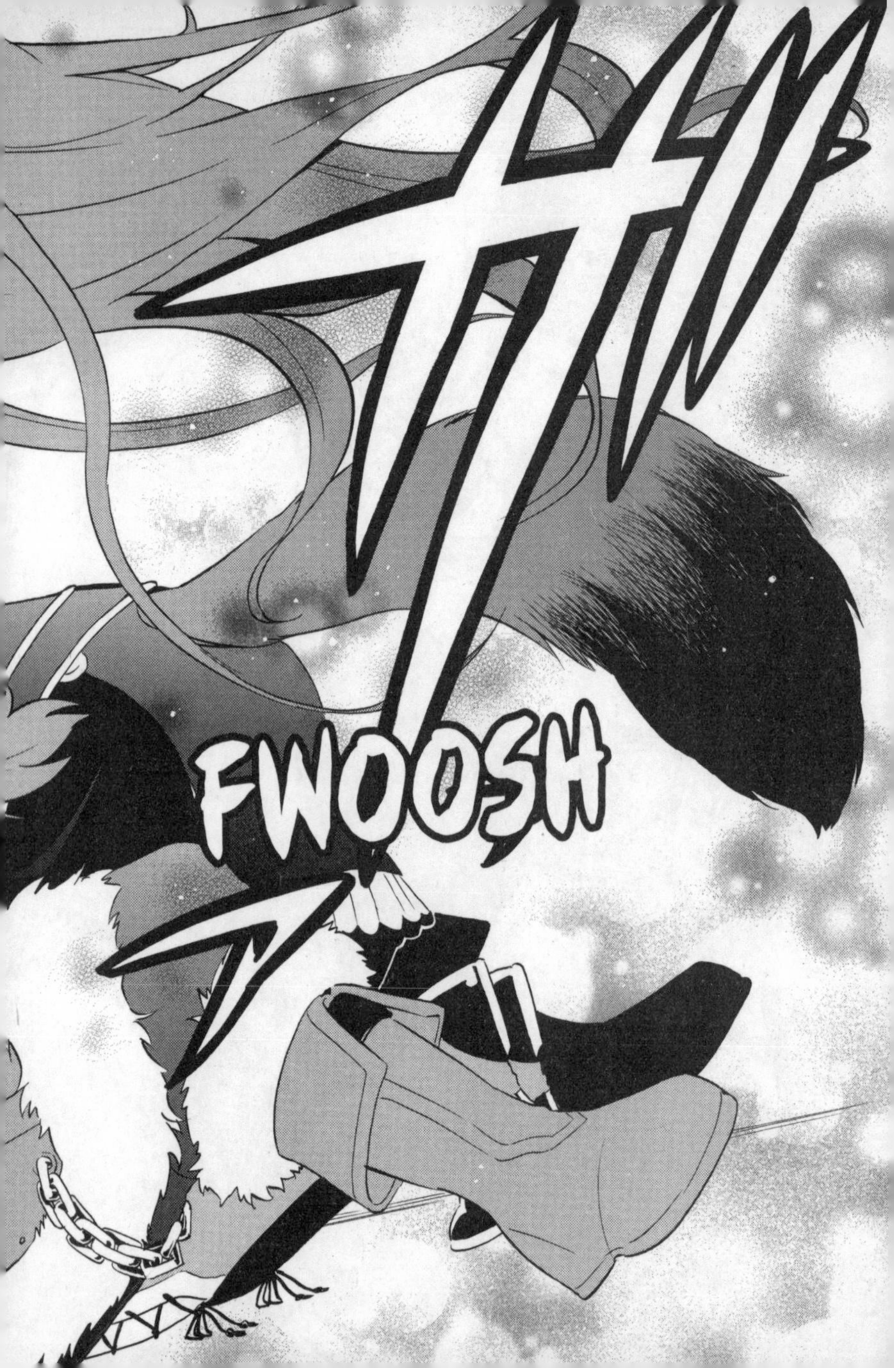
FWOOSH

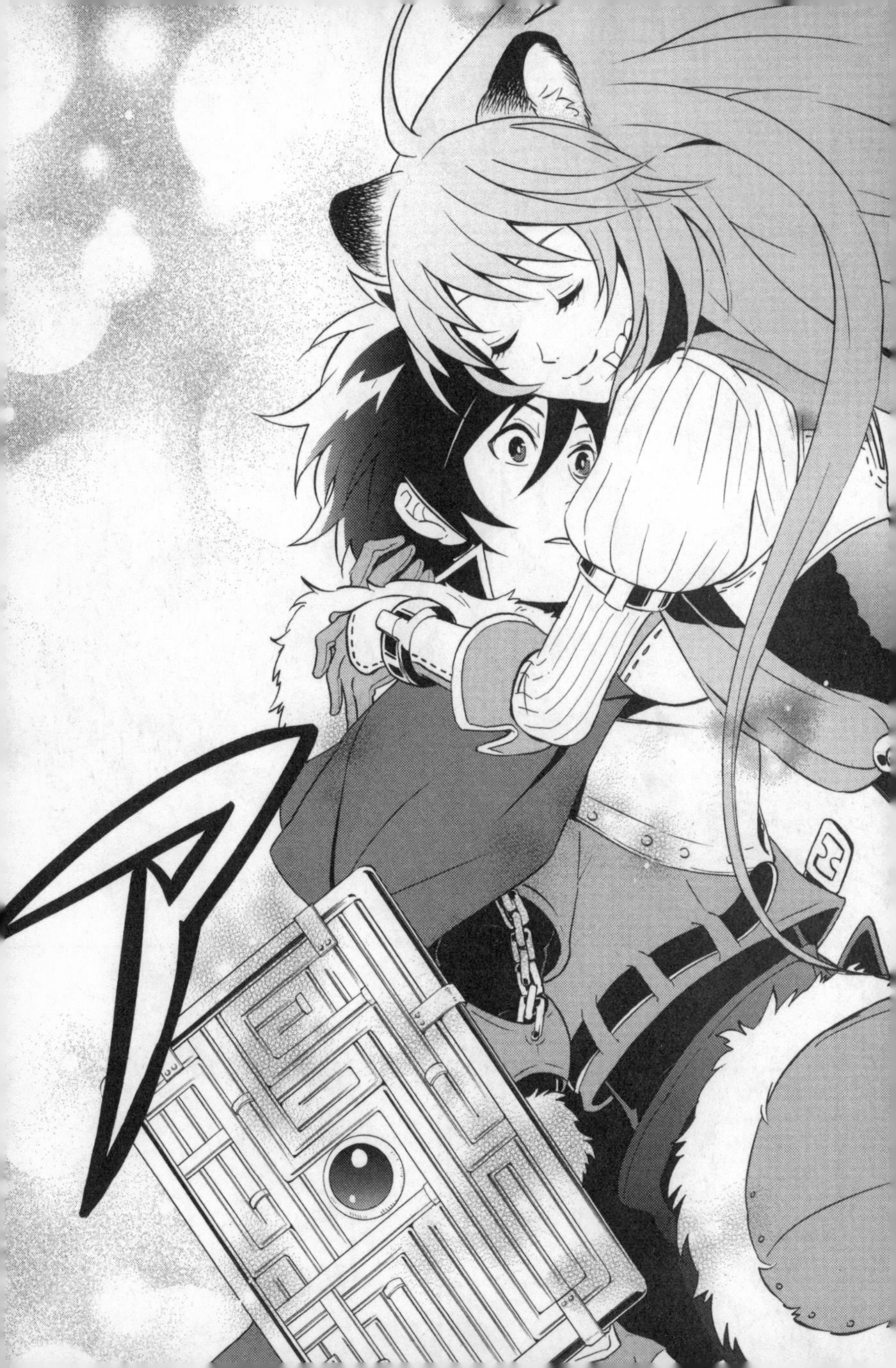

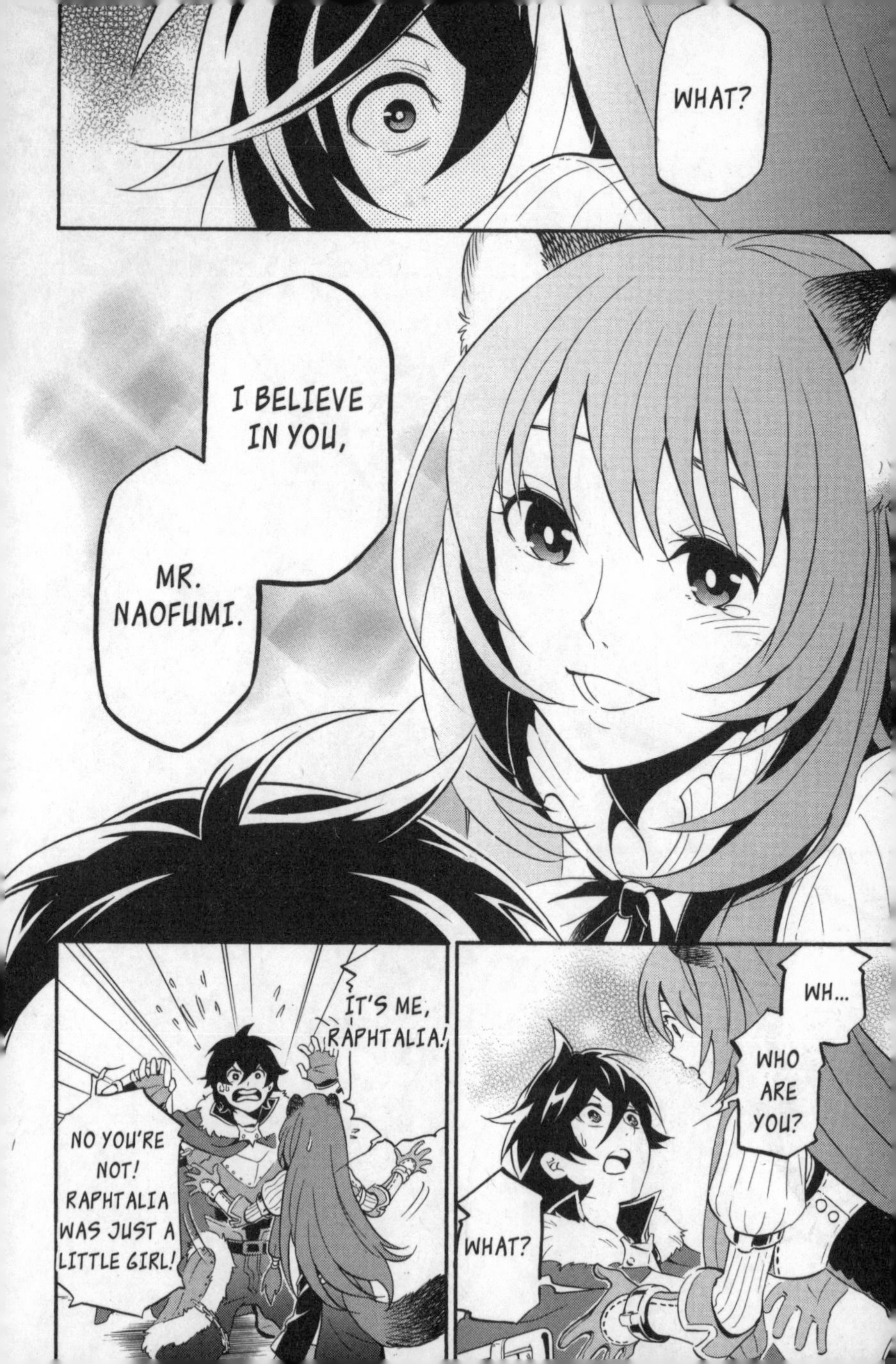
WHAT?
I BELIEVE IN YOU,
MR. NAOFUMI.
WH...
WHO ARE YOU?
WHAT?
IT'S ME, RAPHTALIA!
NO YOU'RE NOT! RAPHTALIA WAS JUST A LITTLE GIRL!

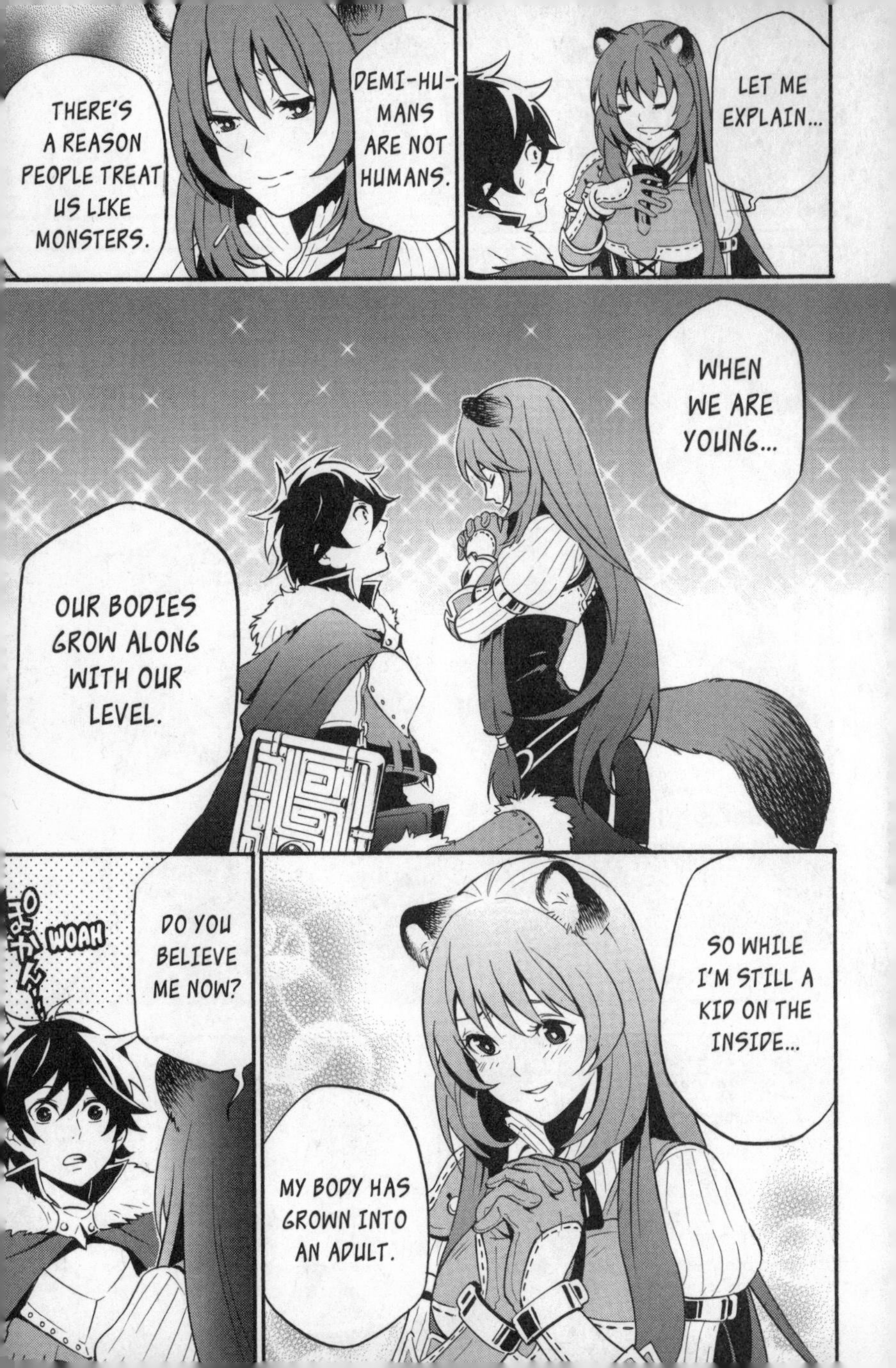
LET ME EXPLAIN...
DEMI-HUMANS ARE NOT HUMANS.
THERE'S A REASON PEOPLE TREAT US LIKE MONSTERS.
WHEN WE ARE YOUNG...
OUR BODIES GROW ALONG WITH OUR LEVEL.
SO WHILE I'M STILL A KID ON THE INSIDE...
MY BODY HAS GROWN INTO AN ADULT.
DO YOU BELIEVE ME NOW?
WOAH

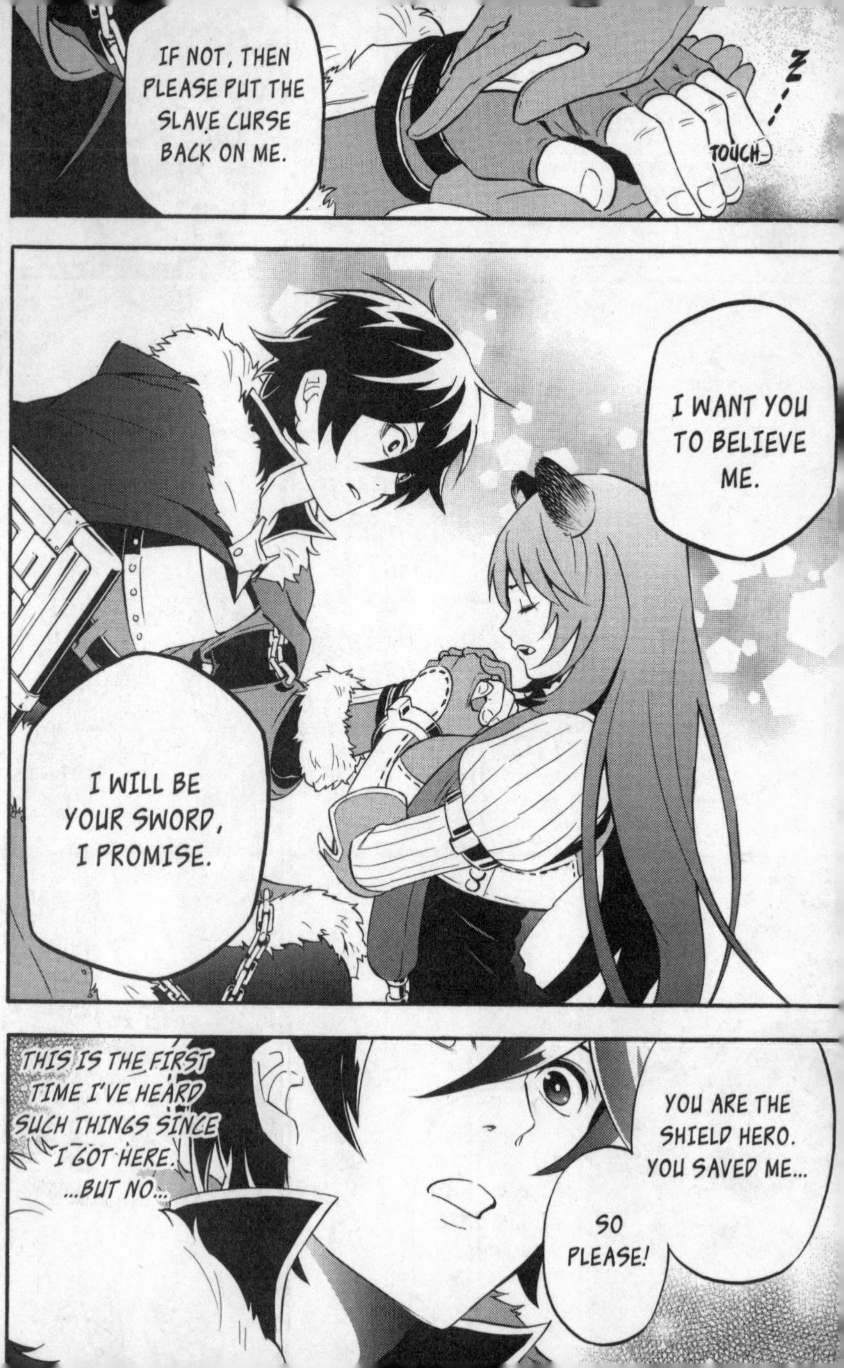
Z- - -
TOUCH
IF NOT, THEN PLEASE PUT THE SLAVE CURSE BACK ON ME.
I WANT YOU TO BELIEVE ME.
I WILL BE YOUR SWORD, I PROMISE.
YOU ARE THE SHIELD HERO. YOU SAVED ME...
SO PLEASE!
THIS IS THE FIRST TIME I'VE HEARD SUCH THINGS SINCE I GOT HERE. ...BUT NO...

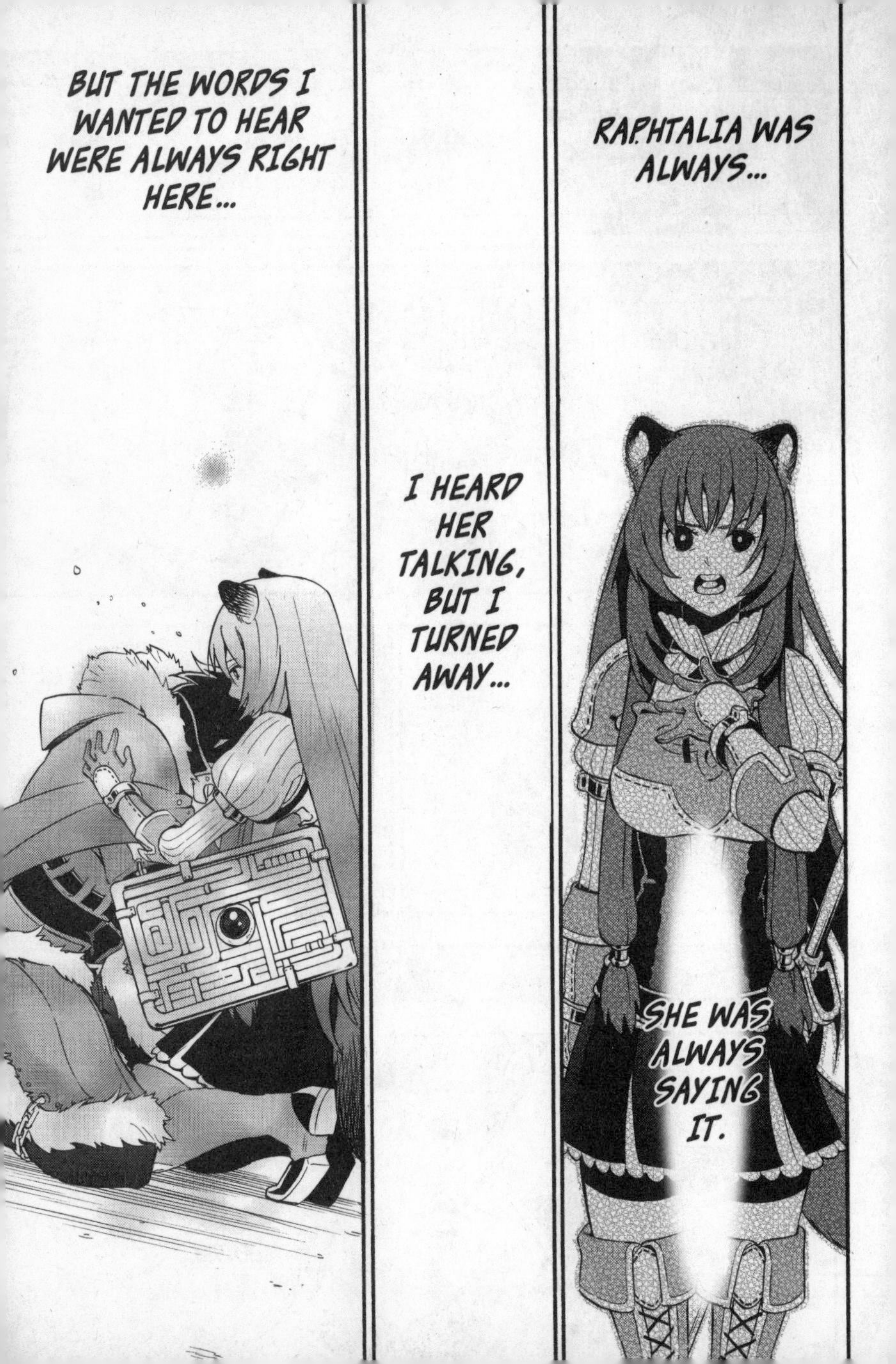
RAPHTALIA WAS ALWAYS...
SHE WAS ALWAYS SAYING IT.
I HEARD HER TALKING, BUT I TURNED AWAY...
BUT THE WORDS I WANTED TO HEAR WERE ALWAYS RIGHT HERE...

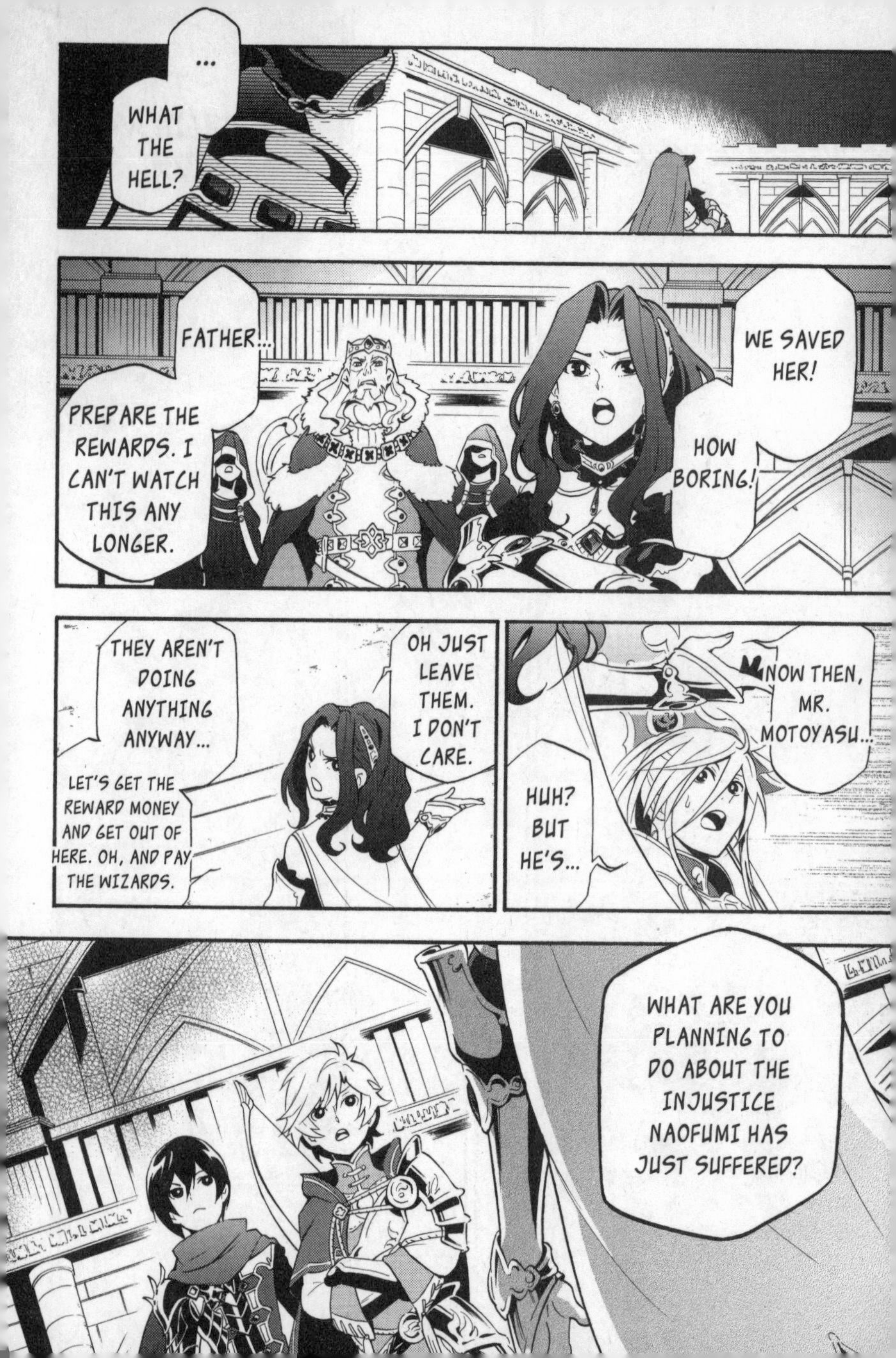
...
WHAT THE HELL?
WE SAVED HER!
HOW BORING!
FATHER...
PREPARE THE REWARDS. I CAN'T WATCH THIS ANY LONGER.
NOW THEN, MR. MOTOYASU...
HUH? BUT HE'S...
OH JUST LEAVE THEM. I DON'T CARE.
THEY AREN'T DOING ANYTHING ANYWAY...
LET'S GET THE REWARD MONEY AND GET OUT OF HERE. OH, AND PAY THE WIZARDS.
WHAT ARE YOU PLANNING TO DO ABOUT THE INJUSTICE NAOFUMI HAS JUST SUFFERED?

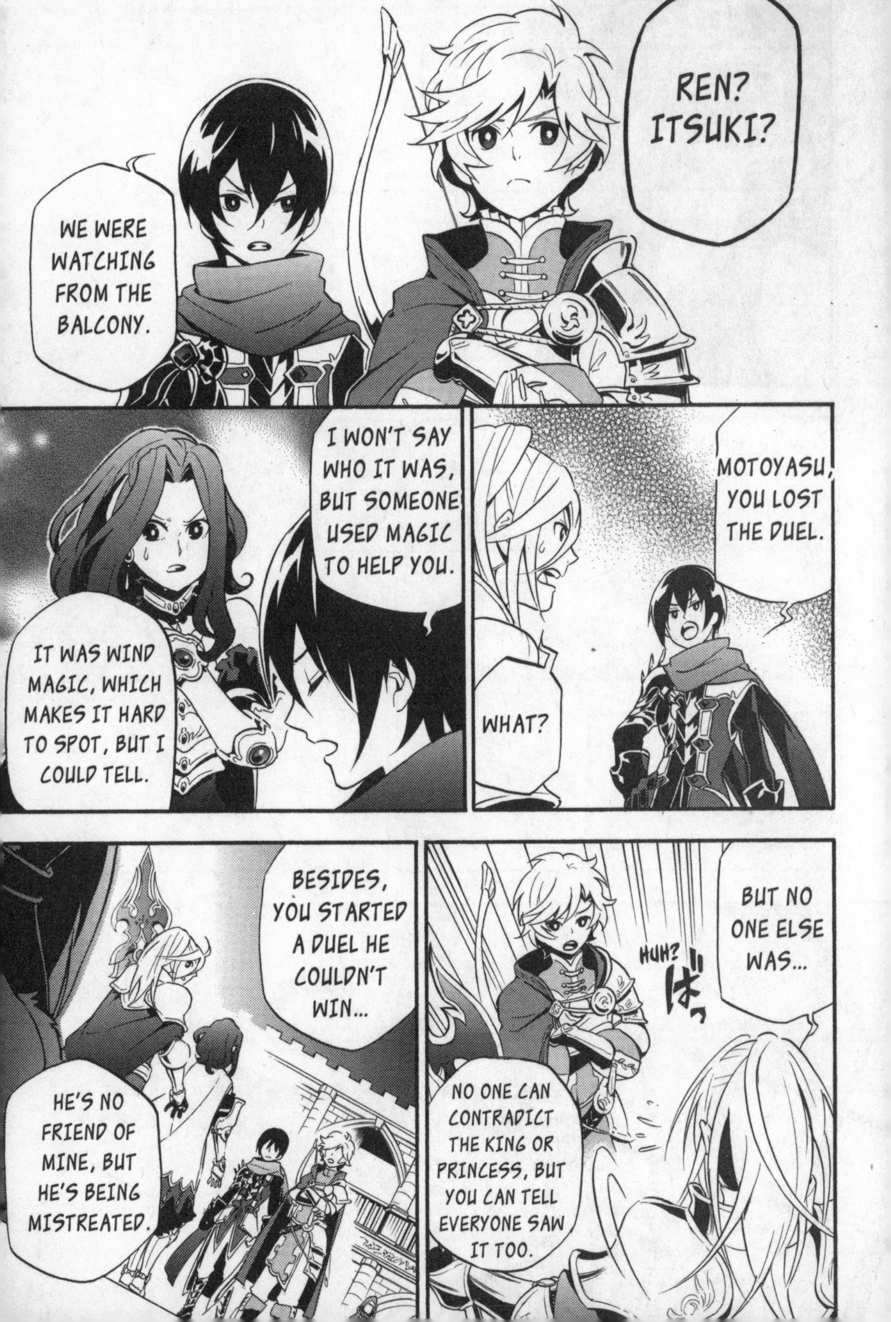
REN? ITSUKI?
WE WERE WATCHING FROM THE BALCONY.
MOTOYASU, YOU LOST THE DUEL.
WHAT?
I WON'T SAY WHO IT WAS, BUT SOMEONE USED MAGIC TO HELP YOU.
IT WAS WIND MAGIC, WHICH MAKES IT HARD TO SPOT, BUT I COULD TELL.
BUT NO ONE ELSE WAS...
HUH?
ばっ
NO ONE CAN CONTRADICT THE KING OR PRINCESS, BUT YOU CAN TELL EVERYONE SAW IT TOO.
BESIDES, YOU STARTED A DUEL HE COULDN'T WIN...
HE'S NO FRIEND OF MINE, BUT HE'S BEING MISTREATED.

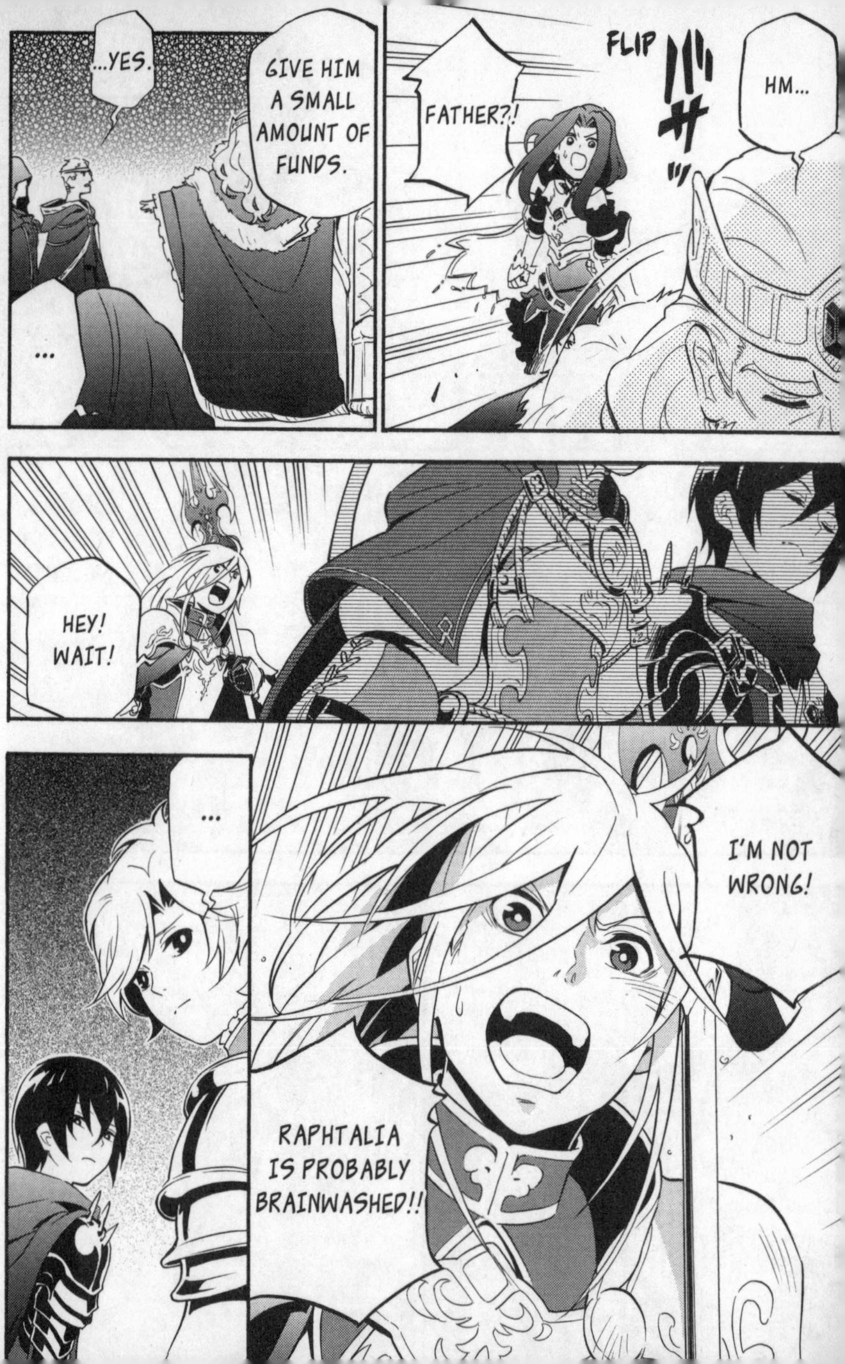
HM...
FLIP
バサッ
FATHER?!
GIVE HIM A SMALL AMOUNT OF FUNDS.
...YES.
...
HEY! WAIT!
I'M NOT WRONG!
RAPHTALIA IS PROBABLY BRAINWASHED!!
...

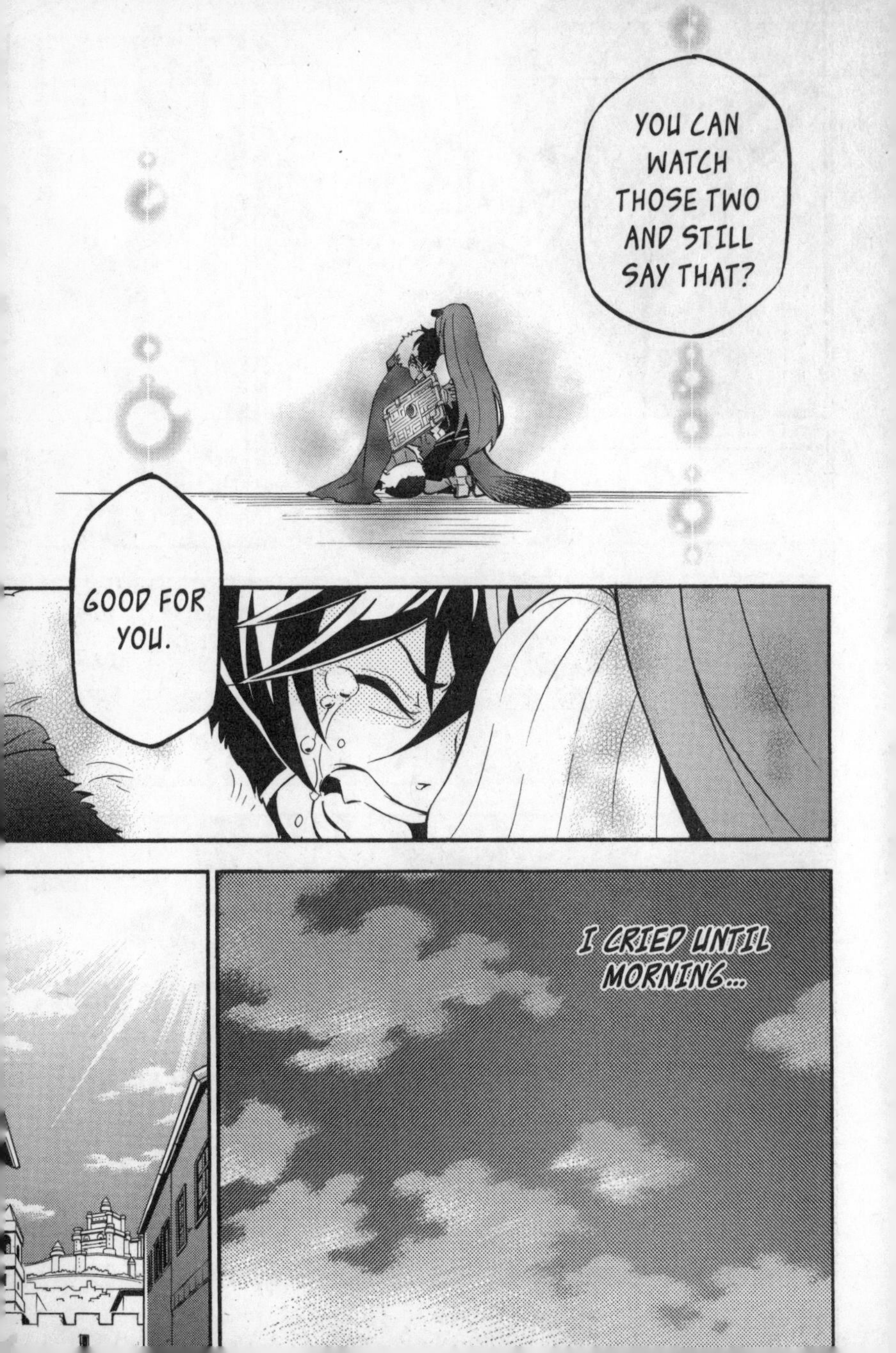
YOU CAN WATCH THOSE TWO AND STILL SAY THAT?
GOOD FOR YOU.
I CRIED UNTIL MORNING...

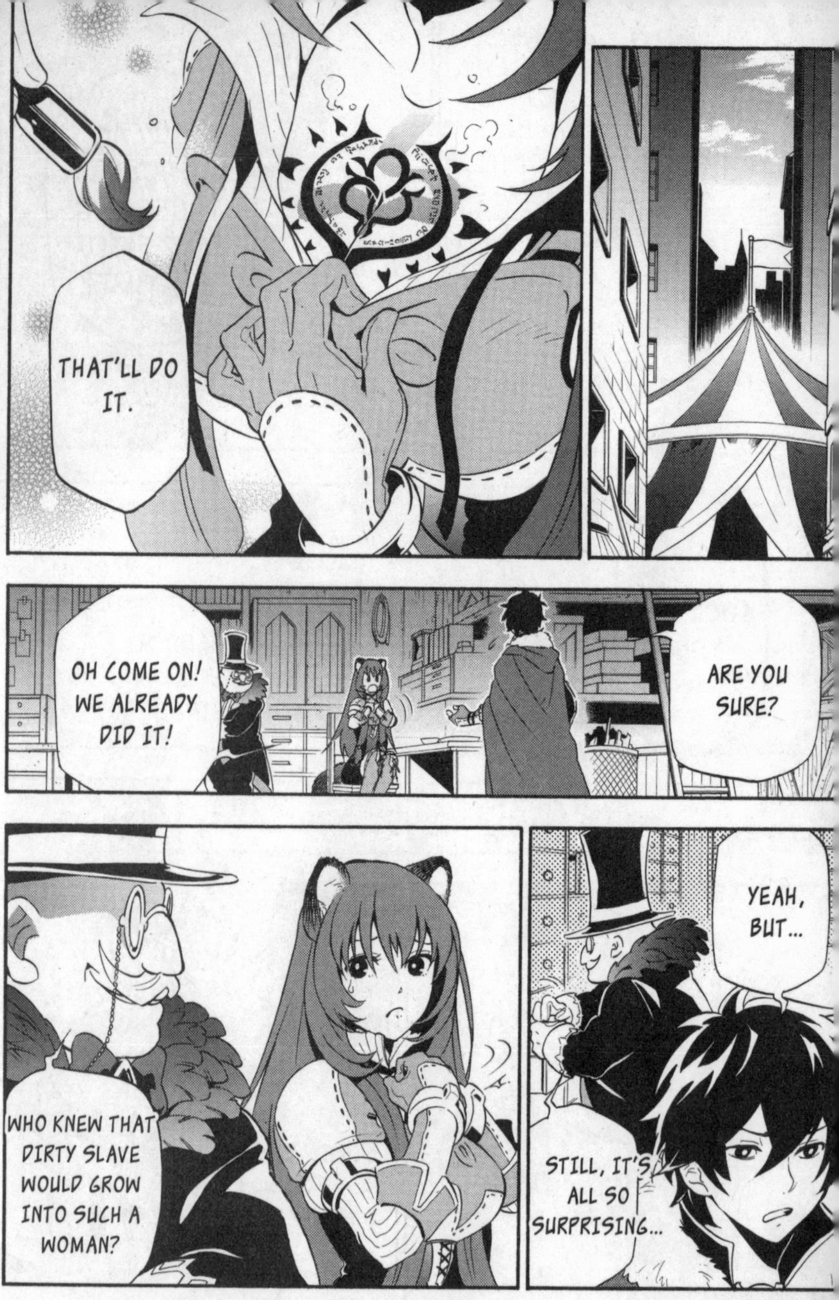
THAT'LL DO IT.
ARE YOU SURE?
OH COME ON! WE ALREADY DID IT!
YEAH, BUT...
STILL, IT'S ALL SO SURPRISING...
WHO KNEW THAT DIRTY SLAVE WOULD GROW INTO SUCH A WOMAN?

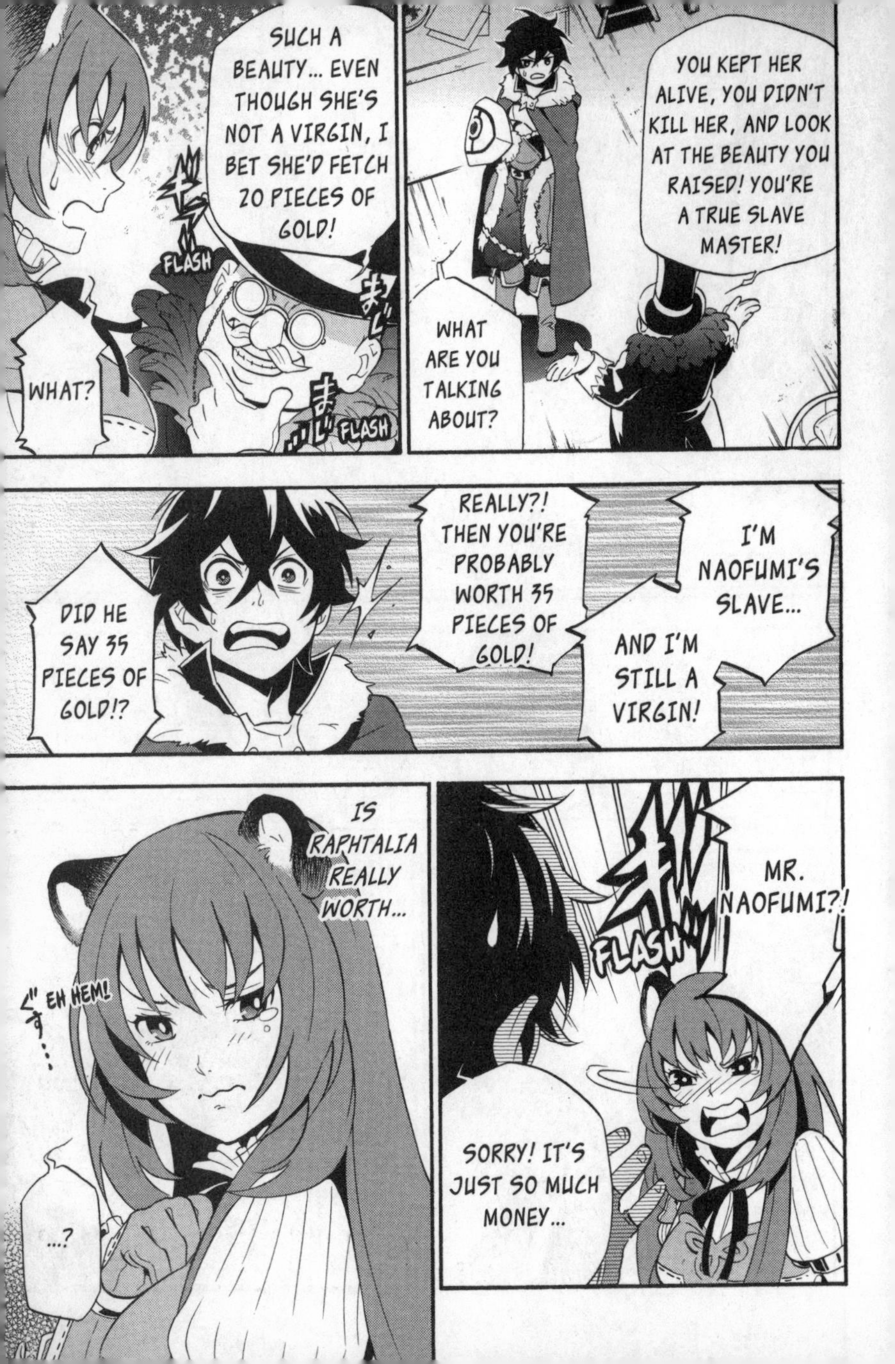
YOU KEPT HER ALIVE, YOU DIDN'T KILL HER, AND LOOK AT THE BEAUTY YOU RAISED! YOU'RE A TRUE SLAVE MASTER!
WHAT ARE YOU TALKING ABOUT?
SUCH A BEAUTY... EVEN THOUGH SHE'S NOT A VIRGIN, I BET SHE'D FETCH 20 PIECES OF GOLD!
FLASH
FLASH
WHAT?
I'M NAOFUMI'S SLAVE...
AND I'M STILL A VIRGIN!
REALLY?! THEN YOU'RE PROBABLY WORTH 35 PIECES OF GOLD!
DID HE SAY 35 PIECES OF GOLD!?
MR. NAOFUMI?!
FLASH
SORRY! IT'S JUST SO MUCH MONEY...
IS RAPHTALIA REALLY WORTH...
EH HEM!
...?

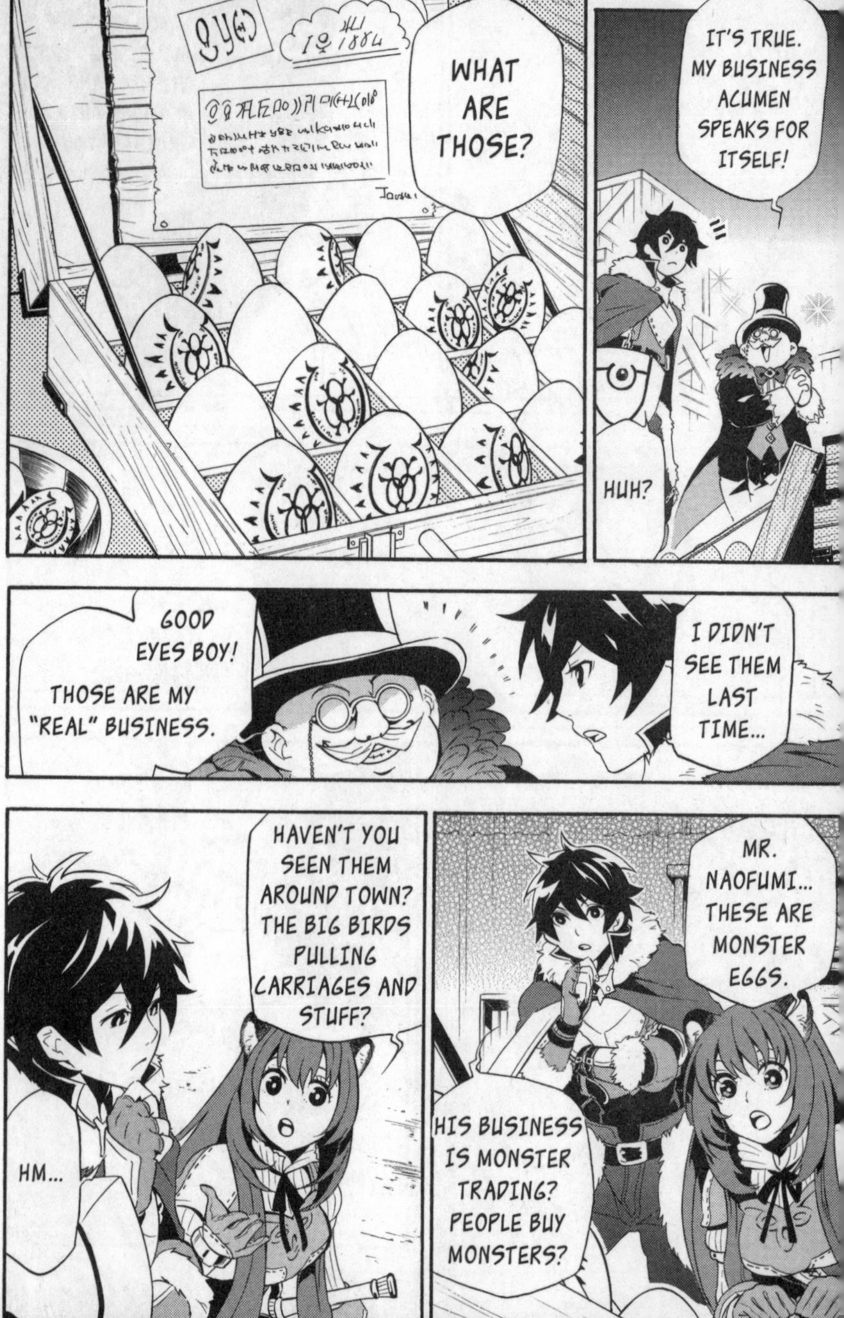
IT'S TRUE. MY BUSINESS ACUMEN SPEAKS FOR ITSELF!
HUH?
WHAT ARE THOSE?
I DIDN'T SEE THEM LAST TIME...
GOOD EYES BOY! THOSE ARE MY "REAL" BUSINESS.
MR. NAOFUMI... THESE ARE MONSTER EGGS.
HIS BUSINESS IS MONSTER TRADING? PEOPLE BUY MONSTERS?
HAVEN'T YOU SEEN THEM AROUND TOWN? THE BIG BIRDS PULLING CARRIAGES AND STUFF?
HM...

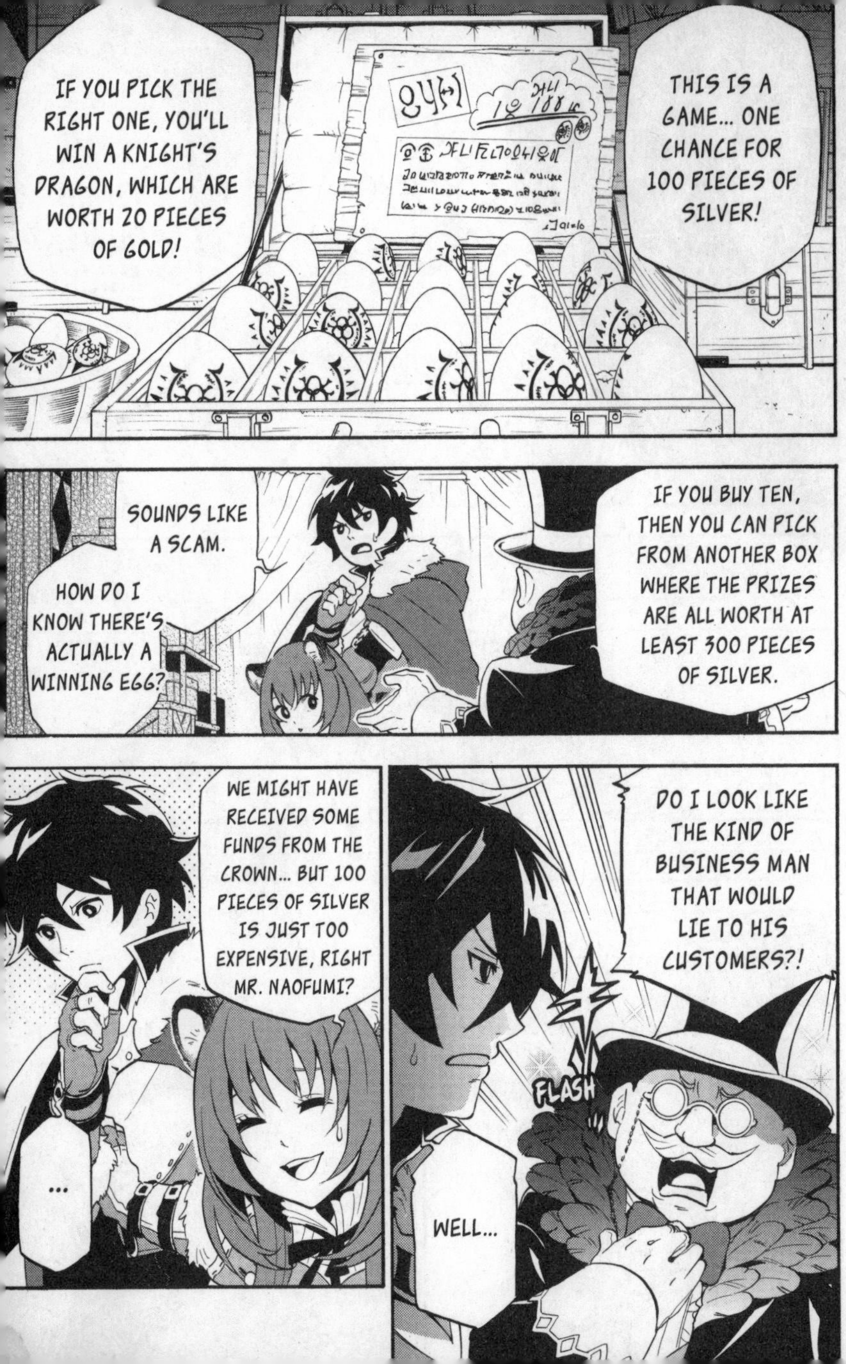
THIS IS A GAME... ONE CHANCE FOR 100 PIECES OF SILVER!
IF YOU PICK THE RIGHT ONE, YOU'LL WIN A KNIGHT'S DRAGON, WHICH ARE WORTH 20 PIECES OF GOLD!
IF YOU BUY TEN, THEN YOU CAN PICK FROM ANOTHER BOX WHERE THE PRIZES ARE ALL WORTH AT LEAST 300 PIECES OF SILVER.
SOUNDS LIKE A SCAM.
HOW DO I KNOW THERE'S ACTUALLY A WINNING EGG?
DO I LOOK LIKE THE KIND OF BUSINESS MAN THAT WOULD LIE TO HIS CUSTOMERS?!
FLASH
WELL...
WE MIGHT HAVE RECEIVED SOME FUNDS FROM THE CROWN... BUT 100 PIECES OF SILVER IS JUST TOO EXPENSIVE, RIGHT MR. NAOFUMI?
...

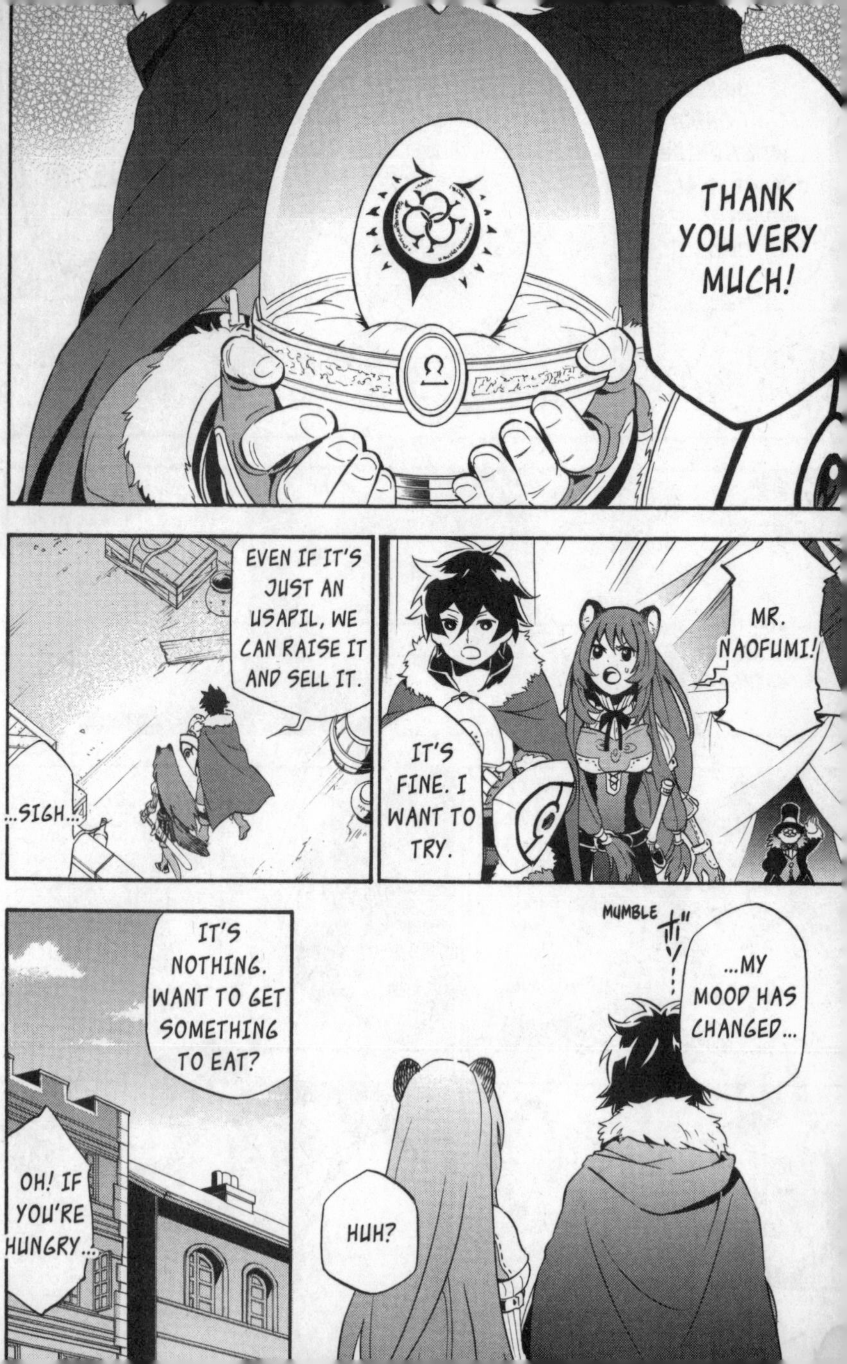
THANK YOU VERY MUCH!
MR. NAOFUMI!
IT'S FINE. I WANT TO TRY.
EVEN IF IT'S JUST AN USAPIL, WE CAN RAISE IT AND SELL IT.
...SIGH...
MUMBLE
...MY MOOD HAS CHANGED...
IT'S NOTHING. WANT TO GET SOMETHING TO EAT?
HUH?
OH! IF YOU'RE HUNGRY...

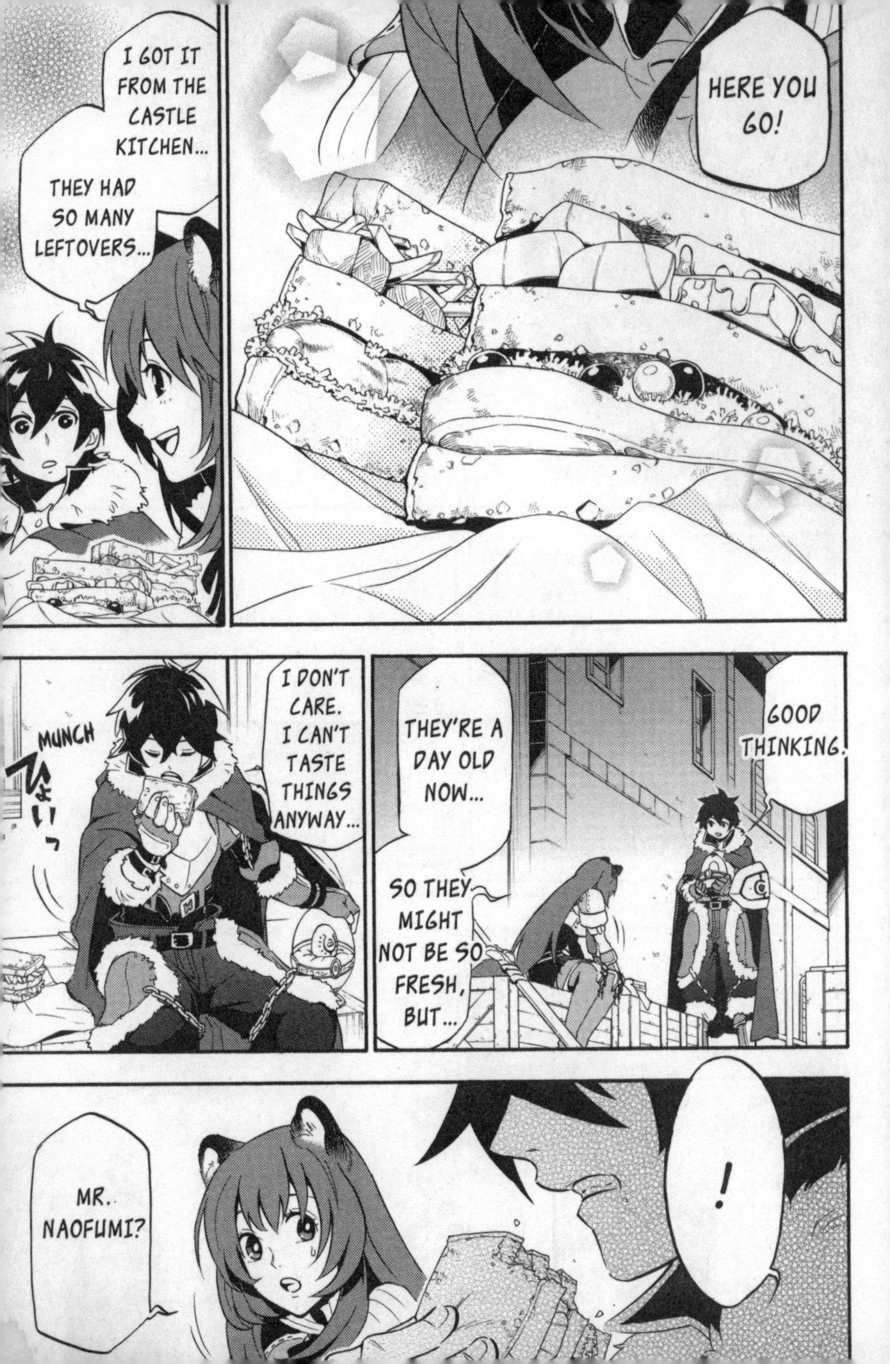
HERE YOU GO!
I GOT IT FROM THE CASTLE KITCHEN...
THEY HAD SO MANY LEFTOVERS...
GOOD THINKING.
THEY'RE A DAY OLD NOW...
SO THEY MIGHT NOT BE SO FRESH, BUT...
I DON'T CARE. I CAN'T TASTE THINGS ANYWAY...
MUNCH
ひょいっ
!
MR. NAOFUMI?

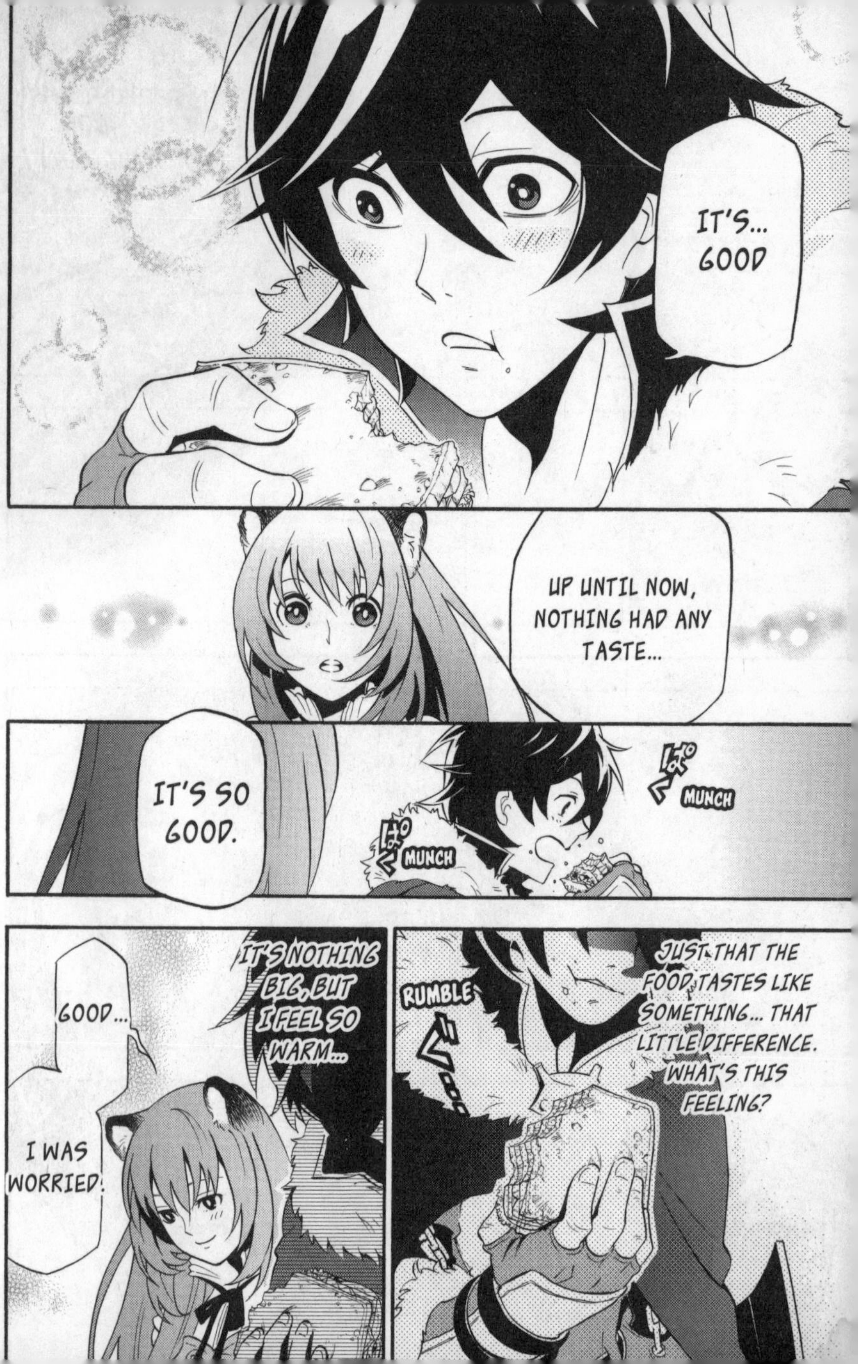
IT'S... GOOD
UP UNTIL NOW, NOTHING HAD ANY TASTE...
MUNCH
MUNCH
IT'S SO GOOD.
JUST THAT THE FOOD TASTES LIKE SOMETHING... THAT LITTLE DIFFERENCE. WHAT'S THIS FEELING?
RUMBLE
IT'S NOTHING BIG, BUT I FEEL SO WARM...
GOOD...
I WAS WORRIED.

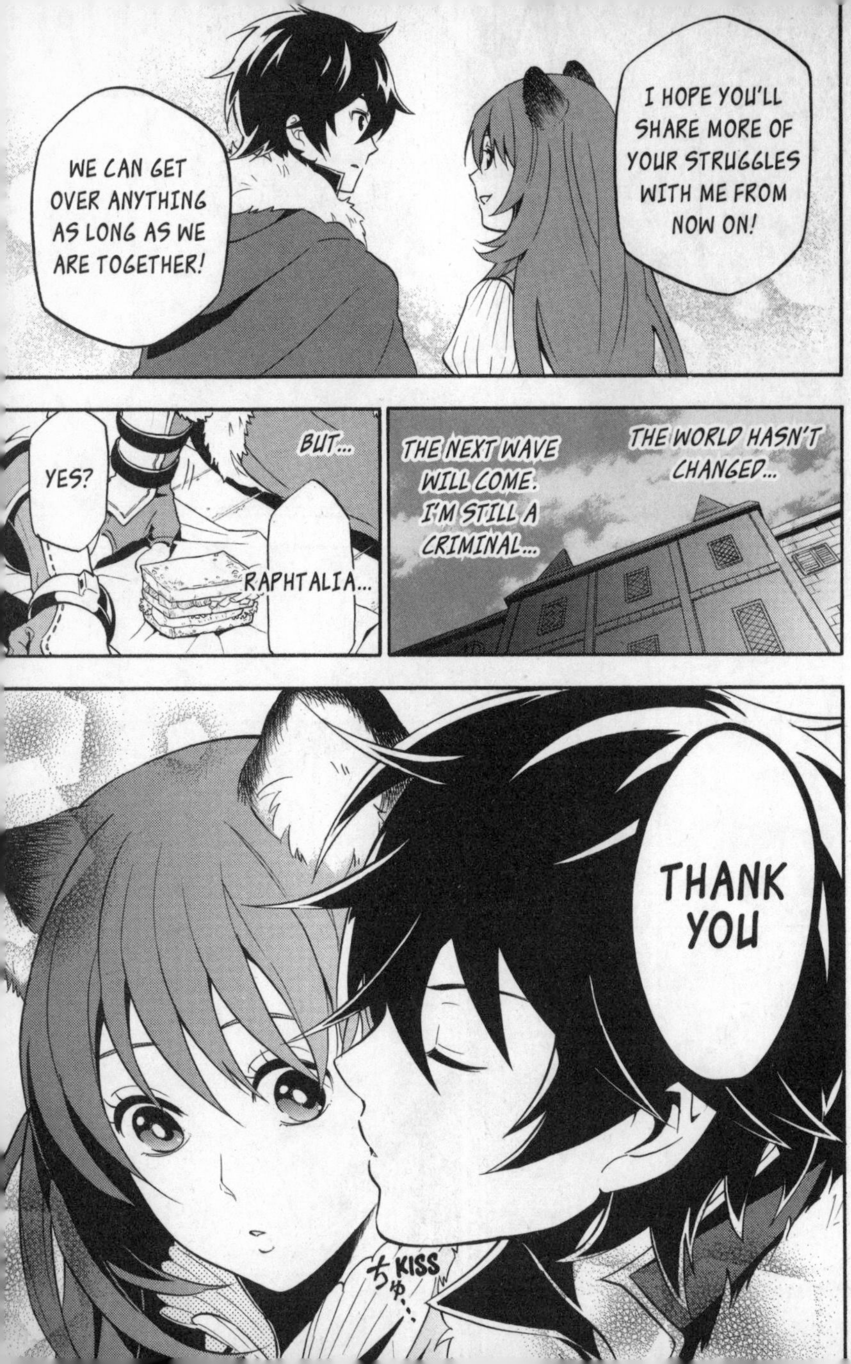
I HOPE YOU'LL SHARE MORE OF YOUR STRUGGLES WITH ME FROM NOW ON!
WE CAN GET OVER ANYTHING AS LONG AS WE ARE TOGETHER!
THE WORLD HASN'T CHANGED...
THE NEXT WAVE WILL COME. I'M STILL A CRIMINAL...
BUT...
RAPHTALIA...
YES?
THANK YOU
KISS
ちゅ…

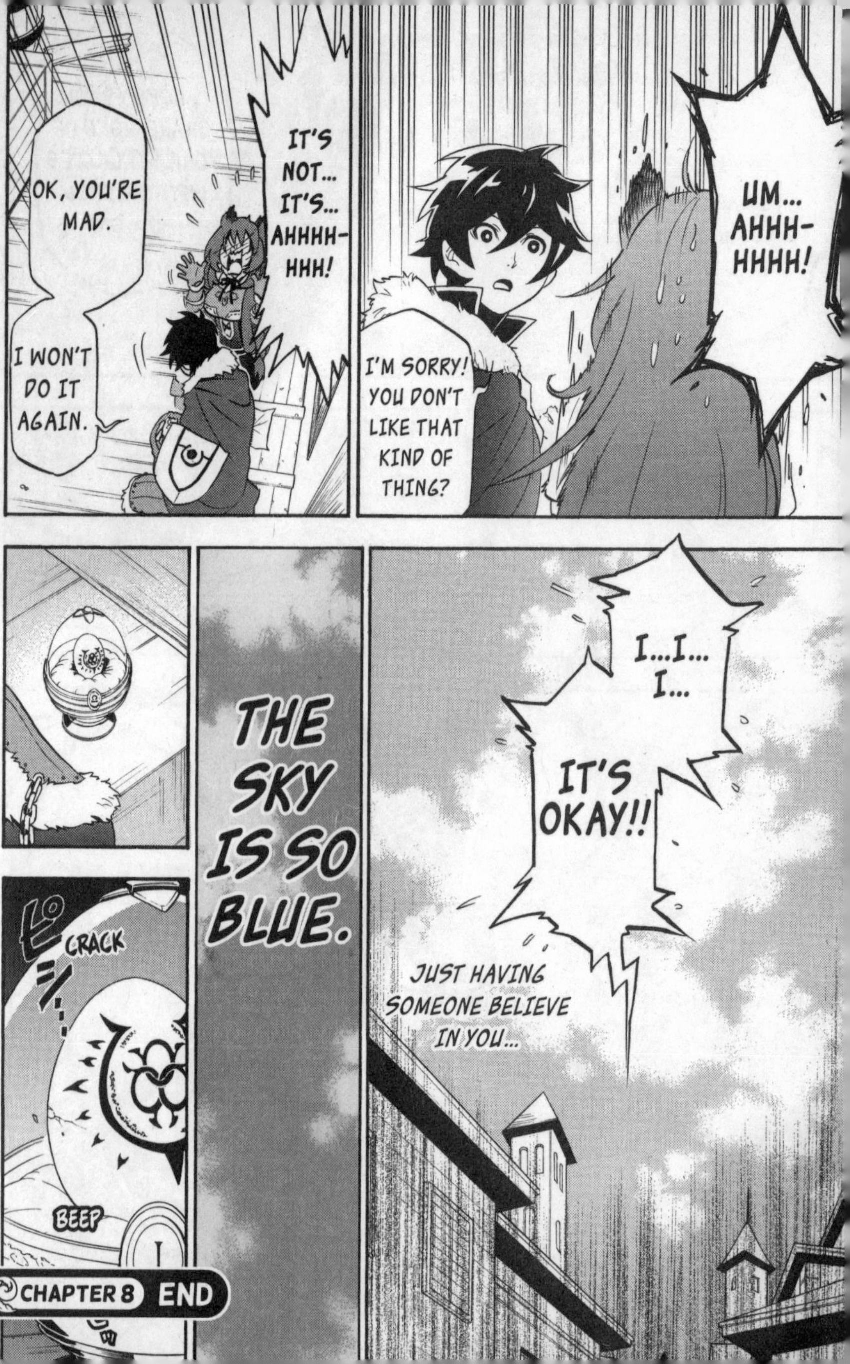
UM... AHHH-HHHH!
I'M SORRY! YOU DON'T LIKE THAT KIND OF THING?
IT'S NOT... IT'S... AHHHH-HHH!
OK, YOU'RE MAD.
I WON'T DO IT AGAIN.
I...I... I...
IT'S OKAY!!
JUST HAVING SOMEONE BELIEVE IN YOU...
THE SKY IS SO BLUE.
CRACK
BEEP
CHAPTER 8 END

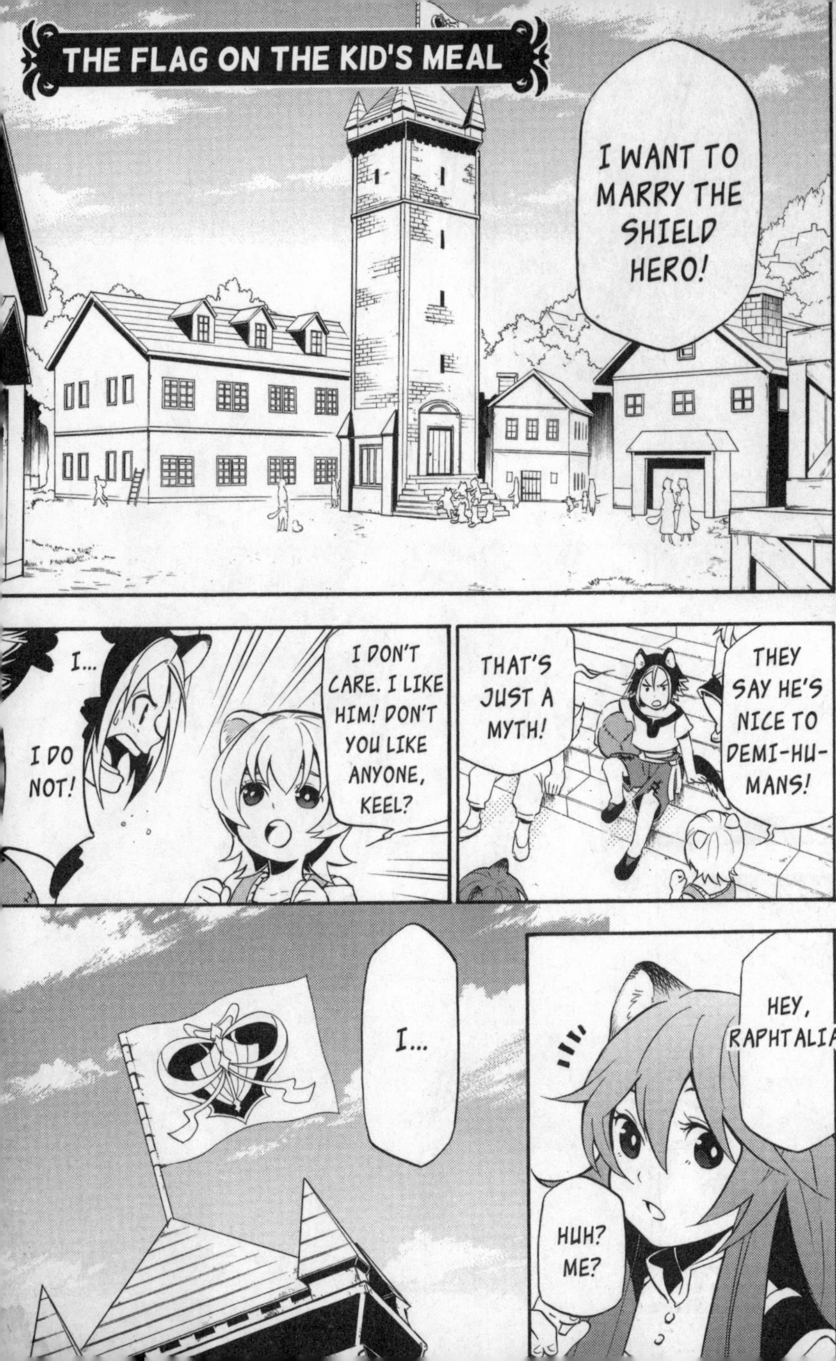
THE FLAG ON THE KID'S MEAL
I WANT TO MARRY THE SHIELD HERO!
THEY SAY HE'S NICE TO DEMI-HUMANS!
THAT'S JUST A MYTH!
I DON'T CARE. I LIKE HIM! DON'T YOU LIKE ANYONE, KEEL?
I...
I DO NOT!
HEY, RAPHTALIA!
HUH? ME?
I...

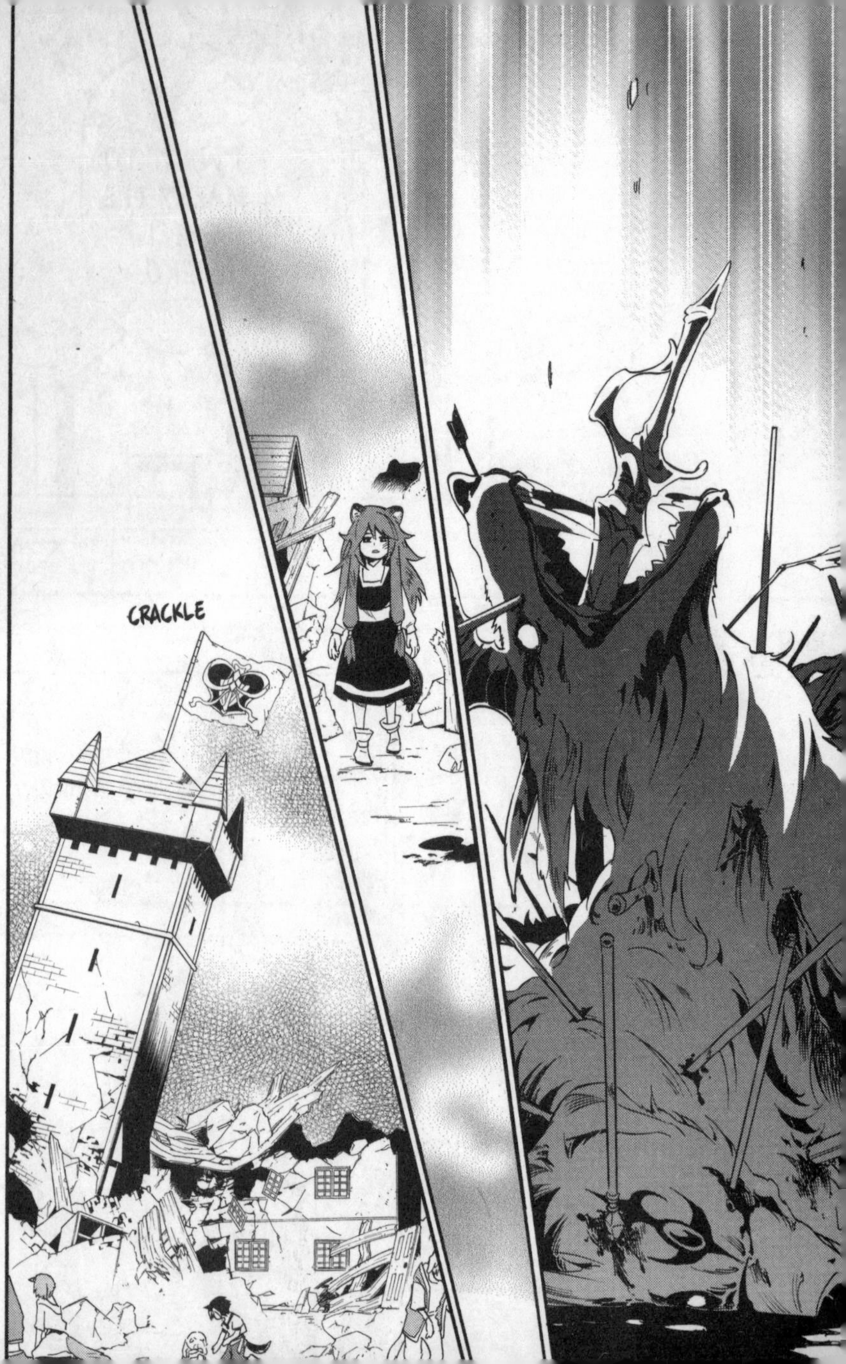
CRACKLE

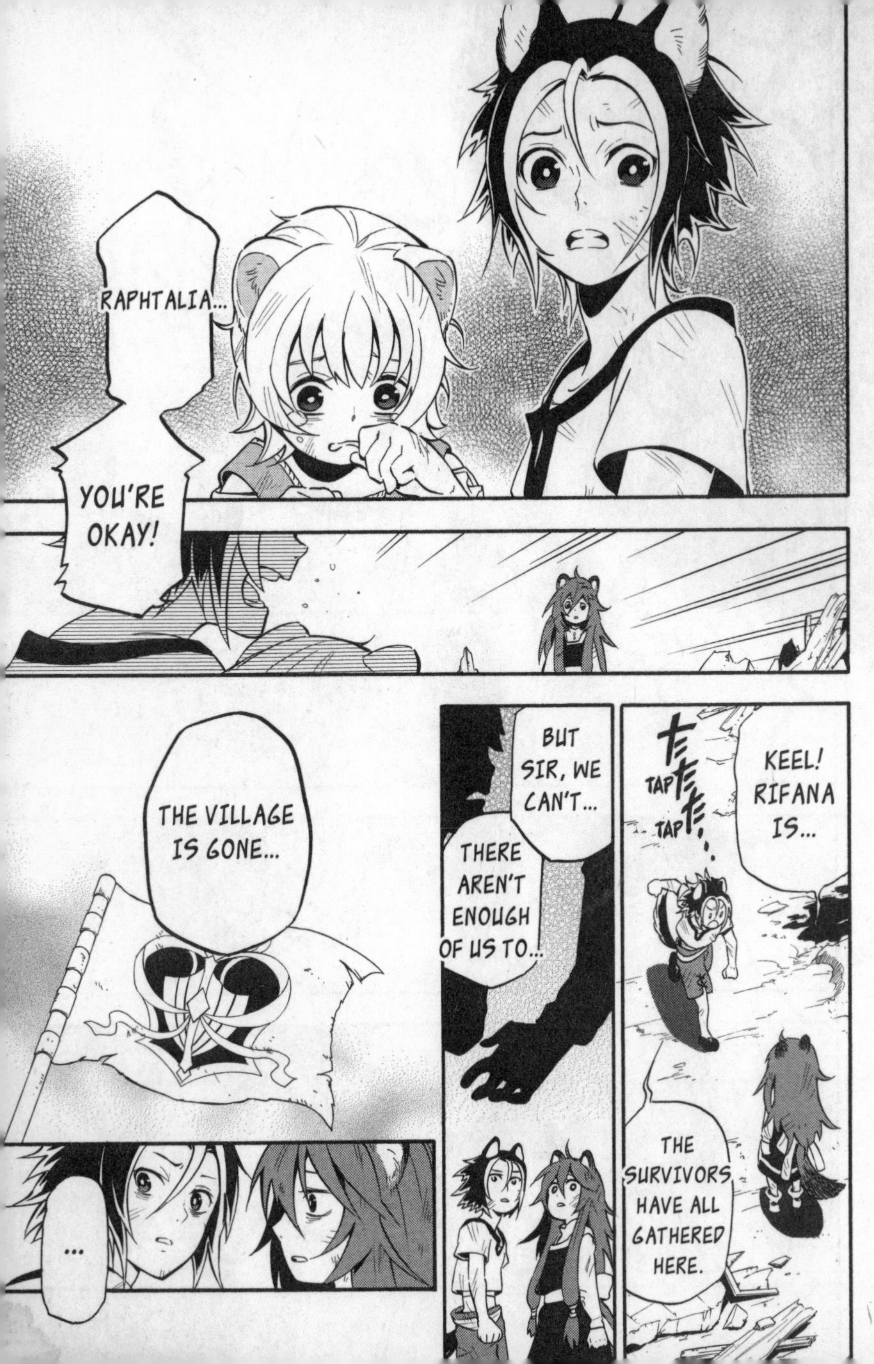
RAPHTALIA...
YOU'RE OKAY!
KEEL! RIFANA IS...
TAP TAP
THE SURVIVORS HAVE ALL GATHERED HERE.
BUT SIR, WE CAN'T...
THERE AREN'T ENOUGH OF US TO...
THE VILLAGE IS GONE...
...

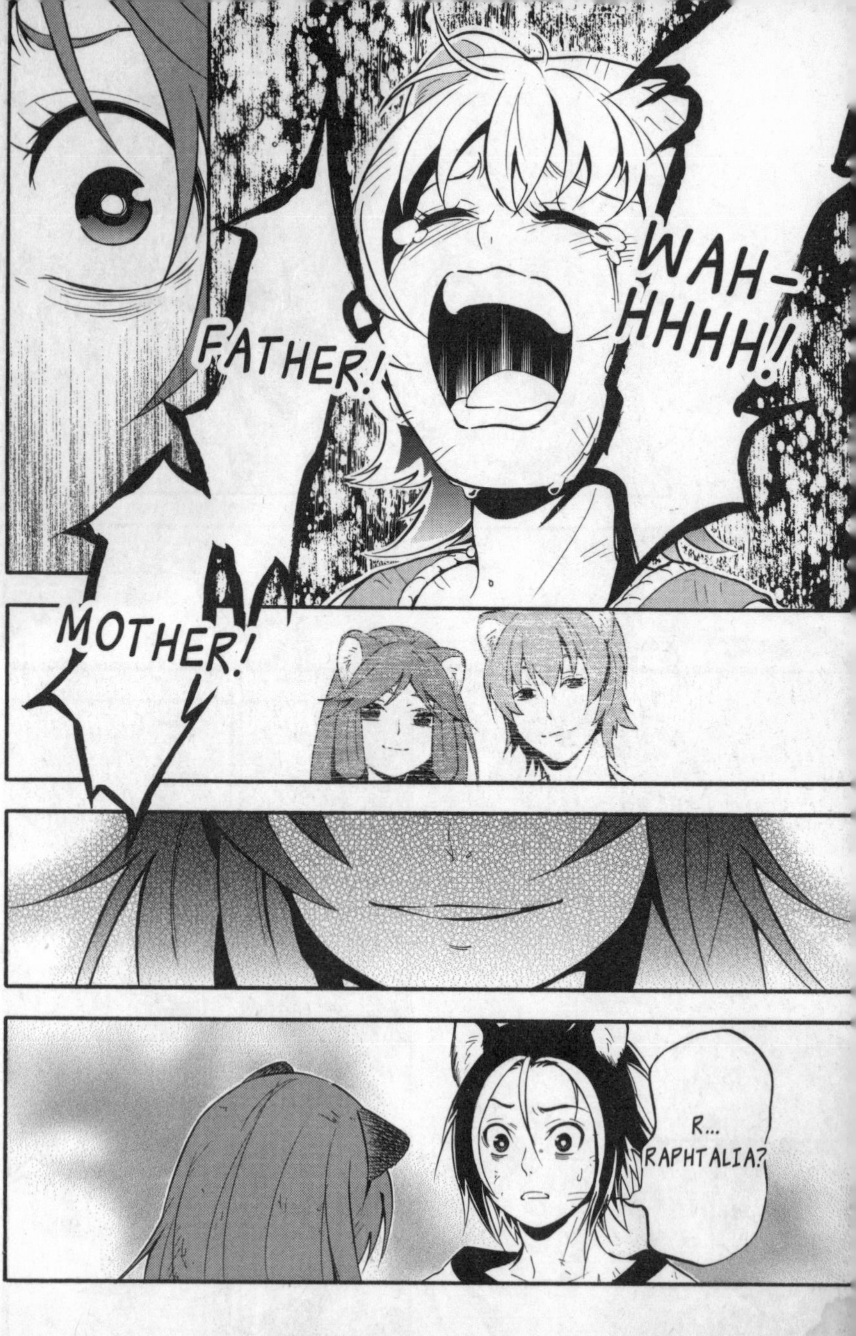
WAH-HHHHH!!
FATHER!
MOTHER!
R...
RAPHTALIA?

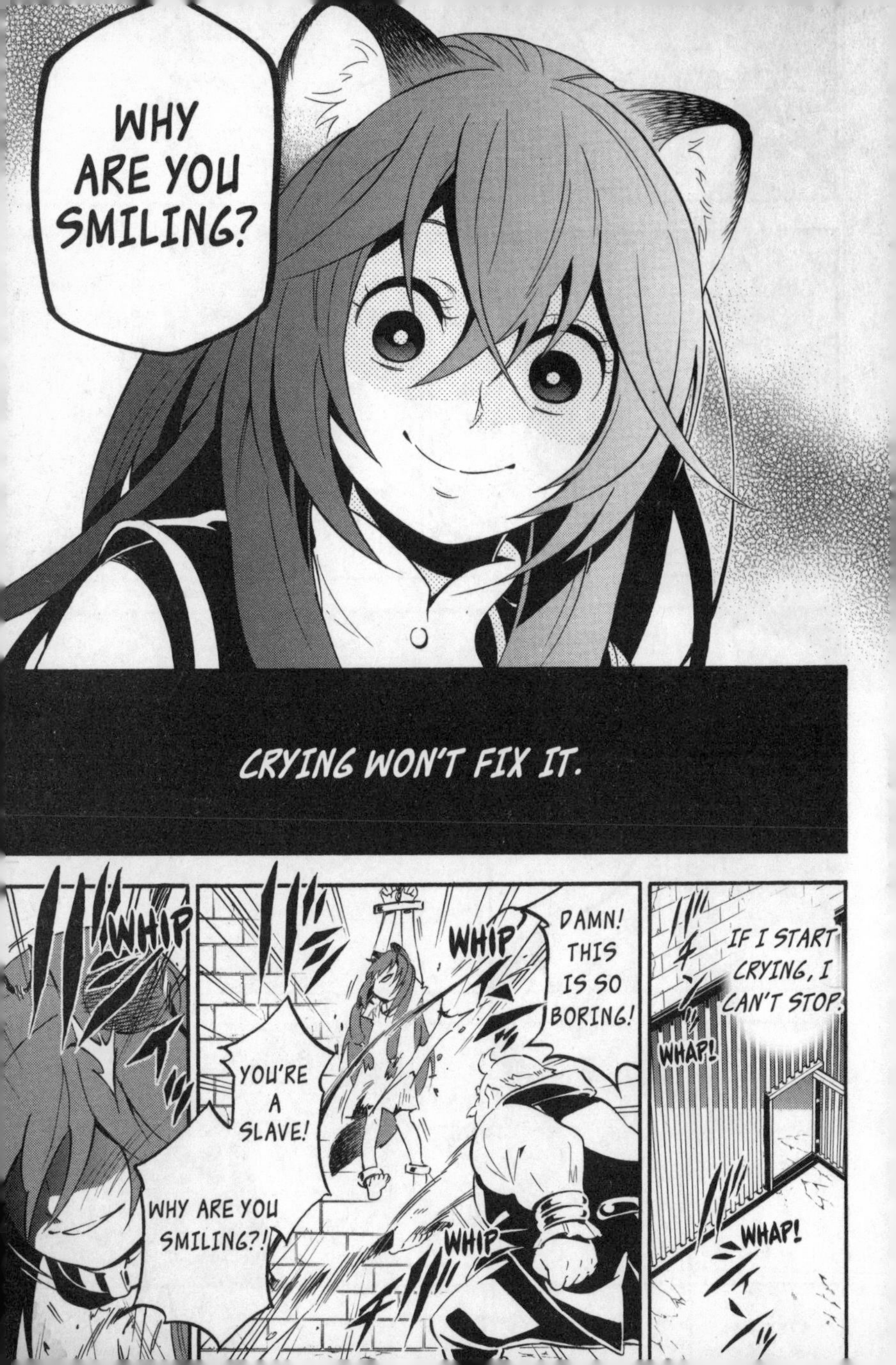
WHY ARE YOU SMILING?
CRYING WON'T FIX IT.
IF I START CRYING, I CAN'T STOP.
WHAP!
WHAP!
DAMN! THIS IS SO BORING!
WHIP
YOU'RE A SLAVE!
WHY ARE YOU SMILING?!
WHIP
WHIP

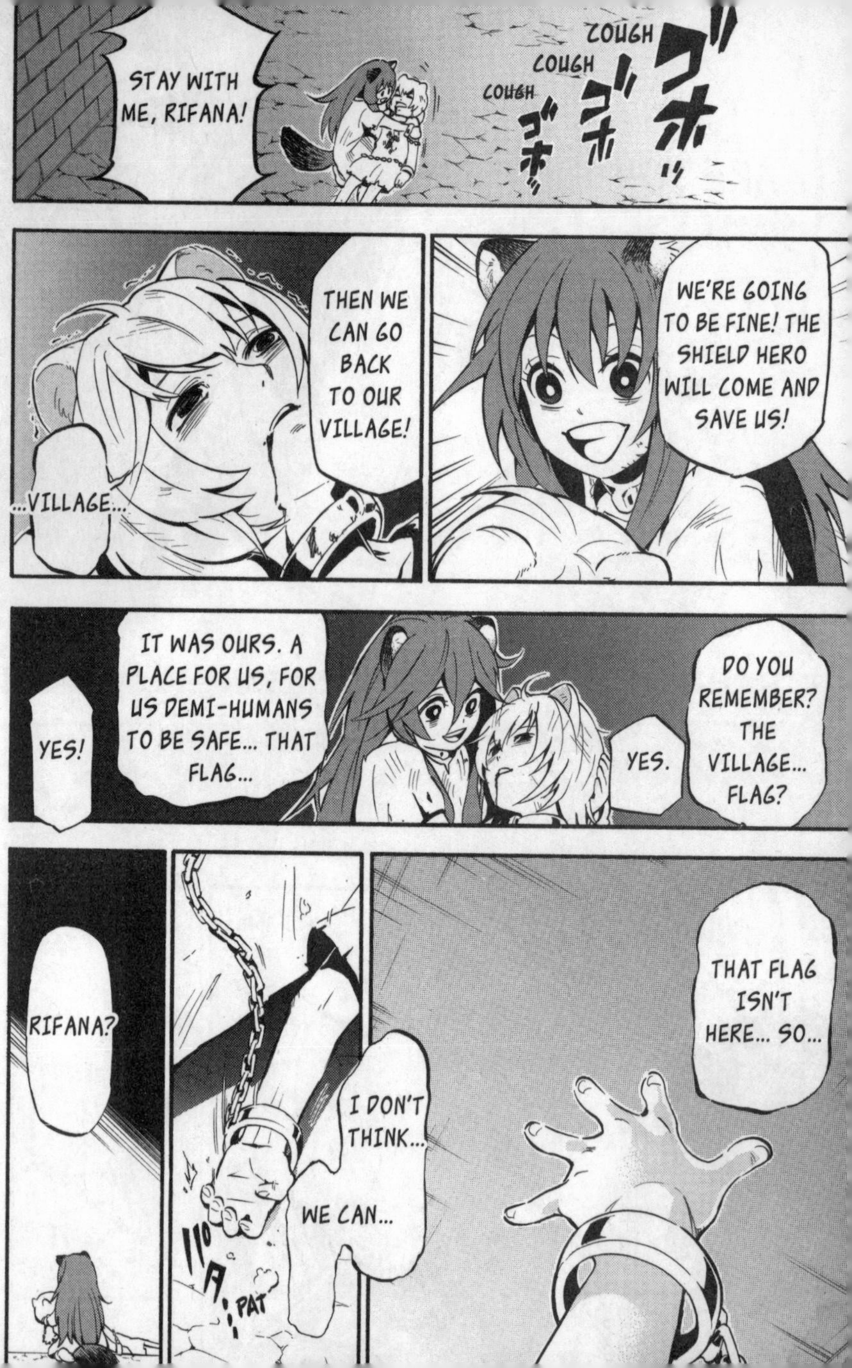
COUGH
COUGH
COUGH
STAY WITH ME, RIFANA!
WE'RE GOING TO BE FINE! THE SHIELD HERO WILL COME AND SAVE US!
THEN WE CAN GO BACK TO OUR VILLAGE!
...VILLAGE...
DO YOU REMEMBER? THE VILLAGE... FLAG?
YES.
IT WAS OURS. A PLACE FOR US, FOR US DEMI-HUMANS TO BE SAFE... THAT FLAG...
YES!
THAT FLAG ISN'T HERE... SO...
I DON'T THINK...
WE CAN...
PAT
RIFANA?

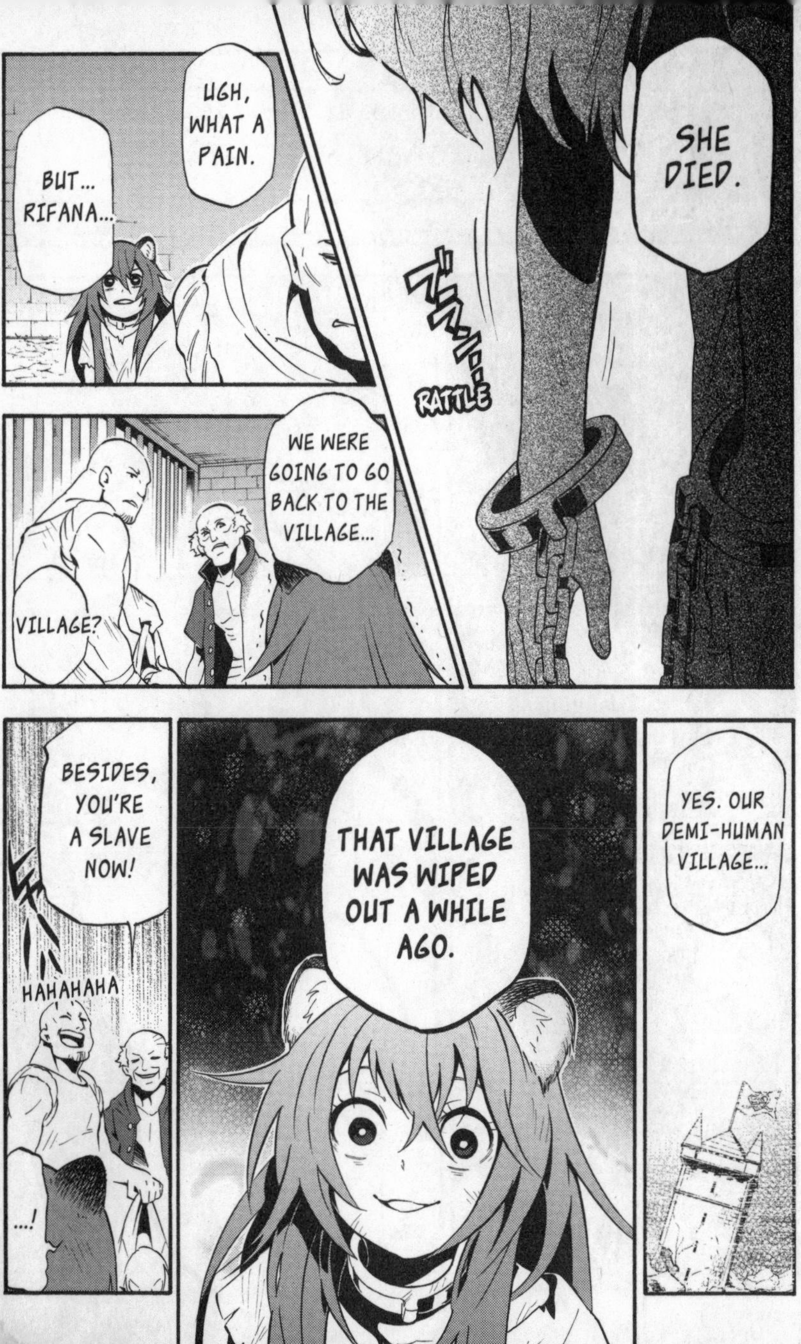
SHE DIED.
RATTLE
UGH, WHAT A PAIN.
BUT... RIFANA...
WE WERE GOING TO GO BACK TO THE VILLAGE...
VILLAGE?
YES. OUR DEMI-HUMAN VILLAGE...
THAT VILLAGE WAS WIPED OUT A WHILE AGO.
BESIDES, YOU'RE A SLAVE NOW!
HAHAHAHA
...!

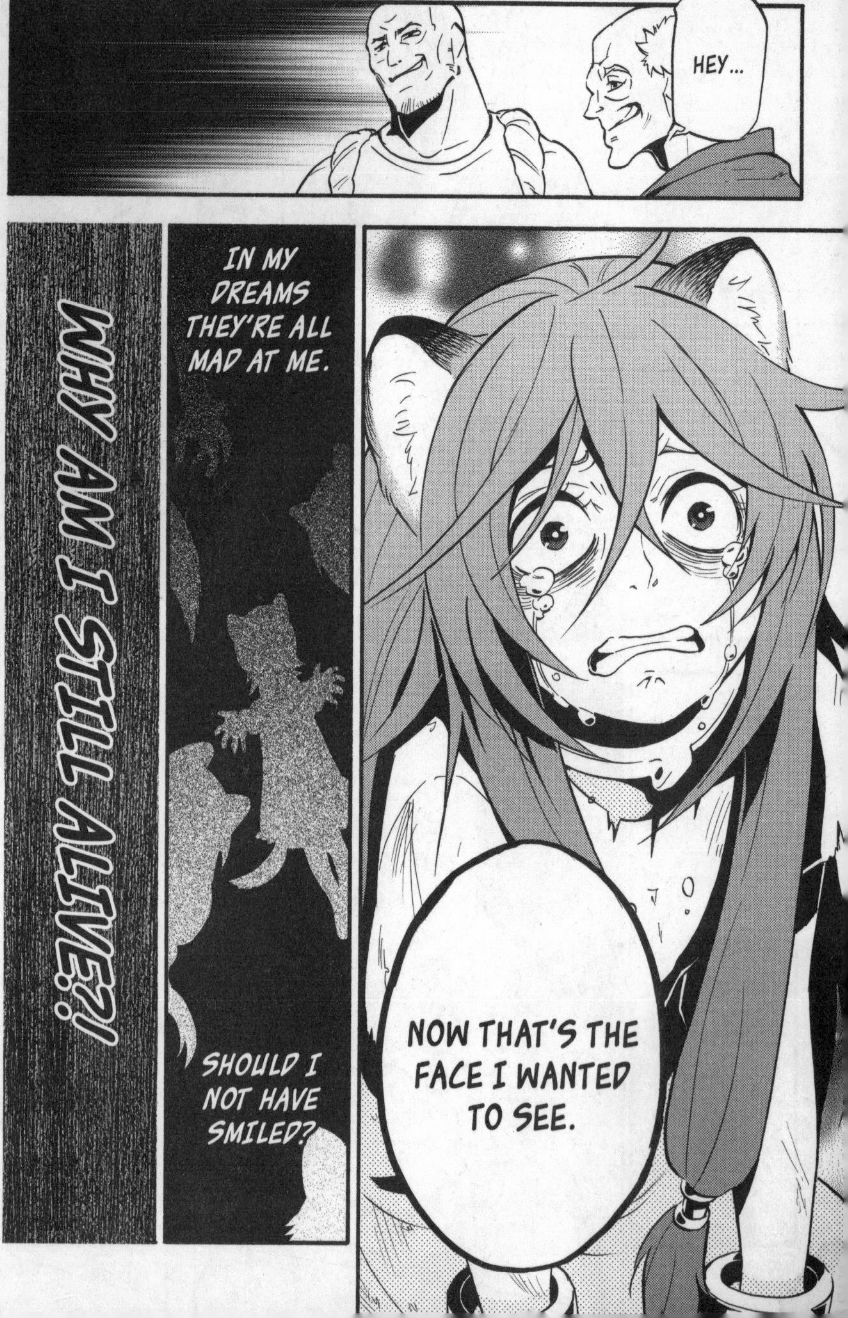
HEY...
NOW THAT'S THE FACE I WANTED TO SEE.
IN MY DREAMS THEY'RE ALL MAD AT ME.
SHOULD I NOT HAVE SMILED?
WHY AM I STILL ALIVE?!

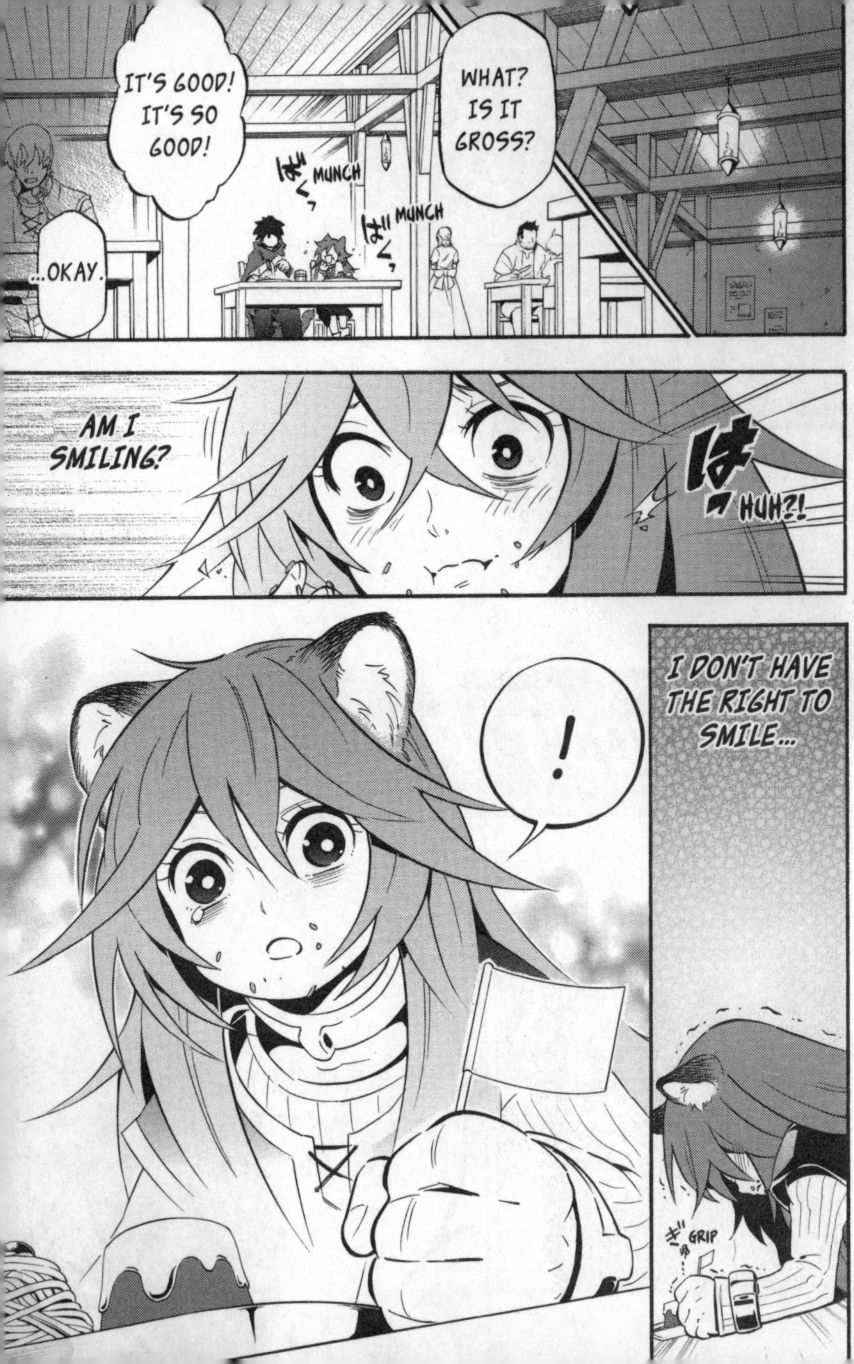
WHAT? IS IT GROSS?
ぱくっ MUNCH
ぱくっ MUNCH
IT'S GOOD! IT'S SO GOOD!
...OKAY.
はっ HUH?!
AM I SMILING?
I DON'T HAVE THE RIGHT TO SMILE...
ぎゅ GRIP
!

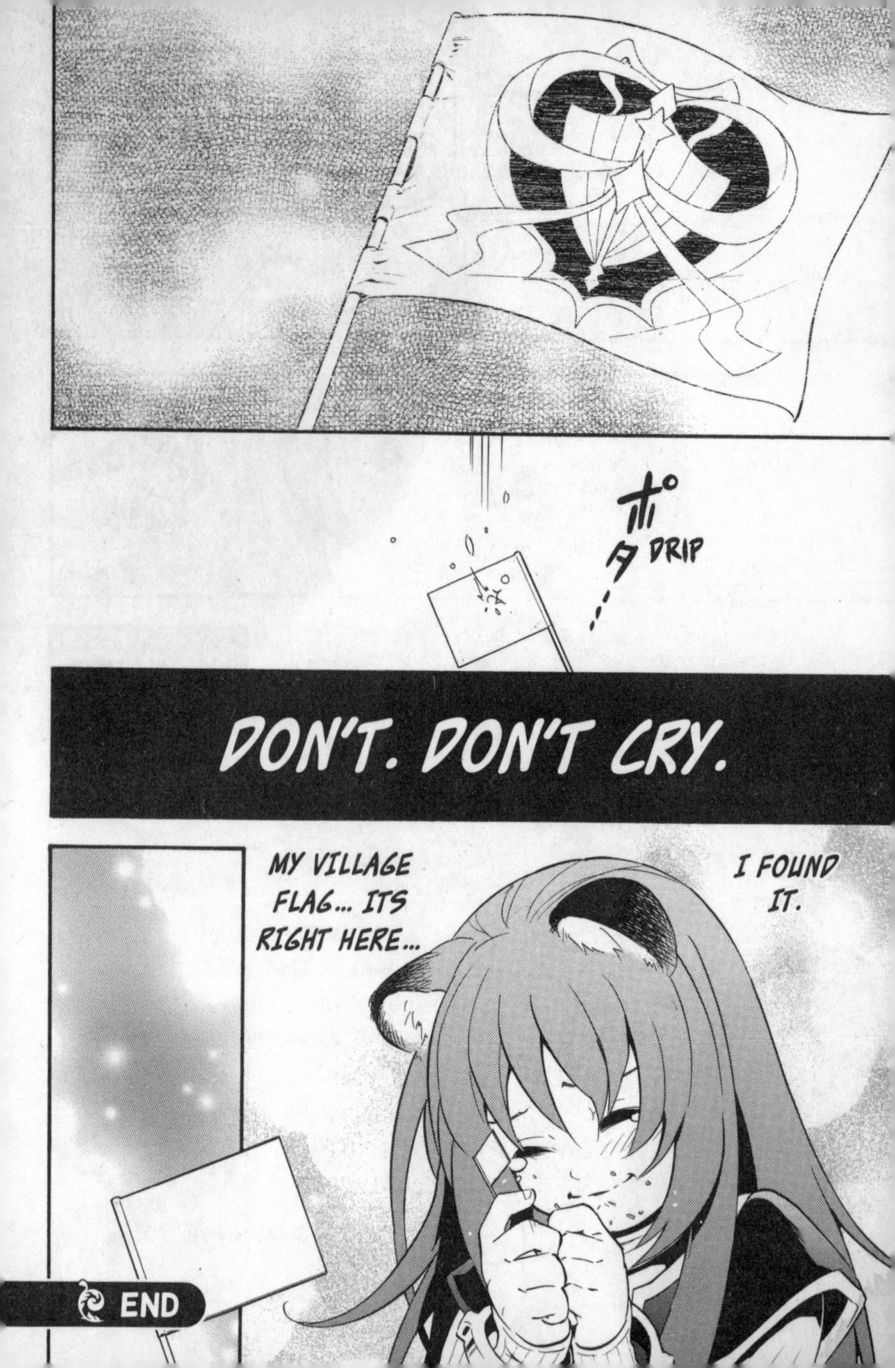
ポタ
DRIP
DON'T. DON'T CRY.
I FOUND IT.
MY VILLAGE FLAG... ITS RIGHT HERE...
END

AFTERWORD

THANK YOU SO MUCH FOR PICKING UP THE SECOND
VOLUME OF THE RISING OF THE SHIELD HERO MANGA!
I'D LIKE TO THANK ANEKO YUSAGI FOR CHECKING
OVER ALL MY WORK AND MINAMI SEIRA FOR HELPING
ME GET THE DESIGN RIGHT.
I LOVE... RAPHTALIA! I HOPE I CAN DRAW HER AS
CUTE AS I ENVISION HER! I'LL CONTINUE TO DO MY
BEST—THANKS FOR READING!

--AIYA KYU